# THE MALE HETEROSEXUAL

This book is dedicated to all men and women
who strive to improve our understanding
of human sexuality

THE **MALE**

HETER⚦SEXUAL

*Lust in
His Loins,
Sin in
His Soul?*

*Larry A. Morris*

SAGE Publications
*International Educational and Professional Publisher*
Thousand Oaks   London   New Delhi

*For information address:*

 SAGE Publications, Inc.
2455 Teller Road
Thousand Oaks, California 91320
E-mail: order@sagepub.com

SAGE Publications Ltd.
6 Bonhill Street
London EC2A 4PU
United Kingdom

SAGE Publications India Pvt. Ltd.
M-32 Market
Greater Kailash I
New Delhi 110 048 India

Printed in the United States of America

*Library of Congress Cataloging-in-Publication Data*

Morris, Larry A.
    The male heterosexual: Lust in his loins, sin in his soul? /
author, Larry A. Morris.
       p.   cm.
    Includes bibliographical references and index.
    ISBN 0-8039-5639-8 (acid-free).—ISBN 0-8039-5640-1 (pbk.: acid-free)
    1. Sex role.  2. Gender identity.  3. Masculinity (Psychology)
4. Men—Psychology.  I. Title.
HQ1075.M69  1997
305.3—dc20                    96-45794

97  98  99  00  01  02  03  10  9  8  7  6  5  4  3  2  1

*Acquiring Editor:* C. Terry Hendrix
*Editorial Assistant:* Dale Grenfell
*Production Editor:* Michèle Lingre
*Production Assistant:* Karen Wiley
*Typesetter & Designer:* Andrea D. Swanson
*Indexer:* Cristina Haley
*Cover Designer:* Lesa Valdez
*Print Buyer:* Anna Chin

# Contents

# Foreword

$M$asculinity is in crisis. During the past several years, the fact that the traditional code of masculinity has collapsed has become increasingly clear. Many men are confused and demoralized in the current climate, and some now react defensively to even a hint of criticism. To respond to the contemporary male crisis, I advocate a "reconstruction of masculinity" (Levant & Kopecky, 1995). In this reconstruction, one would identify those parts of the male code that are still quite valuable and honor those that provide a basis for male pride, while at the same time, one also would specify aspects that are anachronistic or dysfunctional today and find ways to help men change these. These latter aspects include men's difficulties in experiencing emotional empathy and in being attuned to their own emotional processes; the tendency for their vulnerable emotions to be transformed into anger, rage, and violence; and their tendency to be limited to a nonrelational orientation to sexuality.

*Nonrelational sexuality* can be defined as the tendency to experience sex as lust without any requirements for relational intimacy. In this situation, objects of sexual desire are often objectified and sometimes are in fact objects (as in pornographic books and videos); the man pursues these objects in an agentic fashion, partly to meet nurturance needs and partly to satisfy another set of needs related to his sense of adequacy as a man (Brooks, 1995).

A psychological understanding of the problems associated with male sexuality is urgently needed, for this is one of the dimensions of the male code that has fallen the farthest and the fastest. The catalyst has been a seminar on male sexuality conducted by the media over the past few years. This public deconstruction of male entitlement and abuse of power in heterosexual relationships began in 1991 with the broadcasts of Anita Hill's allegations of sexual harassment against Clarence Thomas and the subsequent Senate hearings, and continued with the William Kennedy Smith date rape trail, Mike Tyson's rape trial, the Tailhook scandal, the Woody Allen mess, Judge Sol Wachter's case, the allegations against Senator Bob Packwood and President Bill Clinton, and the O.J. Simpson murder trial.

I want to avoid giving the impression that I view male sexuality as inherently dysfunctional. On the contrary, I believe that men's relative freedom from sexual inhibitions and unbridled lustiness can add a great deal to relationships, and could in fact counterbalance the tendency among women to suppress lust as a result of their gender role socialization. Male sexuality becomes a problem, however, when nonrelational sexuality is the only way that men can relate intimately. When this is the case, nonrelational sexuality is a state of being that is less than fully optimal, arising as a defensive adaptation to a series of socialization experiences and normative developmental traumas.

It should also be pointed out that nonrelational sexuality exists along a continuum, from mild to moderate forms, in which a man may be unable to express caring and affection other than through sexual acts or in which a man must fantasize about tantalizing sexual experiences to make love to his wife to more severe problems such as sexual addiction. In its most severe form, nonrelational sexuality contributes to men's sexual aggression against women and children, including sexual harassment, rape, and child molestation.

In this volume, Larry Morris provides what we most need at this time: a scholarly examination of male (hetero)sexuality in its broadest context. Morris surveys, in turn, the biological, developmental psychological, sociocultural, and historical perspectives on male sexuality, then takes up the issues of sexual dysfunctions, sexually transmitted diseases, and the modern men's movement, and finally offers a new formula for the cultivation of healthy male sexuality. The writing is very clear, the material is presented in an interesting manner, and both the author's breadth of knowledge and his sense of humor come through delightfully. Morris does a good job of critiquing essentialism, sociobiology, and evolutionary psychology and also is sensitive to the cultural "privileging" of male heterosexuality. I found Chapter 5 particularly interesting, in the way that it reviews a wealth of material on ancient mythology, history, pornography, *Playboy*, comic books, TV, and advertising to illustrate the intoxicating "witches' brew" of cultural messages that sustain the myth of nonrelational sexuality.

Morris proposes a reconstruction of male heterosexuality. Although I would argue that this must occur in the context of the reconstruction of masculinity overall, I find his prescriptions compelling. He describes his solution alliteratively using the terms *phallocentrism, performance, promiscuity, paternity, phobia,* and *playfulness.* He argues for an end to phallocentrism, promiscuity, and (homo)phobia; a reframing of sexuality away from performance and toward intimate communication and playfulness; and, last but certainly not least, a reclaiming of paternity.

This is an exciting but difficult time in which to be alive: 30 years after the emergence of the modern women's movement, the reconstruction of masculinity is coming onto the national agenda. Morris lights the way for all of us as we attempt to reconstruct gender roles for a new millennium.

Ronald F. Levant
*Associate Clinical Professor of Psychology,*
*Department of Psychiatry, Harvard Medical School*
*(at Cambridge Hospital)*

# Acknowledgments

First and foremost I want to thank my wife, Patty, for her love, patience, support, understanding, and creative inspiration throughout the lengthy process of writing this book.

Special thanks to a wonderful friend, colleague, mentor, and fellow Grand Canyon Trekker, Ken Marsh, for reviewing an early draft of this manuscript and providing a most valuable critique.

I would like to express my gratitude to Ron Levant, the intrepid trailblazer for a new psychology of men, for his review of the manuscript and for taking time from a very busy schedule to write the Foreword to this book.

I am also grateful to David Lisak, Mic Hunter, and Beth Erikson for their comprehensive reviews of the manuscript and for their valuable suggestions for improving the presentation.

Thanks also to Trish Morris whose computer expertise and creative clerical manipulations resurrected most of the manuscript during the dark days of the hard-drive crash. I am also grateful to my good friend, Tom Volgy, who told me about Trish and her magic.

I would also like to thank the many patients, colleagues, family members, and friends who had the courage to share their personal stories with me about growing up sexual in America.

And special love and thanks to Peaches, our loving golden retriever, who sat by my feet with leash in mouth, waiting patiently for her turn.

# 1

# A Sexual Gender Journey

## *The Itinerary*

Scientists speculate that sexual behavior emerged about 2 billion years ago. One can only imagine the initial encounter between the first sexual beings. Perhaps they were driven by some newly developed biological urge to cruise the primordial soup in search of a mate, much the way singles now cruise bars and other habitats in search of Mr. or Ms. Right. Maybe they were yet unaware of their potential, and a chance encounter awakened latent sexual urges that produced a tidal wave of passion and the birth of the world's first peak sexual experience.

Although there is much that we do not know about the original sexual beings and their first romantic trysts, we do know that their actions marked the beginning of the most controversial behavior in the known universe. Few activities associated with reproductive processes have spawned such concern as sexual behavior. Philosophers, romantics, scientists, and religious zealots have all staked a claim. Declared ownership often begets proprietary rights and regulatory control. Genetics, biology, and physiology become the battleground for social, political, religious, and personal agendas. If our sexual ancestors had realized what they were about to propagate, besides themselves, I wonder if they would have bothered. After all, most primitive reproductive schemes were much less complicated and still worked very well. And single cell division, although seemingly autoerotic, remained socially acceptable, even in the best of neighborhoods.

This book is about the development of sexuality in one half of this sexual partnership: males. It is a journey along a circuitous route from ancient biological stirrings to modern interpretations of masculinity and sexuality. Along the way I will visit a number of important issues related to a basic question: Are male heterosexuals a homogeneous group doomed by a legacy of sin and lust? Some would have us believe that males are sexually savage beasts always poised to penetrate any female who happens by their lairs. Are males charged by powerful primitive urges forever festering deep inside their souls? Others believe that the destiny of males to become sex-lust beings may have been sealed when the first man lost control of himself and was found guilty of complicity associated with participating in a forbidden act of carnal sin with the world's first lady. Although women have borne the brunt of spiritual condemnation for this most serious transgression, males also have suffered more than their share of grief from this rather inauspicious beginning.

You will discover that a wide range of notions about sexual matters has occurred over the short history of humankind. Human sexual behavior, especially male heterosexual behavior, has never quite recovered from all this meddling. The overall result is a kind of "witches' brew" of ideas consisting of a strong dose of religious dogma occasionally laced with changing biological "facts," stirred intermittently by sociopolitical activism. Those who drink deep of the potion come under its spell and are compelled to act out its commands. Although both genders appear to be equally beguiled by the concoction, much of what is played out and perpetuated in our society is done so through historically male-dominated purveyors of cultural beliefs and values. I will examine closely the contents of the cauldron and its effect on the development of sexuality in what is generally believed to be the most powerful group of people in the United States: male heterosexuals. Of course, it is not possible to study male sexuality without also examining female sexuality, homosexuality, and bisexuality, but my primary focus will be on the development of male heterosexuality. Through this type of close scrutiny of male sexuality, Americans may begin to develop a better understanding of the way our culture reproduces a confusing and potentially harmful mixture of notions about gender roles and sexuality, regardless of sexual orientation. My hope is that positive changes will follow.

I begin the journey in Chapter 2 by extracting and examining the biological essence of sexuality: genes and hormones. Although the popular view is that gender is determined at the moment of conception and gender-appropriate sexual behavior naturally follows, the schematic is much more complex than simple genetic determinism would have one believe. Even the role biological juices, especially testosterone, appear to play in the development of sexuality has become controversial and subject to sociopolitical interpretation. Recent discoveries related to sexual differentiation, sexual orientation, and the brain are increasing our understanding of the development of sexual responses.

In Chapter 3, I examine developmental variables affecting the maturation of male sexuality from birth throughout the life cycle. Historically, displays of childhood sexuality in the United States have been discouraged and much less is known about the normal development of sexuality than other developmental tasks, such as acquiring language. Seldom is a child in Western society provided with the opportunity to learn about and experience his or her developing sexuality within a supportive, nurturing, understanding, and informative environment. Instead, a child's sexual curiosity and experimentation are met mostly with no information, misinformation, myths, or punitive responses from the child's caretakers. I view this societal call to deter children from exploring normal developmental tasks associated with sexuality a serious form of child abuse and have previously described it as "the abuse of sexuality" (Bolton, Morris, & MacEachron, 1989). A similar type of abuse of sexuality also rears its ugly head when society begins to impose itself in the sexual affairs of the elderly. Sexually active elders are often treated much like children and are discouraged from engaging in developmentally appropriate sexual activities. By removing the shroud of cultural proscriptions associated with sexual activities, the potential for rich developmental experiences unfolds.

The next stop on the journey is a tour of the ancient underground labyrinth of philosophical and "scientific" suppositions supporting Western civilization's ideas about gender roles, love, marriage, and sexual behavior. Two ancient civilizations, Greek and Roman, are especially influential on Western culture and receive close examination, as are the ancient Hebrews' teachings about gender roles and sexuality. The amalgamation of these philosophic attitudes eventually became the driving force behind traditional Judeo-Christian religious beliefs. These convictions provide the foundation for the collective cultural mentality regarding sexual commerce in the United States. Although the resultant social standard is certainly a force with which to be reckoned, it is by no means unified in its messages, power, or consequences, as I will show in Chapter 4. On this stop, you will also learn that, since about the 19th century, concepts about sexuality that have been promulgated by various scientific disciplines sometimes support and at other times refute mainstream Western beliefs about human sexuality. Agreement within the scientific community about the relative importance of genetics, biology, evolution, and sociocultural factors on sexual behavior remains elusive.

Although some people portray conventionally gendered male heterosexuality as some form of cultural privileging, the male sexual experience can be much more complex and difficult than it seems. In Chapter 5, I show that cultural expectations about masculinity and sexuality have fluctuated over time and are often laden with conflicting messages. For example, fertility symbols from the Stone Age suggest the worship of a woman's ability to bear children. Art objects from this period often emphasize women's breasts, wide hips, and external sexual organs. Around 9000 BC, when ancient people seemed to shift from a hunter-and-gatherer organizational structure to one consisting mostly of farmers and sheepherders, a shift of focus regarding sexuality also seemed to occur. At about this time, a knowledge of paternity appears to have developed and phallic worship began to replace the previous focus on maternity. Representations of external male sexual structures began to play an increasingly larger role in religious ceremonies and art in many ancient civilizations, such as in India, Egypt, Greece, and Rome. These civilizations in particular seemed to have deified the penis and openly celebrated the masculinization of sexual life and society. In a number of subtle ways, penis worship has found its way into Western thought about sexuality and manhood. Males are exposed to strong beliefs associated with judging self-worth by not only the size of the penis but what a male does with it. That is, achieving manhood is yoked to achieving sexual prowess, a potentially troublesome connection. The historical foundation supporting the various sociocultural prescriptions for masculinity and male sexuality, as well as interpretations of these messages communicated through works of art, the media, and an assortment of publications, is documented and discussed.

Learning how to be a well-functioning male heterosexual sometimes feels like negotiating a mine field with a faulty map. With danger lurking at nearly every step, one moves slowly, steps gently, and tries to plan ahead. Even so, one false step and one's genitals and masculinity are history. The various wounds males incur on their seemingly perilous journey toward sexual maturity are examined in three sections. The first chapter on this topic (Chapter 6) provides front row seats at what is commonly, but erroneously, called "performance" problems. Sexual behavior is not a performance, even though most men have been conditioned to believe that it is. So when problems, even minor deviations from an expected norm, occur, many men react with terror. They anguish over the loss of their perceived badge of manhood. But the presence of a sexual dysfunction does not always foretell the death of a man's sexuality or his masculinity. I also examine the various ways some males have sexually misbehaved, although most males learn to develop some form of acceptable sexuality that does not include such sexual misconduct as rape, sexual harassment, or child sexual abuse. Attempts to identify specific variables responsible for inappropriate sexual behavior are also examined.

The next installment (Chapter 7) in this series takes you into unfamiliar ground for most people: the sexual victimization of males. Males are socialized to be strong and to protect themselves. For males, the term *victim* is associated with weakness and is reserved for females. Sexually maltreated males are reluctant to disclose their victimization experiences for fear of being seen as soft, weak, unmanly, and, in some cases, homosexual. You will learn that sexual victimization is not for females only and many males suffer gender-related negative effects from the sexual misconduct of others. Because many men view the routine use of circumcision as a form of child sexual abuse, a discussion of this practice and the possible effect circumcision has on males is also offered in this segment.

Information about various sexually transmitted diseases (STDs) is presented next (Chapter 8) to complete the series on wounds incurred by the sexually active male. Although some males may be quite knowledgeable about STDs, many have absorbed a lot of myths and misinformation about this very important health and sexuality issue. Others have chosen to ignore this aspect of sexuality entirely, believing, perhaps, that they are somehow "immune" to it all. Of particular importance to heterosexual males is the understanding that the AIDS virus was not created by an angry deity to punish homosexuals: AIDS is gender and sexual-orientation blind. Safer sex procedures for males are available, but males must learn to modify a lot of old ideas about their sexuality.

In addition to the various wounds described above, many men suffer a social crisis. The time-honored code of masculinity appears to have eroded and is on the verge of collapse. Males are now expected to express themselves and act in ways that seem counter to their self-image as a real man and are often beyond their skills. With pressures from women to be treated equally in all respects, many males embraced feminism and have become partners with women in their attack on traditional concepts of gender roles. Other men find the feminist movement a threat to their manhood and have retreated to the trenches of masculinist ideologies. Other men are turning to movements promising a resurgence of traditional masculinity based on ancient stories and masculine archetypes. Writings and workshops by Robert Bly, Sam Keen, Robert Moore, and Douglas Gillette represent the most influential of the so-called mythopoetic men's movements. But leading advocates for professional men's studies such as Ron Levant, Gary Brooks, and William Pollack express concern that the mythopoetic men's movements may be atavistic and will ultimately produce more problems than solutions for males in search of their lost masculinity. Chapter 9 presents a review of the various men's movements and a discussion of how they portray and influence the development of masculinity and male sexuality.

Chapter 10 offers a discussion of the most salient points issued from the inquiry into the development of the male heterosexual. Using this information as a guide, I argue that the witches' brew is no love potion. Instead, it is poor chemistry with a toxic result. As such, it should require the following government warning label:

> According to the Socialization General, consumption of this concoction impairs your ability to achieve mature masculinity and may interfere with the development of healthy sexuality.

But all is not lost. Some elements of the mixture are not virulent, and in another mix they may actually be beneficial. In fact, many men have avoided the toxicity of the mixture and have managed to develop reasonably healthy sex lives.

Moving from deconstruction to reconstruction, I offer a revised formula for the cultivation of healthy personal and social male sexuality. The journey exposes those elements of male heterosexuality that are harmful and must be discarded and those that are useful and should be retained. Other helpful elements of sexuality long since forsaken by ancient philosophers or only hinted at by developmental factors are then added to the mix. The journey ends with a look at sex and the new real man.

# 2

# Biological Beginnings

## *Genes and Juices*

At one time or another, most of us have been told that we resemble our parents or other family members. Statements such as "You have your father's eyes, but your mother's nose" are all too familiar to those who recoil from any comparisons with their parents. A parent frustrated with a child's misbehavior may shame the child with comments such as "You are just like your mother." As we mature, we often find ourselves having ideas or engaging in behavior similar to those displayed by a parent. Our thoughts are often "My Gosh, I am becoming just like my father!" Of course, parents usually have a lot of positive attributes too, but we tend not to acknowledge those characteristics as readily as the negative ones. Some of us even fear that we may never be able to escape our perceived legacy of "bad genes."

The genetic template is certainly an important part of each of us. But are we destined to become only what the template dictates? What role do other factors such as hormones play in our development? The purpose of this chapter is to examine how genes and juices, individually and collectively, influence the development of male heterosexuality.

## ❏ The Genetic Code

When Gregor Mendel developed a scheme to describe how traits are transmitted from generation to generation, he did so through the observation of the final product: the adult pea plant's characteristics. Genes themselves were never directly observed by Mendel and his colleagues. Instead, Mendel described factors that would explain the results of his experimental manipulations. These factors were subsequently named genes, and certain rules of genetic transmission were postulated.

One of the most important discoveries by Mendel was that some genes are dominant and others are recessive. This observation helps explain how two parents with very similar physical characteristics (phenotypes) can produce a child with dissimilar features. For example, some brown-eyed parents may produce blue-eyed offspring. This difference may have negative social consequences as tongues begin to wag about the paternity of the child. But Mendelian rules can silence the gossip through the simple explanation that some parents carry recessive genes; when paired, the recessive phenotype (blue eyes) may appear. In other words, the genetic material associated with blue eyes was introduced into the parents' lineages sometime in the past and remains a part of their genetic makeup, even though the parents may not manifest the trait themselves. Later, when circumstances are correct, the overall parental genetic pool may produce a variation from the dominant phenotype.

During the century since Mendel's landmark work, geneticists have been able to isolate what is currently accepted as the chemical substrate of heredity: deoxyribonucleic acid (DNA). This large molecule is a graceful double helix chain, the structure of which forms a code describing the organism. When cells divide, the DNA replicates itself, thus transmitting and preserving the genetic code. Except for identical twins and clones, no two organisms have exactly the same DNA genetic structure.

Studies by geneticists have not only provided a better understanding of how traits are transmitted from generation to generation, but they also have produced commentary linking genetics with all sorts of human characteristics, not the least of which are gender superiority and sexual behavior. Although this notion is not new, some scientific discoveries have been used to bolster the proposal that one gender may engage in certain behaviors more than the other primarily for genetic reasons. Implied in this idea is the thought that a genetic inheritance of a behavioral propensity or trait means permanency of that characteristic. It is a short jump from biological determinism to almost any other type of "ism."

Fausto-Sterling (1985) argues that biological determinism is one of the roots of political discrimination against women. She also states that male-dominated science has a tendency to interpret scientific findings to support conservative rather than egalitarian views of women and their "place" in society. She argues:

> Genes alone do not produce biological phenotypes. Instead an individual's developmental and environmental history in combination with his or her total genetic endowment (all the genetic information encoded in the DNA), as well as chance, contribute to the final phenotype. By the same token, genes alone do not determine human behavior. They work in the presence and under the influence of a set of environments. (p. 71)

Let's see how this plays out in the development of male sexuality.

## ❑ Genes and Sexual Differentiation

The human body is made from billions of cells. The majority of these cells contain 23 pairs of chromosomes. These threadlike structures contain the genetic information transmitted to the new organism by his or her parents. Each parent contributes an equal amount of chromosomes: 23. Among the 23 chromosomes produced by the female parent, one is an X sex chromosome. The male produces an X sex chromosome or a Y sex chromosome. At conception, one sperm penetrates an ovum. The male's 23 chromosomes then combine with the female's 23 chromosomes, producing 23 pairs of chromosomes. Gender is determined by a gene called *testis-determining factor* (TDF) located only on the Y chromosome (Koopman, Gubbay, Vivian, Goodfellow, & Lovell-Badge, 1991; Sinclair et al., 1990). If the successful sperm bears an X sex chromosome, the offspring will be female (XX combination without TDF). A combination of an X chromosome from the mother and an intact Y chromosome from the father will yield a male offspring (XY combination with TDF). Thus, the role of the father's sperm, either X or Y bearing, appears primary in determining the offspring's sex.

Driven by a set of genes common to both sexes, genetic male and genetic female embryos develop identical sex structures during the first 6 weeks of gestation. Each develops internal structures consisting of an indifferent sex gland, a set of Wolffian (male) ducts, and a set of Mullerian (female) ducts. Each also has external sex structures consisting of a genital tubercle, a urethral fold, and a labioscrotal swelling. Sometime during the 6th week of gestation, genetic information is sent out to turn on the TDF gene. The Y chromosome with TDF responds to the wake-up call and initiates the production of a specialized protein. Although it is uncertain how this specialized substance works, researchers agree that its presence somehow stimulates the transformation of the indifferent sex gland into embryonic testes rather than ovaries (Muller & Urban, 1981, 1982). The fetal embryo's newly formed testes soon begin to produce hormones, two of which are needed to complete the male embryo's sex tissues. One hormone, testosterone, stimulates a period of active growth for the male Wolffian duct system, which will develop into the vas deferens, the seminal vesicles, and the prostate gland. The other hormone, Mullerian Inhibiting Substance (MIS), inhibits the growth of the female Mullerian duct system, which would develop into fallopian tubes, a uterus, and the upper part of the vagina. At about the 8th week of fetal development, another androgen, dihydrotestosterone (DHT), stimulates the development of the external male genitals.

Clearly, fetal hormones play a significant role in the development of a male's sexual organs. Although researchers are less certain regarding the role hormones play in the development of female sexual organs, it is generally assumed that the absence of fetal testosterone leads to a preprogrammed development of the female sexual structures. That is, androgens (testosterone and related steroids) take charge of indifferent sex tissues and transform them into male sexual organs. Without androgens, these tissues would simply follow the existing messages to develop into female sex organs. Even an XY chromosomal fetus would begin to develop female sexual organs in the absence of the TDF gene and subsequent sex-specific hormones. Thus, in the absence of androgens and MIS, the embryo would develop female rather than male sex characteristics. As Money (1993) quips, "the primordial template of development is designed to create Eve not Adam" (p. 13).

Fetal sex structures are not the only organs to undergo changes associated with the prenatal sexual differentiation process; sexual differentiation of brain structures, especially the hypothalamus, occurs during the second trimester (Pillard & Weinrich, 1986). During this period, fetal testosterone produces an insensitivity in male fetuses to estrogen, the female sex hormone. In the absence of fetal testosterone, the hypothalamus of the female fetus develops a sensitivity to estrogen. This form of differentiation is the beginning of a feedback loop involving the brain and the sexual structures necessary for regulating genetic gender-related sexual and reproductive responses.

Several recent studies have suggested that separate centers for the generation of male-typical (more common to males than females) and female-typical (more common to females than males) sexual behavior and feelings develop within the hypothalamus. For example, the destruction of the medial preoptic area of the hypothalamus in male animals produces either a reduction or cessation of male-typical copulatory behavior such as mounting females and, in some, an increase in female-typical sexual behavior such as approaching and exposing genitalia to males. Electrical stimulation of an intact medial preoptic area in males will typically elicit mounting behavior and pelvic thrusting, but not ejaculation (activity in an adjacent area of the hypothalamus, the dorsomedial nucleus, appears to be a subcenter for ejaculatory functions). Measurements of neuronal activity in the medial preoptic area of male monkeys while engaging in sexual behavior suggests a strong relationship between the electrical activity of this area and levels of sexual arousal. The medial preoptic area also contains a high level of receptors for hormones, especially male hormones, and at least one nucleus in this area is larger in human males, on average, than in females. Based on similar studies with females, the corresponding region in the hypothalamus for female-typical sexual behavior appears to be the ventromedial nucleus (for a review, see LeVay, 1993).

Fetal testosterone is largely responsible for transforming the original ambisexual tissues into male internal and external sex structures. Testosterone also plays another important role in the development and maintenance of male sexuality. Testosterone is secreted by the testes into the blood stream and is circulated to the brain, specifically the hypothalamus. If the hypothalamus detects a low level of testosterone, it secrets a hormone called LH-releasing hormone (LH-

RH) that triggers the pituitary glad to secrete an interstitial cell-stimulating hormone (ICSH) back to the testes. ICSH then stimulates Leydig cells in the testes to release more testosterone into the blood system. Once an acceptable level of testosterone in the blood system is reached, the hypothalamus signals the pituitary gland to stop releasing ICSH. This feedback loop involving three endocrine glands—the testes, the hypothalamus, and the pituitary gland—regulates the level of testosterone in the blood, ensuring that a genetic male will develop as a biologic male.

## ❏ Genes and Sexual Orientation

Although it is generally assumed that biologic males and females will be "naturally" attracted to their opposite sex, primarily for procreational purposes, reality presents a rather different story. History has shown that human sexual behavior can be quite diverse and certainly not limited to procreational activities between males and females. The range of people's sexuality can be captured in four categories of sexual interest, commonly referred to as *sexual orientation*. Individuals who appear totally disinterested in any type of sexual activity with either sex, in spite of possessing perfectly healthy sexual equipment, are typically seen as having no sexual orientation (asexual). Heterosexuality includes individuals whose sexual feelings or behaviors are directed toward individuals of the opposite sex. Homosexuality includes individuals whose sexual feelings or behaviors are directed toward individuals of the same sex. Bisexuality includes various combinations of heterosexual and homosexual sexual feelings or behavior. It should be noted that some individuals may have sexual feelings reflecting one sexual orientation but behavior reflecting another. As you will see later in this volume, political, social, and religious forces play a significant role in the expression of sexual feelings.

Since scholars first noticed sexual diversity, a number of wide-ranging explanations for sexual orientation have been offered. A growing body of research seems to point to a strong genetic and biologic connection. Well-executed statistical studies of twins and other family members suggest that homosexuality may be genetically linked within the family. For example, it appears that the likelihood of being gay with a gay monozygotic (identical) twin is

50% to 60%, whereas the likelihood of being gay with a gay dizygotic (fraternal) twin is reduced to 25% to 30% (Bailey & Pillard, 1991; Whitam, Diamond, & Martin, 1993). Pillard and Weinrich (1986) found that about 25% of brothers of gay men were also gay, a rate about 15 to 20 percentage points higher than the estimated 5% to 10% rate of male homosexuals in the general population (see Michael, Gagnon, Laumann, & Kolata, 1994). The genetic effect appears present but weaker for females, with about 48% of identical twin sisters of lesbians also lesbian, and only 16% of fraternal twin sisters also lesbian, a rate comparable to that found for nontwin sisters of gay women (Bailey, Pillard, Neale, & Agyei, 1993).

When a group of researchers at the National Institutes of Health found an increased incidence of male homosexuality in maternal relatives (e.g., maternal uncles, sons of maternal aunts), a search for a gene on the X chromosome that might be responsible for sexual orientation in men was launched. Although the gene itself has not yet been isolated, one region of the X chromosome appears to contain a cluster of DNA markers shared by gay brothers at a rate significantly higher than 50%. This finding suggests that a gene or genes that influence sexual orientation in men may, indeed, be located on the X chromosome and inherited by men from their mother's genetic pool (Hamer, Hu, Magnuson, Hu, & Pattatucci, 1993).

Support for the notion that genetic factors may affect sexual orientation can also be found in studies of men with an extra X chromosome. Overall, XXY men tend to be taller, produce less testosterone, show more sex-atypical traits as children, and have lower IQs than their XY counterparts. Their testes also fail to produce sperm, a condition known as Klinefelter's syndrome. Homosexuality among XXY men in Denmark was found to be significantly higher than an excellent control sample of XY men. The extra X chromosome in these men may have influenced sexual orientation through genetic encoding or by related prenatal hormonal factors (Schiavi, Theilgaard, Owen, & White, 1988).

Other studies suggest that the brains of homosexual men may develop in a sex-atypical manner, perhaps under the influence of genetic factors. For example, gay men tend to score less like heterosexual men but more like heterosexual women on tests of spatial ability, such as mental rotation and water-level tasks (Gladue, Beatty, Larson, & Staton, 1990; Lindesay, 1987; McCormick & Witelson, 1991; Sanders & Ross-Field, 1986). Homosexual men and women may also tend to be less consistently right-handed (they either prefer the left hand or perform some tasks with the left hand and other tasks with the right) than heterosexuals (McCormick, Witelson, & Kingstone, 1990).

The most compelling evidence that sexual orientation may be related to structural differences in the brain is found in comparative studies of brains of gay men, straight men, and women. LeVay (1991, 1993) found that one of four groups of neurons forming the interstitial nuclei of the anterior hypothalamus (a portion of the medial preoptic region of the hypothalamus thought to be associated with male-typical sexual feelings and behavior) was on average two to three times larger in heterosexual men than in women, whereas this group of neurons in gay men was, on average, the same size as in women.

Although LeVay (1993) suggests that the structural differences between the brains of homosexual and heterosexual men are most likely a function of the prenatal sexual differentiation process, he does not exclude the possibility that the changes may be the result of adult sexual behavior. Support for the prenatal hypothesis comes from other studies, however. For example, Allen and Gorski (1992) found that the anterior commissure (an axonal connection between the right and left sides of the cerebral cortex) was on average larger in homosexual men than in heterosexual men, whereas this area in gay men was comparable in relative size to that found in women. Because the anterior commissure is not known to be associated in a regulatory fashion to sexual behavior, adult sexual behavior would seem to have little or no effect on its size. Thus, the sex difference in brain structures appears connected to prenatal sexual differentiation processes, which appear to be genetically driven (LeVay, 1993).

## ❑  Genes, Hormones, and Sexual Identity

When hormonal errors occur during prenatal development, the sex structures can be affected in a variety of ways. Regardless of genetic gender, some fetuses develop gonadal tissues of both genders. That is, they may have an ovary and a testicle or gonads that have a combination of ovarian and testicular tissues. This rare condition is referred to as true hermaphroditism. For males, the Mullerian duct develops as well as the post-Wolffian structures. A failure in the sequence involving the Mullerian-inhibiting substance seems to occur, resulting in the development of both male and female internal sex structures.

Prenatal hormonal errors can also produce pseudohermaphroditism. Unlike true hermaphrodites, pseudohermaphrodites have either testes or ovaries but not both, and their testes or ovaries match their genetic gender. That is, genetic females have ovaries and genetic males have testes; however, internal and external sex structures may be poorly formed or resemble those of the opposite genetic gender.

One type of pseudohermaphroditism, called androgenital syndrome, occurs in genetic females when the fetus is exposed to excessive levels of androgens, either through the fetus's own adrenal glands or through synthetic androgens administered to the mother during pregnancy. Although the female fetus with this syndrome has internal sexual structures consistent with her genetic gender, her external structures, especially the clitoris, are masculinized. In most cases, the clitoris is the size of a small penis.

Fortunately, androgenital syndrome is usually diagnosed in infancy, allowing for early hormonal and surgical procedures to correct the masculination of the external genitalia. In this way, females with this syndrome have the opportunity to develop a feminine sexual identity consistent with their genetic gender. If early intervention does not occur, these genetic females may be reared as boys due to their masculinized external sex structures. Further masculinization may be performed through surgery during childhood and hormone treatments at puberty. The result is a genetic female with female internal sexual structures, masculinized external genitals and secondary sex characteristics, and a male gender identity. Money and Ehrhardt (1972) studied two children with androgenital syndrome who received different treatments. One child received early intervention oriented toward feminizing her, whereas the other received treatment oriented toward masculinization at about the age of 3 years and again at puberty. The "feminized" girl adopted a female gender identity, including sexual attraction to males. The masculinized girl continued to maintain the male gender identity established prior to the therapeutic procedures. At sexual maturation, the masculinized girl reported sexual attraction to females consistent with "his" adopted male gender identification.

Some XY males experience an unusually low sensitivity to androgens during fetal development. As a result, another type of pseudohermaphroditism, androgen-insensitivity syndrome, is produced. Because the developing male sexual structures are insensitive to the hormones necessary for appropriate development, they become poorly formed. External genitals are feminized and may include a small vagina. Testes are typically undescended at birth. In addition, the male duct system, consisting of the vas deferens, seminal vesicles, ejaculatory ducts, and epididymis, does not develop with this syndrome. Internal female sexual structures such as a uterus or Fallopian tubes do not develop, however, because the fetal testes are not prevented by this syndrome from producing Mullerian-inhibiting substance. The result is a genetic male with clearly feminized external genitals, poorly developed testes, and no female reproductive system or male duct system. Studies of individuals with androgen-insensitivity syndrome suggest that these genetic males typically begin to develop female gender identities early in childhood and maintain feminine interests thereafter (Brooks-Gunn & Matthews, 1979; Money, 1968; Money & Ehrhardt, 1972).

A third type of pseudohermaphroditism was first discovered in young boys in the Dominican Republic by Julianne Imperato-McGinley and a number of her colleagues. These boys suffered from a rare genetic enzyme disorder known as 5-alpha-reductase deficiency that significantly reduced their ability to convert testosterone into dihydrotestosterone, the androgen responsible for masculinizing the fetal external sexual structures during the period when testosterone levels are low. Although the boys were born with normally masculinized internal sexual and, presumably, related brain structures, their penises resembled clitorises and their scrotums resembled female labia. Partially formed vaginas were also present.

Because these genetic males had ambiguous external genitals resembling female rather than male genitals at birth, most were raised as girls and assumed a female identity during childhood. But at the onset of puberty, their testes began to produce the normal amount of testosterone for that period. The result was not only the emergence of typical masculine secondary sex characteristics, but the development of masculinized external sexual structures as well. To everyone's surprise, these "girls" changed into adolescent males. They developed facial hair, their voices deepened, their testes descended, and what appeared to be clitorises developed into full functioning penises. Once the transformation began to occur, most of these boys reared as girls adopted a male, rather than a female, gender identity. One of the boys who adopted a male gender identity continued to maintain his previous feminine gender role, however. That is, he accepted the fact that he was a male but continued to function as a female, including wearing female clothing and performing culturally determined feminine roles. One boy maintained the female gender identification presented to him since birth. He subsequently sought sex reassignment surgery to reverse the masculinization of his external sex structures that occurred at puberty (Imperato-McGinley, Guerrero, Gautier, & Peterson, 1974; Imperato-McGinley, Peterson, Gautier, & Sterla, 1979).

Several years later, a similar group of boys was found in the Eastern Highlands of Papua New Guinea. Again, a majority of these boys reared as girls changed their gender identities from female to male at puberty in spite of serious cultural barriers, including being previously excluded from the requisite prepubertal male initiation rites (Imperato-McGinley et al., 1991).

The establishment of gender identity is a complex process involving genetic encoding, prenatal and adolescent hormones, and sociocultural factors. Support is found in these studies for the position that gender identity is not firmly established during childhood, however, in spite of the focus on socializing one gender identity or the other, and that genetics and sex hormones may be the most important factors in establishing gender identity (LeVay, 1993).

## ❏ Hormones and Puberty

The hypothalamic-pituitary-gonadal feedback loop system established during fetal development becomes active briefly during the early postnatal months, the purpose of which is uncertain (Money, 1993). Sex steroid activity is then suppressed in both males and females by a negative feedback mechanism until late childhood. Estrogen and androgen production levels by prepubertal males and females are essentially the same. Sex steroid secretion is then reactivated in the prepubertal and pubertal periods through two independent processes: adrenarche and gonadarche. Adrenarche normally precedes gonadarche by approximately 2 years and is marked by androgen production by the *zona reticularis* of the adrenal cortex. Gonadarche is marked by the reactivation of the hypothalamic-pituitary-gonadal feedback loop system.

As the gonads develop, an increase in androgens is found in males. In females, both androgens and estrogens increase. Incremental amounts of serum estrogen are also found in females, which eventually stimulates menarche. Although the concentration of hormones varies during the day for males, a progressive and linear increase in the levels of serum testosterone and follicle-stimulating hormone (FSH) coincides with the period of puberty (Winter, 1978). By comparison, for females the increase in circulating androgens occurs during puberty, but the maximum level finally reached is typically about one tenth of that reached by males (Smith, 1989).

Puberty is generally considered that period during which reproductive maturation occurs. That is, the male testes begin to produce sperm and the female begins to ovulate. For most females, the onset of puberty is marked by a single readily identifiable event: menarche. This event normally occurs between the ages of 10 and 16 years and reflects the maturity of the female reproductive system. The average age of menarche in the United States is believed to be between 12.5 and 13 years (Muuss, 1970; Roche, 1979). Physical changes called *secondary sex characteristics* also occur during puberty. Most notable for females is the development of breasts and pubic hair. Hips often round with fatty tissue as well.

The signs of puberty for the male are more subtle and are marked mostly by emerging secondary sex characteristics. For males, the beginning of facial, pubic, and other body hair, as well as the lowering of the voice due to the lengthening of the vocal cords, are the most prominent changes denoting the onset of puberty. Even so, no one event, equivalent to the female's menarche, signals that the young male's sperm is capable of reproduction. During puberty, the hypothalamus and the pituitary glands combine to stimulate the maturing testes into producing sperm capable of reproduction. The testes are also stimulated to produce large amounts of testosterone, which is primarily responsible for the secondary sex characteristics as well as the enlargement of the testes and the shaft of the penis. Most males also experience a growth spurt during this period, including an increase in height, weight, musculature, and physical strength (Reinisch, 1990).

For the adolescent male, signs of sexual maturity may include nocturnal emissions, often called "wet dreams," the beginning of masturbation to ejaculation, and an increased interest in the opposite sex. Beach (1974) found that the dramatic rise in these behaviors by young males was closely related to a rapid increase in male plasma testosterone levels during puberty. The development of pubic hair and the emergence of ejaculation in males also appear closely related (Kinsey, Pomeroy, & Martin, 1948).

Male adolescents are often described as "raging hormone machines" or "hormones on wheels." This sudden increase in hormones at puberty, following a low level of activity during childhood, typically produces a rather stressful and tumultuous period for the adolescent. Psychologist G. S. Hall (1904) calls this period, "sturm und drang" (storm and stress). Others posit that hormonal changes during puberty produce sexual libidinal changes that, in turn, stimulate psychological defenses mechanisms to address the emerging strong sexual drives. Smith (1989) clarifies this biosocial model of adolescent behavior and development:

> There does, however, appear to be enough evidence to conclude that puberty onset heightens libido as well as shapes the individual as an attractive and appropriate sexual partner. Social processes also affect sexual involvement by influencing an adolescent's attitudes, presenting role prescribing and reinforcing behavior, and affording opportunities. Culture, as an all-inclusive concept, works through a variety of social channels, including peers and parents, to develop standards of sexual behavior to which an adolescent ascribes. The incorporation of all three of these elements—biological, social, and cultural—within one framework provides a fruitful means to explain both individual and group differences in sexual behavior. (p. 162)

## ❑ Hormones and Sexual Behavior

Clearly, hormones play a key role in the final development of one's gender. But do sex hormones also regulate human sexual feelings and behavior? The answer to this question is elusive because most of the research in this area has been conducted with lower animals and may not generalize to humans (Ellis & Ames, 1987). Most animal studies show that the experimental control of sex hormones produces varying levels of sexual behavior depending on the level of testosterone. For example, male rats, once castrated, show a decrease in normal sexual behavior, such as attempts to mount female rats, but their sexual behavior resumes when normal testosterone levels are again achieved through injections. If testosterone is administered to female rodents before the sexual differentiation of the brain occurs, typical masculine, rather than feminine, sexual behavior emerges in adulthood. Similarly, female rat fetuses exposed to increased levels of testosterone often develop somewhat masculinized sexual organs as well as a predisposition for male mating behavior in adulthood.

Although a reduction in testosterone levels in men may also produce a gradual reduction in sexual drive for some males, other men show little negative effect (Leshner, 1978). This finding suggests that human sexual behavior is much more complex than can be predicted simply by measuring hormones. Even so, the role of testosterone in activating sexual behavior has been well documented. For example, adult males who display a lowered level of sexual interest and behavior due to a low level of testosterone often resume their premorbid level of sexual drive and behavior following testosterone injections (Cunningham, Cordero, & Thornby, 1989). Some studies also found a positive correlation between testosterone levels in adult males and the frequency of sexual intercourse (Dabbs & Morris, 1990; Knussman, Christiansen, & Couwenbergs, 1986).

For adolescent males, free (circulating) testosterone levels also seem to predict sexual interest, masturbation rates, and the early onset of sexual intercourse (Udry, 1988; Udry & Billy, 1987; Udry, Billy, Morris, Groff, & Raj, 1985). In a study by Halpern, Udry, Campbell, and Suchindran (1993), the pubertal development of 100 adolescent boys was examined over a 3-year period. Results show a significant relationship between testosterone levels and coital status. Although testosterone levels also proved to be a good predictor of the boys' transition to sexual intercourse, changes in hormone levels over the course of the study did not predict changes in thinking about sex or noncoital sexual behavior. It should be noted, however, that sexual behavior may be related to the level of testosterone, but this relationship does not appear to continue above an absolute concentration of 300 nanograms of the hormone per 100 milliliter of blood (Nieschlag, 1979).

For female adolescents, free testosterone, DHEA, DHEAS, and androstesnedione have been shown to be good predictors of motivation for future sexual behavior, masturbation, and thoughts about sexual behavior but not coital activity itself (Udry, Talbert, & Morris, 1986). Thus, it appears that females respond to an increase in hormones by showing an increased interest in sexual behavior, but this interest does not lead to actual sexual intercourse as frequently as seen for male adolescents. Other studies suggest that an increase in androgen production in females coincides with increased sexual arousal, sexual initiation, and the frequency of sexual behavior (Adams, Gold, & Burt, 1978; Englander-Golden, Change, Whitmore, & Dienstbier, 1980; Persky, Lief, Strauss, Miller, & O'Brien, 1978). For example, testosterone levels are typically at their peak during the time of ovulation, the period during which women often report being the most sexually interested and active. Carney, Bancroft, and Matthews (1978) also found that testosterone therapy with females produced several positive results such as an increase in sexually arousing thoughts, satisfaction with sexual activities, frequency of orgasms, and even the perceived attractiveness of the male sexual partner.

Clinical studies of women who have undergone surgery to remove ovaries and/or adrenal glands suggest that the removal of the ovaries does not produce the reduction in sexual interest typically produced by an adrenalectomy (Waxenburg, Drellich, & Sutherland, 1959). Further evidence of the importance of testosterone in the sexual behavior of females is found in studies of women who received androgens as part of a therapy regimen. Money and Ehrhardt (1972) found increased sexual responses in women who had been administered exogenous androgen for the treatment of estrogen-dependent carcinomas.

It is not an uncommon practice to remove the testes of male animals surgically to "settle them down." In animals, castration has been shown to be an effective procedure to reduce the level of testosterone production. And castrated male animals often become less aggressive and less sexually active following the procedure.

Castration is sometimes used as one method to assist in the treatment of cancer or other diseases of the male reproductive system. Although castrated men show a wide variety of responses to having their testes removed, most report a gradual loss of sexual desire. The ability to attain erections and to ejaculate is also affected in a negative manner over time. Leshner (1978) found that men who were sexually experienced before castration had a more gradual reduction in sexual interest and activities than men who were less experienced at the time of castration. For inexperienced men, the loss of interest in sexual activities was more pronounced. The interplay between the decrease in testosterone due to castration and previous learning experiences regarding sexual behavior is posited as the main reason for the differences found between these two groups.

Attempts to reduce testosterone in sexual perpetrators have been seen by many as the keystone to the successful treatment of repeat offenders (Blair & Lanyon, 1981), even though research has not supported the notion that sexual offenders, as a group, have excessive amounts of testosterone (Bradford, 1983; Lang, Langevin, Bain, Frenzel, & Wright, 1989). Although surgical castration has been employed, with limited success, in the treatment of sexual offenders (Berlin & Coyle, 1981; Freund, 1980; Hein, 1981; Wille & Beier, 1989), most somatic therapies rely on the use of various medical interventions, rather than orchiectomies, to assist in reducing deviant sexual arousal (Maletzky, 1991). For example, cyproterone acetate, a synthetic form of the female hormone progesterone, has been shown to reduce circulating levels of testosterone effectively and leads to subsequent reduction of sexual arousal in male sexual offenders (see Berlin & Coyle, 1981; Cooper, 1981; Zbytovsky & Zapletálek, 1979). Some males experience side effects, which include some feminizing physical changes such as breast enlargement and an elevation in voice pitch. Some other males report a reduction of their angry feelings and aggressive behavior (Zbytovsky & Zapletálek, 1979).

Another hormonal agent, medroxyprogesterone acetate (trade name Provera), has been shown to reduce circulating testosterone levels in males as well as to block testosterone itself (Freund, 1980; Gagne, 1981). The use of Provera, either in its injectable form (depo-Provera) or in its oral form (oral-Provera) produces a decrease in the frequency of sexual daydreams, sexual arousal, masturbation, and sexual intercourse. This effect is more dramatic when testosterone levels are reduced to approximately 50% of baseline measurements. As with the use of cyproterone acetate, some males experience enlarged breasts, a voice pitch change, and a reduction of aggressive feelings and behavior.

Neuroleptic medications such as thioridazine (Burnstein, 1983) and haloperidol (Comings & Comings, 1982) have been shown to suppress sexual arousal in males as a side effect. Interestingly, thioridazine also produces an antiarousal effect in females, but the effect is not as great as seen in males.

## ❑ Genes, Hormones, and Aggressive Behavior

At the time of writing this book, the U.S. Navy had just assigned women to the nuclear powered aircraft carrier the *U.S.S. Eisenhower.* Although women have been involved in military service for decades, this was the first time females were actually trained for combat, placed on a warship, and allowed to perform roles directly related to battle. At the cost of several million dollars, the mighty *Eisenhower* was retrofitted to accommodate the needs of this new type of combat sailor. For example, many urinals were torn out and replaced with more appropriate facilities, separate sleeping quarters were constructed, and preparations were made for the acquisition and disposal of sanitary napkins. Some quipped that the ship's medical personnel had to enroll in crash courses related to gynecology or risk transfer to the submarine fleet.

Certainly times are changing, but what is all the fuss about? Historically, women who have served in the military have done so with honor and distinction. In 1942, Congress authorized a program called Women Accepted for Volunteer Emergency Service (WAVES) and the Women's Army Auxiliary Corps (WAACs) to replace men who were shifted to combat duty during World War II. Women who enlisted in these programs served in various noncombat, but vital, military positions. Many women were skilled pilots and became members of the Women Air Services Program (WASP), used in training missions and to transport military aircraft. But WASPs also were not allowed to fight. In fact, the U.S. government attempted to keep WASP a secret because it feared that the use of women as military pilots might appear as a sign of weakness and desperation to the enemy. Traditional values still held that only men were strong and capable of waging war successfully and women were weaker and less aggressive. Males were thought to be genetically predisposed toward aggression and primarily responsible for wars in the first place. Men, therefore, should fight among themselves. Women should not be placed in harm's way.

Also related to the persistent belief that males are more aggressive than females is the notion that this predisposition to violent behavior is somehow related to male hormones, especially testosterone. Because testosterone is also linked to male sexual behavior, it is not surprising that the media, the public, and even some researchers frequently use the terms *sex* and *violence* in tandem. It is important, therefore, to examine the evidence purportedly supporting the notion that males are genetic- and hormone-driven war machines.

The search brings us first to studies associated with genetic abnormalities. The flip side to having too many X chromosomes (XXY men, discussed earlier) is having too many Y chromosomes, the XYY genotype. Although the extra Y chromosome does not appear to affect physical sexual structures, some researchers have posited a causal relationship between the extra Y chromosome and criminal behavior. For several years, the XYY syndrome was often identified as the criminal genotype. Some violent male criminals have been found to have the XYY genotype, but the link between the extra Y chromosome and violent behavior is tenuous at best. For example, Meyer-Bahlburg's (1978) review of the literature produced a conclusion that criminal behavior displayed by many XYY males was not related to an increase in androgens. Most researchers now appear to agree that an extra Y or an extra X chromosome affects normal development, including intelligence, more than aggressive behavior; lowered intelligence often shows a positive correlation with criminal behavior.

Although exceptions can be found, males appear to be more aggressive than females of most species. Many social scientists use the animal studies as a foundation for inferring that human males may also be more aggressive than females because of biology, but some are more cautious in their interpretations. Others are vocal in their criticisms about the utility of generalizing the results from studies of animals to humans.

Early support for the idea that human males are more aggressive than females due to biological factors can be found in the ground breaking book, *The Psychology of Sex Differences* (Maccoby & Jacklin, 1974). After an exhaustive review of the literature related to the work on sex differences, Maccoby and Jacklin (1974) found few variables that show a consistent difference between the two sexes. One exception was that males appeared to be more aggressive than females. Postulated as the culprit is male sex hormones. The conclusions reached by Maccoby and Jacklin have been challenged along several dimensions (see Block, 1976; Tieger, 1980). In 1980, Maccoby and Jacklin responded to their critics by reiterating their position that studies support their conclusion regarding sex differences in aggression. More recently, Maccoby (1990) reports, "studies continue to find that men are more often agents of aggression than are women" (p. 513).

Other social scientists who reviewed the same or similar research have reached different conclusions. For example, Pleck's (1981) review of the research related to the relationship of testosterone and male aggressive behavior fails to find the strong link between male hormones and aggression posited by Maccoby and Jacklin (1974). Although Pleck agrees that a biological connection with aggressive behavior in animals has been established by research findings, he finds no comparable evidence for this connection in studies with humans.

Studies using individuals who have been convicted of violent crimes or individuals who have been convicted of other crimes but who may appear to be violent persons may be useful here. Dabbs, Jurkovic, and Frady (1991) measured salivary testosterone and cortisol concentrations in late adolescent male offenders. The results showed a positive relationship between huge levels of testosterone and the commission of more violent crimes, a higher rate of violating prison rules, and harsher treatment by the parole board. No significant relationship between the level of hormones and the results of personality and delinquency inventories was found. Cortisol was found to act as a moderator between testosterone and the violence involved in the crimes.

When Dabbs, Frady, Carr, and Besch (1987) compared free testosterone in the saliva of young adult male prison inmates, they found a strong relationship between higher testosterone concentrations and convictions for violent crimes, as well as a strong relationship between lower testosterone concentrations and convictions for nonviolent crimes. A positive relationship between high levels of testosterone in nonviolent offenders and a higher frequency of prison rule infractions was also found. Peers also rated inmates with higher concentrations of testosterone as "tougher" than other inmates.

Dabbs, Ruback, Frady, and Hopper (1988) compared saliva testosterone concentrations of adult female inmates and female undergraduate college students. The highest level of testosterone was found in inmates convicted of unprovoked violence. Inmates with convictions associated with defensive violence showed the lowest level of testosterone. The inmates' mean level of testosterone was similar to the college sample.

Among a sample of combative African Bushmen, Christiansen and Winkler (1992) found significantly positive correlations between violent behavior and high levels of serum 5α-dihydrotestosterone, free non-sex-hormone-binding-globulin-bound salivary testosterone, and total serum testosterone ratio. Indirect hormonal effects on aggression were also suggested by higher mean ratings of physical robustness obtained by the more violent Bushmen.

Investigating the possible causal effect of circulating plasma testosterone on aggressive behavior by male adolescents, Olweus, Mattsson, Schalling, and Low (1988) found that a high level of testosterone had a direct causal effect on provoked aggressive behavior. High testosterone levels also produce a higher level of impatience and irritability, which appears to increase aggressive and destructive behavior.

Working from a biosocial model, Udry (1990) investigated problem behavior exhibited by male adolescents. Results show a strong relationship between problem behavior and hormones. Indirect effects on problem behavior were also found with social and biological variables.

A recent review of the research related to the role of physiological processes in puberty led to this conclusion:

> Current research suggests that physiological processes during the early adolescence life phase contribute to interindividual variation in aggressive affect and sexual behavior and arousal (with findings stronger for boys than for girls), and possibly in the areas of depressive affect and mood lability as well. (Paikoff & Brooks-Gunn, 1990, p. 77)

Although the above studies point to a relationship between aggressive and problem behaviors and higher concentrations of testosterone, other studies produce different findings. For example, Bradford and McLean's (1984) study of adult male sexual offenders failed to find a relationship between plasma testosterone and high levels of violence in sexual offenses. Of note, a correlation between low plasma testosterone and depressive neurosis was found. A comparison of adult males who committed violent crimes (murder and assault) with nonviolent offenders failed to establish a significant relationship between blood hormone levels and aggressive behavior (Bain, Langevin, Dickey, & Ben-Aron, 1987).

But what of prenatal development? The production of testosterone and dihydrotestosterone by the male fetus is crucial to the development of both internal and external sex structures. The presence of testosterone, in combination with other variables, guides the male fetus toward developing genitalia consistent with his genetic gender. Does the presence of these hormones during embryonic development also predispose males toward heightened aggressive behavior? Perhaps a related fetal feedback loop similar to the hypothalamus-pituitary-gonad system for sexual development is also organized for the subsequent cultivation of physical activity and aggressive behavior. Again, evidence for this type of hormonal influence on embryonic development and subsequent behavior patterns is well documented in studies of lower animals. Perhaps a similar process occurs in humans.

Because it would be unethical to alter the normal production of hormones in human fetuses experimentally, most research has been limited to examining the effects of abnormal development of the fetal hormonal system, such as found in the adrenogenital syndrome (AGS), and the effect of various drugs administered during pregnancy. In 1972, Money and Ehrhardt published the results of their comparison of AGS females with females whose mothers had been prescribed progestins during pregnancy. They described the masculination of external genitalia of otherwise normal genetic (XX) females and the effect of this on the girls regarding their gender identity. Money and Ehrhardt also discovered a higher frequency of "tomboyism," such as a preference for play, games, and sports typically considered masculine, in the AGS and the progestin-exposed girls, when compared to medically normal females. Although the authors conclude that the higher frequency of tomboy behavior in the androgen-exposed girls is related to the masculinizing effects on the fetal brain, they do not find an increase in what is typically considered aggressive behavior, such as fighting.

Ehrhardt and Baker (1978) studied AGS in girls and boys and found that AGS girls show a lowered interest in doll play but a higher level of intense physical energy when compared to their non-AGS sisters. No difference between the AGS girls and their sisters was discovered regarding the frequency of aggressive behavior, such as initiating or participating in fighting. Although the AGS boys also show a higher level of intense physical energy than their unaffected brothers, no difference was found with regard to the initiation of aggressive behavior. It is interesting to note that the AGS boys also show more interest in nurturant behavior such as care-taking activities with infants than their nonexposed brothers.

The above studies suggest that female fetuses exposed to the male hormone testosterone subsequently develop masculine traits typically considered tomboyish, but not necessarily a heightened level of aggressive behavior during childhood. Males similarly exposed may also develop a heightened level of typically masculine behavior, but not necessarily an increase in aggression.

Some researchers have studied the effect of in utero exposure to "female" hormones, such as synthetic progesterones, on the subsequent development of aggressive behavior. The results have been equivocal. For example, Reinisch (1981) reports that boys and girls from progesterone-treated mothers scored higher on a test designed to measure the potential for aggression than their unexposed siblings, whereas other studies have found that progesterone-exposed boys and girls were less physically active than controls and showed no "feminizing" effects on personality questionnaires (Ehrhardt & Meyer-Bahlburg, 1979, 1981). Although Yalom, Green, and Fisk (1973) found that boys from estrogen-treated mothers appeared to be less active, aggressive, and athletically skilled, the results could have been confounded by the mothers' chronic illnesses.

Has the question about the relative importance of genes and raging hormones to the development of male sexual behavior been answered? From what we currently know about human sexual development, it is clear that genes and hormones both play important roles in this process. Genes certainly provide the foundation for the sexual structures plus the hormonal fuel to activate and develop them further. Genes may also provide the foundation for the development of sexual orientation. But there is no evidence that males are genetically destined to misuse their hormonal allotment to wreak sexual havoc on females and the world. Nor is there any solid evidence that an overallotment of sexual juices will consistently override other factors and turn males into savage sexual machines. Although the interplay between genes and hormones, especially testosterone, may provide the direction for sexual feelings and behavior, the actual guidance system may be a malleable contrivance constructed from complex biosocial prescriptions rather than a well-balanced hormonal gyroscope built from genetic blueprints. The role developmental variables play in this drama is discussed next.

# 3

# Developmental Milestones

## *Sexuality Throughout the Life Cycle*

Read any good text on human development and you will discover extensive information about prenatal physical development and responsiveness; neonates' responses to various kinds of stimulation; differences in nutritive sucking behavior in newborns; the development of smiling, laughing, locomotion, visual-motor coordination, visual perception, cognitive maturation, language, social attachment, emotional responses, and social relationships; and many other related topics. Much less is written about the normal childhood development of sexuality. As Masters, Johnson, and Kolodny (1988b) note, "childhood has been called 'the last frontier' in sex research because there is little reliable data about sexual behavior during this formative time" (p. 123).

Similar methodological problems exist in studying childhood sexuality as in examining other childhood developmental variables, but the study of children's sexual behavior is particularly daunting. Ask most parents for permission to observe their children at play to understand better the development of prosocial behavior, and the answer will most likely be yes. On the other hand, ask parents for permission to observe their children exploring each other's private parts to learn about the development of sexuality and the parents may respond by summoning the SWAT team. Attempts at legitimate research regarding the childhood development of sexuality are often defeated by the same sex-negative social attitudes that work toward repressing sexuality in general. Thus, most of what is known about the development of sexuality comes from anatomical and physiological studies, anthropological studies of so-called primitive societies where sexual repression is mostly absent, and retrospective studies of adults who are willing to share their memories about childhood sexual experiences. Even though some of the information is sketchy, controversial, and not very well formulated, a more explicit consideration of what is generally known about the developmental roots of human sexuality may prove rewarding in the quest to understand male heterosexuality.

## ❏ Early Sexual Stirrings

Parents are often surprised when they discover that their infant son is having erections. What many parents do not know is that physiological erectile responses are common biological reflexes in neonates of both genders. Although erections are more obvious because of the external sexual structures of boys than girls, swelling in the clitoris (erection) and vaginal lubrication occur in newborn girls. Baby boys and girls also show signs of sexual arousal while being breast-fed, and pelvic thrusting has been observed in human infants of both genders and other primates (see Bowlby, 1969; Lewis & Kagan, 1965; Martinson, 1981).

Masturbation is seen by some as sinful or morally reprehensible, but this form of self-stimulation is typical among primates. For humans, the behavior begins at age 6 to 12 months. Boys appear to engage in masturbatory activities at a somewhat earlier age than girls. Initially, both genders seem to rub their genitals against teddy bears, blankets, pillows, towels, or other soft objects. Some children become reluctant to surrender these comforting objects and may use them in more directed masturbatory actions by rubbing the item on the genitals. Later, once manual dexterity is better developed, fingers and hands are used to stimulate the genitals directly. Sometimes masturbation to orgasm occurs as early as 5 months for boys and 4 months for girls, but orgasmic responses are rare until about age 2 years (Reinisch, 1990). It appears that human infants have the basic sexual equipment in place at birth and begin to experiment with it early on, much the way experimentation occurs with the infant's other equipment such as fingers, toes, and noses.

Findings from cross-cultural studies suggest that societal attitudes and practices regarding sexuality significantly influence the child's normal expression of early sexuality. Ford and Beach (1951) found that in more sexually permissive cultures, in which masturbation is allowed by infants and young children, masturbatory activities seem to have a "normal" progression from occasional genital touching at very young ages to more purposeful manipulation of the genitals by age 6 to 8 years. In sexually repressive cultures, masturbation is discouraged and even punished by having children's genitals, especially the penis, thrashed with switches.

## ❏ Childhood Sexual Curiosity and Experimentation

Young children are very efficient learning machines capable of absorbing considerably more information than they can communicate. For example, child development experts point to the first 3 years of life as the most important in developing the foundation for culturally transmitted gender role stereotypes and subsequent adult attitudes and behavior. Yet these young children do not have the ability to communicate their newly formulated ideas about themselves and the world around them. Much of this early learning about prosocial behavior occurs through a child's natural curiosity about nearly everything, including other people's bodies. It is not uncommon for children of this age group to engage in activities such as kissing, touching, hugging, and exploring other children's genitals. These activities occur naturally and become important rehearsals for later prosocial and sexual behavior. During this period, children are not motivated for sexual gratification in an adult manner but simply include sexual play in their normal routine of learning about themselves and those about them.

At about age 3, boys and girls are quite aware of the feelings they have when they stimulate their genitals. Although they have not yet developed the cognitive structures to interpret their feelings and behavior as erotic or sexual, children at this age can and will explain how genital stimulation feels. Because they have not yet figured out that open talk about sex in our culture is discouraged, young children often embarrass adults with candid stories about self-stimulation.

Soon enough, however, many parents and other caretakers become vocal in their disapproval of genital experimentation and play.

Although most sexologists agree that it is important for parents to teach children that exhibiting or playing with one's genitals in public is not socially appropriate in our culture, negative messages may teach children that they are bad and that sexual pleasure may also be bad. Most sex educators also agree that negative messages and punishment will usually not stop children from future genital play, but such messages may be among some of the primary causes of later difficulties in establishing intimate or sexual relationships (Calderone & Johnson, 1989; Masters et al., 1988b; Reinisch, 1990). Many of the adult males I have treated for sexual dysfunctions or intimacy problems describe the development of strong guilt and shame responses associated with parental punishment of early childhood masturbation. Some of these males also learned to become very secretive about their sexual feelings and as adults encountered difficulties discussing sexual matters with partners or expressing their sexuality openly in appropriate ways. Thus, at an early age, children are faced with a serious conflict between what may be the normal development of sexuality and societal expectations. Society usually wins the battle by driving normal childhood sexual responses underground, but it loses the war by producing emotionally and sexually dysfunctional adult males.

It is also natural for young children to express curiosity about genitals other than their own. Most of us are familiar with the game often called "Show me yours and I will show you mine." Playing "doctor" is also a common childhood activity that leads naturally to examining the body, including the genitals of the "patient." These and similar interactive games are common between the ages of 6 and 10 years and become harmless opportunities for children to learn of sexual matters appropriate for their developmental levels. In the absence of useful information about sexual matters from caretakers, these childhood exploratory activities provide the first opportunities to learn that male and female bodies are different. Masters and colleagues (1988b) advise that "childhood sex play is not psychologically harmful under ordinary circumstances and is probably a valuable psychosocial experience in developmental terms" (p. 129).

By the age of about 4, most children begin to express curiosity about procreation. Children of both genders seem to have a natural interest in babies and their origin. American society has adopted a convenient way of avoiding discussions about sex and procreation by telling children delightful stories about the magical arrival of babies. One such story is the "bundle of joy dropped down the chimney by a stork" creation myth. Some parents are a bit more forthcoming and offer factual, but rather agrarian, explanations about a seed germinating in the mother's stomach. Others offer no explanation at all, preferring instead to tell the child not to ask those kinds of questions until he or she is older. Although many parents are uncomfortable with their child's interest in sex and babies, children who are curious about procreation are not expressing some evil motivation to copulate. They are only displaying the natural curiosity that almost all young children have about the wonders of the world around them.

By the time children are about 8 or 9 years old, they have developed an awareness of the erotic nature of sexual activities. Play activities with incidental genital contact and purely physiological arousal are gradually replaced with more purposeful sexual activities, including erotic arousal. Children in this age group often begin to develop feelings of "love" for peers, older children, and, sometimes, adults. Sexual fantasies may accompany the child's romantic interests, although most young children possess a rather limited repertoire of sexual notions.

Freud postulated that interest in sexual matters generally becomes latent during the late childhood period, but cross-cultural studies do not support this conceptualization. For example, Goldman and Goldman (1982) found that children from the ages of about 5 years to 15 years from Australia, North America, Britain, and Sweden actually show an increase in interest in sexual matters as a function of increasing age. The early Kinsey studies (Kinsey et al., 1948; Kinsey, Pomeroy, Martin, & Gebhard, 1953) also suggest that sexual experimentation does not decrease during the so-called latency period, with masturbation becoming the primary method of achieving orgasm regardless of gender. Mutual displays of genitals, with or without touching, seem common for preadolescents (Leitenberg, Greenwald, & Tarran, 1989). To explain the so-called latency period behavior displayed by some children, researchers suggest that children of this general age group may appear progressively less interested in sexual topics because they have learned adult rules about repressing sexual matters and simply become more secretive and private about their sexual thoughts, feelings, and behavior (see Gadpaille, 1974; Money, 1980). As one of my male patients said,

> As a kid, I soon learned not to ask my parents about sex. I was very careful about what I said and did and looked elsewhere for information. On the surface I looked just like most kids my age. Nobody knew what I was doing.

Behind the facade, this young man attempted to learn about sex by engaging in secret voyeuristic activities. By the time he was an adult, a dysfunctional pattern of sexual stimulation through clandestine voyeuristic behavior was in place. Although most latency-age children may become secretive about their sexual feelings and behavior without drifting into dysfunctional sexual activities, negative responses from society associated with childhood sexual behaviors circumvents most children's natural inclinations to explore their developing sexuality openly and to seek accurate information from any available resource.

Few displays of sexual behavior are more troublesome for parents than childhood same-sex exploratory activities. Because children are naturally curious about genitals—anybody's genitals—it is not unusual for young children to engage in sex play with either gender. For most preadolescents, same-sex contact occurs naturally within the same-gender social groups they tend to form during this period. Sexual activities tend to be single or infrequent episodes of touching each other's genitals or mutual masturbation. In spite of parental angst, same-sex experimentation may be more common than opposite-sex experimentation for young children and preadolescents and does not necessarily indicate that the child is developing a homosexual orientation (see Comfort, 1963; Hunt, 1974; Leitenberg et al., 1989; Masters et al., 1988b; Reinisch, 1990).

Another source of anxiety for parents is sex play among siblings. Finkelhor (1980) found that 13% of college students admitted to childhood experimentation with a sibling. Although this study revealed that most of the sibling sexual contact appeared similar to typical sexual exploratory behavior exhibited by curious nonsiblings, some sibling sexual behavior was clearly inappropriate. For example, 15% of females and 10% of males reported that their sexual experiences with a sibling were unwanted and involved some form of force or coercion by a sibling who was older by 5 years or more. In cases such as these, experimentation may have given way to exploitation. Even normal sexual responses among siblings may be transformed into inappropriate expressions under certain circumstances.

## ❏ Sexual Challenges of Adolescence

In spite of strong soiciocultural prohibitions against autoerotic practices, masturbation appears a strong developmental variable and soon becomes the primary sexual activity for most adolescents. Even culturally implanted feelings of guilt and shame do not deter most adolescents from masturbating; they just learn to feel bad about it and themselves. And young boys may feel bad frequently because they tend to masturbate two to three times a week, whereas girls may masturbate approximately once a month. The onset of "serious" masturbatory behavior typically occurs between 11 and 12 years, coinciding with the onset of puberty in most cases. Nearly 50% of boys and 25% of girls begin masturbating during early adolescence; by the time they enter adulthood nearly all males and close to 70% of females have masturbated to orgasm (see Coles & Stokes, 1985; Hass, 1979; Hunt, 1974).

When not masturbating, most adolescents appear to show a normative developmental pattern of heterosexual behavior. Hand holding and light embracing typically emerges with the first date and continues through several dates and while going steady. For about one half of adolescents, necking, deep kissing, and general body contact may begin on the first date but then quickly escalates after several dates and going steady. Few adolescents appear to engage in mutual masturbation or simulated intercourse on the first date, whereas nearly half or slightly more may engage in these behaviors after several dates or while going steady. Adolescent males tend to express a desire for more sexual intimacy on the first date than females. Teenagers who date before age 14 are more likely to become involved in steady relationships and engage in sexual intercourse before age 18 than teens who get a later start at dating. Younger teens also appear to be at a higher risk for pregnancy because they are less likely to use any form of effective contraception; an early introduction to sexual intercourse does not necessarily lead to unplanned pregnancies (see Berger 1988; McCabe & Collins, 1984; Miller, McCoy, & Olson, 1986; Thornton, 1990).

Using a longitudinal and cross-sectional design, Smith and Udry (1985) found a predictable progression of sexual activity leading from necking to sexual intercourse among white adolescents but a different and less predictable progression among black adolescents. Although a higher percentage of black male adolescents reported engaging in precoital sexual behavior (necking, petting, fondling genitalia) than reported by white male adolescents overall, the most striking difference was found in the significantly higher number of black (76%) than white (29%) male adolescents reporting having engaged in sexual intercourse. Similarly, 41% of black but only 11% of white adolescent females reported engaging in intercourse. To explain the apparent ethnic differences in adolescent sexual activities, Furstenberg, Morgan, Moore, and Peterson (1987) suggest that white and black adolescents embrace different norms regarding sexual behavior. Majors and Billson (1992) describe black males' early introduction to sexual behavior as a form of "cool pose" used to establish their male identity: "African-American males may consciously and unconsciously reinforce with their brothers the idea that sexual promiscuity and procreation are cool because they symbolize manhood" (p. 16).

The first experience of sexual intercourse dramatically marks the transition from mere childhood sexual curiosity and experimentation to participating in an advanced act of sexual intimacy with another person. And moving from virgin to nonvirgin status forever changes a person's approach to sexuality. Although much exploration and learning remains, one can never return to the innocent phase of childhood sexual play. Often, the first coital experience establishes feelings about sexuality that linger for years. For some, feelings of uncertainty, guilt, and shame, as well as concern about possible negative consequences, follow their first sexual intercourse. For others, bells and whistles go off and they think they have discovered the greatest thing on earth. Obviously these two groups will most likely engage in future sexual activities with different attitudes about themselves and sexual behavior.

Feelings about first sexual experiences often reflect gender differences, with males typically reporting more readiness for sex as well as less ambivalence about and more satisfaction with their first sexual intercourse than females (Coles & Stokes, 1985; Darling & Davidson, 1986; Michael et al., 1994). Even so, many males are disappointed with their first sexual intercourse experience due to unrealistic expectations or some form of sexual dysfunction. As one of my male patients reported, "I expected this great experience, but it was over before I knew it. I was so excited that I was going to finally do it that I came right away. I was so embarrassed." Other males relate stories of being so anxious that they were unable to get an erection:

I had been trying to get laid for years. When my girlfriend
finally agreed to let me go all the way, I couldn't get it up.
Here she was ready to go and all I could do was apologize
for a limp dick. I thought I never would be able to have sex
with anyone.

Some males describe losing their virginity with the help of a
sexually skilled female:

She was experienced and I wasn't. She knew what she was
doing and guided me. One of the things she did that helped
a lot was slowing me down. I was so excited about getting
laid for the first time that I was rushing things. She showed
me how to go slower and enjoy each step. I still came really
fast, but she told me not to worry about it since it was my
first time. We had a lot of great sexual experiences after that.
I was very sad when she moved to another city.

Unlike many developmental variables, such as walking and
talking, it is difficult to determine the age at which most children can
accomplish the developmental task of sexual intercourse. Precoital
sexual behaviors occur early in childhood and seem to escalate to
sexual intercourse at varying ages depending on sociocultural factors. Biologically, humans can engage in sexual intercourse at very
early ages, but they are usually prevented from doing so by societal
prohibitions.

As societal views of sexuality change, so does sexual behavior.
For example, the incidence of premarital intercourse has increased
and the age of first sexual intercourse has decreased since the 1940s.
This is especially the case with females and may reflect a weakening
of the traditional double standard regarding acceptable sexual behavior by males versus females. The increase in sexual behavior by
females may also reflect a trend toward more egalitarian attitudes
toward women, in general, since World War II. Kinsey and his
associates (1948, 1953) found that the double standard was alive and
well in the 1940s and early 1950s, when more than 75% of single
males but less than 25% of single females reported that they had
engaged in sexual intercourse by the age of 20 years. A dramatic
increase in premarital sexual intercourse by females, nearly equaling
the male rate, was found about two decades later, and the effect of

**Table 3.1** Trend in Premarital Sexual Intercourse (1940-1990)

| Source | Period | Age | Percentage | |
|---|---|---|---|---|
| | | | Males | Females |
| Kinsey et al. (1948) | 1940s and 1950s | By 20 years | 77 | 20 |
| Kinsey et al. (1953) | 1940s and 1950s | By 25 years | 83 | 33 |
| Hunt (1974) | 1970s | 18-24 years | 95 | 81 |
| Zeman (1990) (Also see Kantner & Zelnick, 1972; Sorensen, 1973; Zelnick & Kantner, 1980) | 1970s | By 19 years | 78 | 65 |
| Zeman (1990) (Also see Miller, Christopherson, & King, 1993; Pratt & Eglash, 1990; Sonenstein, Pleck, & Ku, 1989, 1990) | 1980s | By 19 years | 86 | 78 |

these more liberated ideas about sexual behavior for females continued into the 1980s and early 1990s. The feminist initiative over the past three decades apparently has been influential in changing the way our society views women and their sexuality. And different ideas about female sexuality certainly influence male sexuality. Having more females available for sexual contact is a long-standing male fantasy. Table 3.1 summarizes the changing trend in premarital sexual intercourse from the 1940s to the 1990s.

Related to an overall increase in the number of adolescents who engage in premarital sexual activities, regardless of gender, is a decline in the age of first intercourse. Although Kinsey and his associates (1953) found that less than about 10% of white females had engaged in coitus by the age of 16, current estimates suggest that nearly 40% of unmarried females have their first coital experience by the time they are "sweet 16." Although adolescent females may be engaging in their first sexual intercourse at younger ages than a few decades ago, less dramatic changes over time are found in the age of first coital experiences by adolescent males. Kinsey et al. (1948) found that 39% of their sample of adult males reported having engaged in

**Table 3.2** Trend in First Sexual Intercourse by Age 15-16

|                              |                 | Approximate Percentage | |
| Source                       | Time Period     | Males   | Females |
| ---------------------------- | --------------- | ------- | ------- |
| Kinsey et al. (1948);        |                 |         |         |
| Kinsey et al. (1953)         | 1940s and 1950s | 35-45   | 5-10    |
| Elliot & Morse (1989);       |                 |         |         |
| Sonnenstein et al.           |                 |         |         |
| (1989); Zeman (1990)         | 1970s and 1980s | 25-50   | 20-35   |

their first intercourse by age 15. More recent studies of teenage sexual behavior suggest a similar rate of about 25% to 30% of adolescent males reaching nonvirgin status by age 15 years. Table 3.2 summarizes trends in age of first sexual intercourse.

Although the average age in the United States for first coital behavior seems to be between 15 and 17 years (Alan Guttmacher Institute, 1991; Reinisch, 1990), strong ethnic differences in the age of first sexual intercourse are found. Overall, black males report experiencing their first sexual intercourse by age 13, whereas Hispanic and white males report that their first sexual intercourse occurred by age 15 (see Brooks-Gunn & Furstenberg, 1989; Furstenberg et al., 1987; Mott & Haurin, 1988; Sonenstein, Pleck, & Ku, 1991; Wyatt, Peters, & Guthrie, 1988a, 1988b; Zelnik & Shah, 1983). In addition, Padilla and O'Grady (1987) found that male and female Hispanic undergraduates report fewer sexual experiences, overall, than their white classmates.

Recent studies not only point to a general decline in the age at first intercourse, but associate the lowered age of reaching nonvirgin status with the number of lifetime sexual partners. For example, Sonenstein et al. (1991) found that 19-year-old black males report an average of 11 lifetime heterosexual partners compared to an average of 2 or 3 sexual partners for 15-year-old Hispanic and white males. Most of this difference is attributed to the 2-year head start by black males over white and Hispanic males in reaching nonvirgin status. Pratt and Eglash (1990) also found a strong association between early sexual intercourse by females and number of lifetime partners. They found that 20% of females who reached nonvirgin status before age 18 reported an average of 10 or more lifetime heterosexual partners, whereas only 5% of females who had their first sexual intercourse by at least age 20 years reported a similar number of sexual partners. It makes sense that an early start could produce more opportunities for sexual partners over time. The early start could also represent either a higher interest in sexual behavior in general or lowered cultural standards regarding premarital sexual behavior.

Does an increase in sexual behavior in adolescence increase the probability of premature parenthood? From the early 1970s to the mid-1980s, the overall rate of births to teenagers declined, but it rose again between 1986 and 1988, reaching its highest level for 15- to 17-year-olds since 1977 (see Alan Guttmacher Institute, 1991; Moore, Wenk, Hofferth, & Haves, 1987). It appears that, in the United States, more children are becoming pregnant at younger ages than ever before (Freeman & Rickels, 1993). Ethnic differences in teenage pregnancy are also present. For example, Matney and Johnson (1993) found that teenage pregnancy rates were twice as high among blacks (163 per 1,000) as among whites (83 per 1,000).

Although studies suggest that about 13% of all women giving birth are teenagers (National Center for Health Statistics, 1988), less is known about the fathers. Fathers are often unknown, absent, or unreliable reporters of their fertility histories (Zabin & Hayward, 1983). One study, based on birth certificates, suggests that about 14% of all fathers are under the age of 20 years, with fathers generally older than the mothers. White fathers are, on average, 4 years older than mothers, whereas black fathers tend to be only 2 to 3 years older than mothers (Hardy & Zabin, 1991). Some studies of young black males suggest that impregnating women and producing children is an effort to compensate for the perceived failure to achieve manhood through traditional economic and family channels. For these black males, fatherhood is a statement of manhood even though they may never participate in rearing their progeny (see Liebow, 1967; Majors & Billson, 1992).

The problem of early childbearing seems to be increasing overall, with teenagers more likely than older age groups to use no method of contraception (Alan Guttmacher Institute, 1991). Recent studies of male adolescent sexual behavior suggest that ineffective contraceptive use decreased, however, whereas effective contraceptive use increased considerably during the last decade. One exception is black teenagers at first coitus. For all groups of teenagers, an increase in the use of the condom has been substantial and has generally replaced nonuse, rather than the pill or other medical contraceptive devices (Sonenstein et al., 1989).

The human organism is apparently well designed and suited for sexual behavior, either for pleasure or for procreation, but some adolescents choose to delay engaging in sexual intercourse and some select a nonsexual lifestyle altogether. Most young persons in the United States who abstain from sexual behavior do so due to strong religious beliefs, moral reasons, or concerns about unwanted parenthood and sexually transmitted diseases. Embracing more traditional values, many young men and women elect abstinence from sexual intercourse until they marry, planning then to establish a satisfactory sexual relationship with a spouse. Others plan to forgo sexual behavior in favor of a life within religious organizations that prohibit sexual activities by their devotees. Masters et al. (1988b) describe a group of sexually experienced teenagers who decided to revert to sexual abstinence following dissatisfying sexual relationships. Most of these "unhappy nonvirgins" plan to wait until they are older or until they meet someone better suited for their romantic and sexual styles before resuming sexual activities.

## ❏ Sexual Challenges of Young Adulthood

Early adulthood is a period of time immediately following adolescence (at about age 20) and ending with the onset of middle adulthood (at about age 40). This developmental phase is marked not so much by any dramatic physiological or anatomical changes as by the playing out of the sexual information, attitudes, and behavior learned from birth. Our culture expects people at about age 20 to begin putting aside childhood and adolescent lifestyles, often reflected by playfulness and irresponsibility, and to become more "adult." This societal call for maturity often requires young people to select an occupation and a marital partner. It is also generally expected that sexual behavior and procreation will occur only within the confines of a marital relationship. During the next 20 years or so, the young adult is expected to behave responsibly and be a devoted member of his or her newly established family. Although this is the ideal, the reality is quite different.

As we have seen, many young people do not subscribe to the traditional values of chastity until marriage. Many enter early adulthood sexually experienced and with children by at least one nonmarital partner. Some choose to continue their adolescent sexual lifestyle by remaining single and engaging in sexual activities with additional partners. Others may choose to remain single but establish a live-in relationship with someone without the formality of a marriage ceremony. Also during this period, first marriages are terminated and the divorced person is thrust back into the world of the singles. Each of these events—marriage, singlehood, parenthood, and divorce—presents developmental challenges. As such, a look at their effect on the development of adult male sexuality is warranted.

### ■ Sex and the Single Life

According to the U.S. Bureau of Census (1990), the percentage of single men between the ages of 20 and 24 increased by about one quarter (55% to 79%) during the period of 1970 to 1988, whereas the percentage of single females in the same age range and time period nearly doubled (36% to 61%). Clearly, the trend for young adults is to remain single or at least to postpone marriage until they are older. The number of never-married singles between the ages of 25 to 29 nearly doubled over the past two decades, yet the majority of males (67%) and females (70%) in this age group are married.

Many reasons may account for the increased preference to remain single. Some individuals see adult singlehood as an extended opportunity to engage in as many sexual experiences as possible. These individuals seem to have little regard for developing quality sexual relationships and vigorously pursue variety and frequency instead. It would not be uncommon for these individuals to have numerous sexual partners before they reach the age of 30 years. Males in this category are often viewed with envy by other men because of their sexual conquests. Females are judged less favorably and are often called promiscuous, sluts, loose women, and other similarly negative terms. Masters et al. (1988b) label these industrious sexual people *experimenters.*

Developmentally, moving from virgin to nonvirgin status is an important stage for becoming a man. The next step in the developmental chain is to affirm manhood by engaging in frequent sexual conquests. If one sexual conquest makes you a man, many will make you a superman. Sexually successful men are revered by most other men. Vicarious pleasure and envy abound when Mr. Stud tells his tales of sexual triumphs. Although the sexual champion seldom reveals the less glamorous and less exciting side of his escapades, all is not what it seems in the land of the singles. For example, many singles complain of loneliness and the absence of a stable, emotionally supportive relationship with one person (see Kammeyer, 1990; Simenauer & Carroll, 1982).

Sometimes it appears that males cannot decide what kind of relationship they prefer. Men in stable relationships often hunger for more sexual freedom, whereas many experimenters secretly dream of establishing a meaningful relationship with one person. Many single men in therapy complain of not being able to find a quality woman with whom to establish a satisfying relationship. Some of these men become so frustrated in their quest that they stop looking and begin to date infrequently. Others become so desperate in their search that they expend most of their energy rummaging through all available resources for the elusive Ms. Right. Sorting through these conflicts is a difficult task for many young single adult males, but in spite of the unresolved conflicts, many singles report being satisfied with their chosen lifestyle (Austrom & Hanel, 1985).

Some singles prefer the swinging singles lifestyle. Others remain single but establish a sexual relationship with one person at a time. This type of serial monogamy appears common and does not always involve cohabitation. For singles who chose to live separately, "dates" often involve overnights or weekends at one or the other's home. During other times, each partner pursues his or her individual lifestyle, but sexual faithfulness is expected by each partner. This type of arrangement eventually leads to cohabitation and even marriage for some couples.

### ■ Sex and Cohabitation

Perhaps the greatest trend in sexual relationships for young adults in the United States today is cohabitation. The U.S. Bureau of Census (1990) reports an 80% increase in cohabiting couples from 1980 to 1990. Young adults under the age of 35 appear to represent the majority of cohabiting couples (60% males and 70% females). Approximately 50% of cohabitors have never been married (55% males and 70% females), whereas about a third report being divorced. Reasons for cohabiting are various. Macklin (1978) points to changing ideas about sexuality, relationships, and the function of marriage; an increase in the number of divorces; improved contraception; and the influence of the woman's movement as some of the more influential factors leading to more young people choosing cohabitation rather than a traditional lifestyle. Renzetti and Curran (1989) found that many couples prefer not to have the legal restrictions of marriage but desire the stability of an intimate relationship with one person. Studies also show that persons who choose to cohabit instead of marry tend to express more personal independence, are less committed to traditional values associated with relationship roles and marriage, and are less religious than those who do not select cohabitation (see Bennett, Blanc, & Bloom, 1988; Bernard, 1982; Blumstein & Schwartz, 1983; Kammeyer, 1990).

Although increasing numbers of couples are choosing cohabitation as an alternative to marriage, the relationship between the cohabitors quickly begins to mirror the early stages of marital relationships. Couples who cohabit often experience the same type of "spill-over" effects of problems in nonsexual areas into their sexual relationships as found in marriages. That is, conflicts in areas not related to sexual matters often create stress and problems in the cohabitors' bed much the same as found in the nuptial chamber. Also found is a tendency for the frequency of sexual activities to decline over time, a phenomenon common with most married couples. This decrease appears to occur in spite of a tendency for cohabitants to have a slightly higher average frequency of sexual relations (8 per month) than married couples (7 per month). Most cohabitants seem to prefer a monogamous relationship, as automatically expected within traditional marriages, but about 30% engage in sexual activities outside of the relationship (see Blumstein & Schwartz, 1983; Cherlin, 1981; Michael et al., 1994).

So, do cohabitors find "marital bliss" in their unconventional lifestyles? The answer is yes and no. Nearly 80% of cohabitants describe their relationships in positive terms and seem satisfied with the arrangement (Risman et al., 1981). About 30% of cohabitants appear so satisfied with their relationships that they choose to marry (Clayton & Voss, 1977). On the other hand, Yamaguchi and Kandel (1985) found that most cohabitants eventually become dissatisfied and terminate their relationships within about 3 years.

Many people choose cohabitation as a way of finding out if they can establish a stable and satisfying relationship with their partners prior to making the societal and legal commitments associated with marriage. Although the premarital opportunities to gain knowledge about the relationship and to resolve problems prior to marriage would seem to be an advantage over establishing a marital relationship without having a dry run first, this advantage may actually become a disadvantage. Nearly twice the number of cohabitants who subsequently marry divorce within a 10-year period than married couples who did not live together before marriage (Riche, 1988). A common theme presented by couples who enter therapy after a year or two of marriage, following a period of cohabitation, is

> It seems that once the marriage contract was official we began to expect each other to perform the roles of husband and wife rather than two people just wanting to love and live with each other. We didn't think that would happen to us.

### ■ Sex and Marriage

Regardless of the couple's premarital history, marriage in our culture poses a different set of expectations regarding interpersonal relationships, sexual behavior, and family responsibilities than found in any other type of relationship. When a person decides to marry, he or she is essentially embracing some of the more traditional aspects of Western thought regarding religious beliefs, moral dogma, and gender roles. Today, few women will promise "to love, honor, and obey," as commanded by ancient marriage vows, but society still tends to survey the institution of marriage within rather traditional boundaries.

Many traditionalists fear that marriage will soon become obsolete and will be replaced by a number of less satisfactory interpersonal and sexual relationship lifestyles. They fear that this erosion of the foundation of stable family life and the weakening of regulations associated with sexual behavior will ultimately result in the collapse of Western culture as we know it. Although it is true that many young adults choose alternative lifestyles, marriage remains the primary lifestyle in the United States. The U.S. Bureau of Census (1990) found that about 5 million people exchange marriage vows each year and about 60% of adult females and 65% of adult males are living with their partners. In addition, Kammeyer (1990) found that before the age of 40, 93% of females and 90% of males in the United States attempt marriage at least once. Marriage is also similarly popular in most other societies (Ember & Ember, 1990).

Western culture continues to portray marriage as the ultimate relationship between man and woman. It is presented as a place for spiritual and personal growth, as well as approved sexual behavior. Familiar are fairy tales with the ubiquitous "and they lived happily ever after" endings. But do marital couples live in marital bliss forever? Is it possible to maintain the sexual excitement typically found at the beginning of most marriages? Did the so-called sexual revolution result in more sexual freedom for marital couples? How about pregnancy and parenthood? What of the effect of trying to survive financially in an economy that essentially requires both partners to work? Perhaps eternal marital bliss is more of a dream than a reality:

> As the novelty of early marital bliss dissolves in the process of learning another's quirks and habits, as early dreams of conquering the world give way to a more practical focus on details of everyday life, sex is likely to become less exciting and sometimes less gratifying for one or both partners. (Masters et al., 1988b, pp. 164-165)

For the young adult male who still places great value on sexual activities, marriage may pose quite a challenge to his sexuality. Many men form expectations that sexual activities will increase and be maintained at a high frequency after marriage. After all, most of the sanctions against sexual behavior are removed once both partners take marriage vows. But the reality is that the frequency of marital sexual intercourse tends to decrease over time. For example, Kinsey et al. (1948, 1953) found that the median weekly frequency of marital coitus was 2.45 for young married couples (16 to 25 years of age) compared to a median of .50 for older couples (56 to 60 years of age). A survey conducted by *Playboy* (Hunt, 1974) found a similar decrease from a median weekly frequency of marital coitus of 3.25 for 18- to 24-year-old couples to a median of 1.00 for couples 55 years and older. This age-related decrease in marital sexual activities occurs in spite of an increase in marital coitus, overall, through all age groups when compared to the Kinsey data. Michael et al. (1994) found that the average frequency of sexual activities in America for young males age 18 to 39 is 7 to 8 times per month. Similarly, young women age 18 to 39 report an average frequency from 6 to 8 times per month. Middle-age men and women (40 to 49 years) report a slight decrease in sex to an average frequency of 6 times a month, whereas older men and women (50 to 59 years) report another decease to 5 times and 4 times a month, respectively. In addition, Blumstein and Schwartz (1990) report that the frequency of sexual behavior tends to decline as a function of the length of time of the marriage regardless of the couple's age. It appears to be a good news, bad news situation. The good news is that marital couples likely tend to engage in a higher frequency of sexual activities now than they did four decades ago. The bad news is that the frequency of marital coitus typically declines with each wedding anniversary and birthday. So much for living happily ever after, if your happiness is yoked to sexual behavior.

But there is more to happiness and sexual satisfaction than just raw sex, even though many males have difficulties getting beyond the frequency criterion. For example, females indicate that their sexual pleasure is often linked to the level of emotional closeness they feel with their spouse and the opportunity to discuss sexual matters openly with their husbands (Banmen & Vogel, 1985; Hunt, 1974; Tavris & Sadd, 1977).

One of the major provisions of the marital contract is fidelity. Once married, it is expected that both partners will engage in sexual behavior only within the marital relationship. To do otherwise is a serious breach of the basic tenets of marriage. Although it is difficult to secure reliable estimates of the number of spouses who have had extramarital sexual experiences, available figures from Kinsey et al. (1948, 1953), Hunt (1974), and Painter (1987) suggest that 13% to 50% of husbands and 7% to 25% of wives admit to extramarital sexual activities. Reinisch, Sanders, and Ziemba-Davis (1988) propose an overall estimate of 37% for husbands and 29% for wives. This suggests that nearly a third of marital partners "cheat" on their spouses at some point in their marriages. Michael et al. (1994) dispute this portrayal of rampant infidelity in American society, however: "More than 80% of women and 65 to 85% of men of every age group report that they had no partners other than their spouse while they were married" (p. 105).

A closer look at the survey results regarding extramarital sex by age indicates that incidence rates have remained fairly stable over time except for young wives under the age of 25. For this group, the incidence rate increased from about 8% in the 1940s and 1950s to about 24% in the 1960s and 1970s. It appears that wives in this age category are gradually approaching the incidence rate of 32% reported by under-25-year-old husbands (see Hunt, 1974; Kinsey et al., 1953).

Many reasons are given for the appearance of extramarital sex. Among the top 10 are a need for variety, hostility toward the other spouse, curiosity, a need for more personal intimacy, personal growth and self-esteem issues, less of a commitment to the institution of marriage, and overall marital dissatisfaction (see Atwater, 1982; Beach, Jouriles, & O'Leary, 1985; Thompson, 1983).

Although our society has become somewhat more liberated about sexual matters through the influences of the feminist movement and the so-called sexual revolution of the 1960s, the double standard regarding extramarital sex for males remains strong. It is almost expected in our society that a male will be unfaithful to his spouse at some point in the marriage. We are not alone. Ember and Ember (1990) found that a double standard regarding extramarital sex is found in many other cultures throughout the world. That is, about 54% of global cultures appear to permit husbands to engage in extramarital sexual activities, but only 11% tolerate similar sexual behavior by wives. For a wife in our society, sexual infidelity is neither condoned nor expected, although some liberalization of these ideas has occurred over the past two decades or so.

Many males are faced with the challenge of resisting the temptation of experimenting outside the marriage at the risk of being seen by other males as weak and under the control of women. Males often encourage other males to "play around a little" if the opportunity presents itself. In many ways, this can be seen as a continuation of the adolescent fantasy about sex and the unfortunate fusion of sexual performance with the masculine self-image. To remain faithful to one woman is consistent with the main culture but is counter to the teachings of the masculine subculture. The developmental task for the young male adult is to resolve these issues satisfactorily so that his sexuality becomes comfortable and satisfying for him without seriously jeopardizing his standing within either the main culture or the masculine subculture. This is no easy task; many males do not negotiate this step very well. Sometimes males risk a loving and sexually satisfying relationship at home for the thrill of a one-night stand with a lovely young woman. Although a man's standing in the male subculture may be enhanced by this act, family members operating within the parameters of the main culture may reject him if his escapade becomes known. On the other hand, his standing in the male subculture may be diminished by his refusal to engage in sexual activities with a willing and attractive sexual partner.

When the frequency of sexual behavior begins its apparently inevitable decline in marriage, many males respond with worry that they are losing their sexual attractiveness. For some males, this is tantamount to the beginning of a systematic dismantling of his positive self-image. To overcome this perceived erosion of manhood, many males begin to put pressure on their wives for additional sexual encounters. Remember, most males believe that if some sex is good, more is better. Less is a disaster. If a wife responds to her husband's badgering about sex in a positive manner, the husband may be temporarily reassured until the next sexual crisis. A less-than-positive response from a wife is confirmation of the husband's worst fears: He has gone from sexual stud to sexual dud. It is at this stage of development that young adult males appear most vulnerable to engaging in behavior that is either designed to mask the pain of the perceived loss of manhood, such as substance abuse, or provides reassurance that his manhood is still intact, such as extramarital sexual activities. As I will discuss later, the risk for this type of crisis increases for men during middle adulthood.

Given the difficult developmental tasks posed by the young adulthood stage and the sorry lack of preparation for these tasks during childhood and adolescence, it is not surprising that many couples are unable to resolve the problems presented by marriage and turn to the divorce court for relief. The divorce rate in the United States increased dramatically from 1960 (about 2.25 per 1,000 population) to 1980 (about 5.20 per 1,000 population) before leveling off (Kemper, 1983; Norton & Moorman, 1987). In 1987, the U.S. Bureau of Census reported that about 50% of marriages were terminated by divorce, with the black divorce rate (220 per 1,000 marriages) double that of whites (107 per 1,000 marriages). Fisher (1987) found that about half of the divorces in the United States occur within the first 7 years of marriage. Perhaps this provides some credibility to the common notion, often called "the 7-year itch," that couples experience a need for novelty after the first several years of marital captivity.

■ Sex and Pregnancy

It is during the period of young adulthood that pregnancy and parenthood are most likely. Sexual activities both produce and are affected by pregnancy, although the effect is not uniform among couples or individuals. If the couple planned for the pregnancy and is prepared both emotionally and economically for the event, their responses tend to be significantly more positive than couples faced with an unplanned or unwanted pregnancy. Significant stress between partners often occurs when one partner of the pregnancy is joyous and the other is unhappy. These and other variables associated with pregnancy can have an influence on the couple's sexual relationship.

Although many males are attempting to learn more about female bodies than just where to stick their penis, most still show a better understanding of the internal combustion engine than about pregnancy and fetal development. A common comment by males to their pregnant partner is, "Well, I did my part. The rest is up to you." Historically, males have shown little interest in the internal workings of pregnancy. Many appear confused about the role of sexual behavior during pregnancy and jokingly express concern that they may be deprived of sexual activities throughout the 9-month gestation period. Others appear misguided and fear that sexual intercourse poses some unknown danger to their partner or the fetus.

Unless the pregnant woman has a history of miscarriages or is experiencing other health problems, sexual coitus poses little threat to her health or the health of the fetus. Most health care professionals recommend, however, that coitus or any other sexual activity that produces orgasms should be avoided by women with a history of miscarriages or women who experience symptoms of vaginal or uterine bleeding during pregnancy, because uterine contractions may exacerbate the condition. Some women express concern that orgasms in the last trimester may trigger premature labor, but this risk remains statistically very small. Masters et al. (1988b) point out that orgasmic responses by pregnant women appear positively associated with lower incidence rates of premature births. On the other hand, Herbst (1979) warns that women at risk for miscarriage or premature delivery should abstain from sexual intercourse during the final trimester of pregnancy.

During the first trimester, some pregnant women experience a decline in sexual interest due primarily to fatigue, nausea, and breast tenderness. Although some males may interpret their pregnant partner's lack of interest in sexual activities as a personal rejection or a harbinger of things to come, most appear sympathetic and patient.

Males who perceive rejection may voice their concern that their partner is malingering to avoid sexual contact. Comments such as "Now that she has what she wants, she's not interested in sex anymore" are all too common among these hurt and "rejected" males. Some males find a fatigued, touchy, and physically ill woman a less-than-desirable sexual partner and engage in some personal rejection of their own. In spite of the initial decline in sexual interest by many pregnant women and the negative responses by some men, the frequency of sexual intercourse usually remains fairly close to the couple's prepregnancy level during the first trimester.

As the couple moves into the second trimester of pregnancy, a majority of pregnant women experience a resurgence of sexual desire and heightened physical responses. Some males become confused by this sudden shift from low to high gear; most welcome the change. As many males say, "I don't know what got into her, but I'm going to enjoy it while I can." The second trimester is also a time when many of the males who have been feeling personally rejected and sexually deprived can begin to calm down and feel more secure.

During the third trimester, the frequency of sexual intercourse may decrease sharply, especially during the 8th and 9th months. This is a time when many pregnant women worry that their physical appearance is unattractive to their partner, although most men deny that the extra weight, bulging stomach, awkward posture, and other physical changes brought on by pregnancy have any negative effect at all. These men explain their seeming lack of interest in sexual intercourse as a concern that sexual activity will be injurious to the fetus, their partner, or both. Privately, however, many males are more honest with their feelings and openly express distaste for a body that is clearly counter to the slim and petite image idealized by Western society.

Although many expectant fathers understand that pregnancy means significant changes will occur in their partner's body, few appear prepared for their own responses to the transformation. It is unfortunate, but some males find their pregnant partner so unattractive that they become stressed by thoughts of sexual contact with her. As one troubled husband explained, "She was so little and sexy before she got pregnant. Now, I can hardly stand to touch her, even though I still love her very much and am excited about the baby." Some males even find it necessary to avoid sexual activities with their undesirable pregnant partner and, instead, seek out sexual pleasure with others.

■ **Sex After Birth**

Many men wonder how long they should wait following child-birth before resuming sexual activities with their partner. The answer to this question varies depending on a number of factors, not the least of which is the emotional and physical condition of the new mother. During the immediate postpartum period, most women express a sense of happiness. Many males join in and share their partner's joy. But it is not uncommon for women to experience mood changes, including feelings of irritability, sadness, and depression, within a few days or weeks after the birth of the baby (Harding, 1989; Samuels & Samuels, 1986). The postpartum period, marked by the so-called baby blues or maternity blues, is relatively brief for most mothers and may be resolved within a few days. For others, the depressive feelings intensify and persist for weeks or months. The more serious type of mood changes and depression following childbirth is gener-ally called *postpartum depression*.

Although much less research has been done on fathers who experience postpartum depression, "paternity blues" appears to ex-ist. For example, Zaslow et al. (1985) found that some new fathers experience mood changes, including depression, during the postpar-tum period. These seemingly troubled fathers tend to withdraw from the parenting role and show a low level of interaction with their babies.

During birth, the baby has to pass through the mother's birth canal on his or her journey to freedom. Sometimes the passageway is quite narrow and some tissue tearing occurs in the mother. A surgical incision, called an episiotomy, may be performed in the area between the vulva and the anus to minimize the possibility of serious random tearing. Even without major tissue damage, most women experience physiological discomfort and soreness for a few weeks following giving birth. Some episiotomies may require additional time to heal properly. Also, a reddish vaginal discharge called lochia is normal and may occur for about 4 weeks postpartum. Most women recover sufficiently from the physiological effects of childbirth to resume coitus by about the 6th week postpartum. Other types of noncoital sexual activities can usually be resumed earlier.

For some women who elect to breast-feed their babies, an overall decrease in vaginal lubrication occurs. This condition of dryness may cause irritation and discomfort when vaginal intercourse is attempted.

Many males, especially first-time fathers, are unaware of this condition and respond as though the lack of vaginal lubrication is a personal rejection or their partner will no longer be interested in sexual activity now that she has given birth. Remember, many males perceive a decrease in sexual activity, regardless of the reason, as a sign that something is amiss with themselves or the sexual relationship. The loss of lubrication is a temporary condition that abates after the mother stops breast-feeding. It is easily remedied during the breast-feeding period by the use of a variety of commercially available lubricants.

Typically, new parents show a decrease in sexual activity in the several months following the birth of a child. It is during this period that both partners, assuming that the parents are married or live together, are faced with the increased tasks associated with parenthood. Although many ill-prepared couples do not quite understand how labor-intensive child care can be, most soon learn that caring for a child seldom resembles the "little bundle of joy" ideas cultivated by mainstream society.

In America, the majority of infant care still remains the responsibility of the female, even though she may also be employed outside the home. With or without outside employment, the new mother is required to expend considerable amounts of time and energy in care-taking chores, unless the couple has the resources to secure relief. Time constraints and fatigue figure prominently in the woman's resumption of interest in sexual activities. Although interested in sexual activities, many women report, "I simply don't have the energy to participate." Males who assist in the care-taking chores may also find themselves more fatigued than usual and less interested in pursuing sexual contact. Some more liberated males comment, "I never realized how much work a baby was until I took over for a whole day to give my wife a break. I now know why she is so tired all the time." Many couples may struggle with finding a place for sex among the increased tasks associated with a new baby, but couples whose sexual adjustment was good prior to pregnancy normally find a way to effect a reasonably satisfying sexual relationship following childbirth. Even so, some couples never return to the frequency and sexual intensity displayed during their preparenthood period. As one young father lamented,

> Our sexual life was great before we had children. After the
> first one we just couldn't seem to find the time and energy

to keep it up. Her level of desire seemed to decrease more than mine, but I became tired and less interested, too.

## ❑ Sexual Challenges of the Middle Years

It happens to all of us, and it happens sooner than we realize. We become middle aged (about 40 to 60 years). The infant son or daughter we were so proud of is now an adolescent or young adult attempting to deal with his or her own sexuality. We have struggled with the rigors of becoming a productive member of our society. Many pursued personal dreams and were successful. Others were not so fortunate. We worry about our bodies and wonder what happened to our youthful appearance. To stay the ravages of time, many have been seduced by a plethora of "youth-enhancing" nutritional, physiological, and medical notions. Others have simply succumbed to the inevitable loss of youth and have attempted to do so gracefully. Now we are 40-something, and the end of our sexual life must be near.

During this period, many males become acutely aware of any signs of erosion in the primary indicators of manhood: sexual attractiveness and sexual performance. A man's once magnificent body of steel is gradually being transformed into a body of flab. Young women seldom notice him anymore, even when he drives around town with the top down on his expensive and flashy sports car. Worse yet, when they do notice him, they call him "sir." Whatever happened to those hordes of giggling teenage girls so eager to pile into his '57 Chevy and challenge the seductive powers of Mr. Stud? Sucking it in becomes increasingly more difficult because there is more to suck in than the day before. It is, after all, quite a chore to suck in something that has managed to wriggle free from the safety of a tightly cinched belt and is now hanging precariously close to the floor. If physical attractiveness is no longer there, sexual attractiveness is surely lost as well.

Although some changes in sexual performance do occur during this period, most males remain without significant alterations in their ability to engage in satisfying sexual activities. Too often, however, males listen to the popular myths, promulgated by a misinformed society, about failing sexuality in males over the age of 40. Once a male becomes overly concerned about his sexual prowess, a self-fulfilling prophecy usually occurs. Yes, it is true that males in their 40s and 50s may require more stimulation than when they were teenagers to reach physiological sexual arousal, but this task is far from the endless quest without gain that most men fear. And, yes, it is also true that most older males require a longer period of recovery following orgasm than younger males before being able to engage in penis-related sexual activities. But it does not take "forever" to recover, as some quip. Other than these relatively innocuous changes in the middle-aged males' sexual prowess, most 40- and 50-something males show little, if any, loss of sexual abilities.

In addition to the concern that most middle-aged males display about their ability to attract sexual partners and to perform adequately, a type of sexual burnout occurs in some long-standing relationships. Sexual burnout? For many males the idea of sexual burnout is contrary to the core message about masculine sexuality: It is not possible for males to engage in so much sexual activity as to produce a burnout. Men are sexually insatiable. Well, aren't they? Not so, according to Masters et al. (1988b), who state that 20% of middle-aged couples begin to satiate on long-standing patterns of infrequently varied sexual activities. Men and women alike may experience feelings of sexual hopelessness, emotional emptiness, fatigue, and negative self-image. A typical comment from these couples is, "The passion is gone out of our sexual relationship." As Bernie Zilbergeld (1992) counsels men, "lust is not as high as it is at the beginning of a relationship" (p. 376). Even so, most long-term sexual relationships are reasonably satisfying and can be invigorated by fostering a positive attitude about sexuality plus introducing variety through playful experimentation. The average frequency of sex per month for males in their 40s appears to be six and decreases only slightly to five during the next decade; only about 10% of couples who experience burnout elect celibacy as a way to resolve their waning feelings of erotic pleasure in the middle years (see Masters et al., 1988b; Michael et al., 1994.)

It is also during this period that many men experience what Gail Sheehy (1976) calls a *midlife crisis*. Many sexologists believe that men are more vulnerable to a sexual midlife crisis than women (Masters et al., 1988b). Many males begin to evaluate their accomplishments and compare themselves to other males with regard to their status in life. They often feel that they have not lived up to society's expectations of them as well as to their own expectations. Many males seem unfulfilled. Time is getting short. Changes need to be made.

As part of the changes, the middle-aged male may try to resurrect a depleted positive self-image by seeking reassurance in clandestine sexual activities, usually with a younger woman. Often, men in crisis turn to behavior that has been socialized as providing comfort and an ego boost. One of these is alcohol and another is sex. If the midlife crisis contains evidence that a man's sexual prowess is on the wane, sexual behavior takes on added importance. In many ways, our current male-dominated society continues to condone liaisons between older males and younger women. This opens this venue to the crisis-crazed male who feels he needs a beautiful young woman on his arm to show that he remains the man he always has been. He perceives his once beautiful partner as aged and he must, therefore, cast her aside like an old suit. Like the suit, the relationship used to fit well but now it is too familiar, a bit frayed, and no longer fashionable. Some partners attempt to tolerate the aberrant behavior of the male in crisis, hoping that the crisis will resolve itself and the male will eventually return to his senses and resume more stable behavior. Many partners do not. As a result, a lot of males ultimately find themselves without either the sexual reassurances from younger women or the support of a long-term partner.

Other men seem to find happiness in the embrace of younger and more sexually exciting women until these women, too, begin to show the ravages of time or until someone more exciting comes along. For these men, the crisis never seems to end because a pattern of masking the problem with a parade of ego boosters is established. Few men have the resources to support their sagging male egos with a large number of young women.

Although it appears somewhat true that some young women find the older elegant man attractive, "elegant" usually means "powerful and wealthy." Beautiful young women, by and large, are not attracted to older males simply because they are older. Older males who demonstrate financial success, political power, or celebrity status are at a distinct advantage over males who are average or below in these important measures of manhood. The male fantasy, however, is that young females will naturally be drawn to mature good looks, a sophisticated manner, and experienced sexual prowess. Sometimes the trappings of success helps; even so, the results can be disappointing. Midlife males who have attempted this type of lifestyle often comment:

> She was beautiful and very sexy in bed. I was in lust with her,
> but I knew that she was really only interested in my financial

stability. She liked being shown off in fancy restaurants, and I liked showing her off. My male friends thought I was the luckiest man in the world, and they all lusted after her, too. Fortunately, I didn't kid myself about her too much because I knew she was not able to offer much in a relationship except a great body and sex. And even the great sex was mostly in my mind. When we broke up, she went immediately to another older man who also had money.

This is not to say that some older males have not been successful in establishing satisfying and stable relationships with younger females. The point is that middle-age men often experience an identity crisis that sends them chasing after false notions of manhood and sexuality.

## ❏ Sexual Challenges of the Silver Years

Depending on which study you read, sexual behavior in the over-60 group decreases, increases, or remains the same (see Ade-Ridder, 1985; Knox, 1988; Palmore, 1981), but Masters et al. (1988b) criticize researchers for focusing on the frequency of sexual intercourse as the primary indicator of sexual behavior among the elderly. In their work with elderly people, Masters et al. note that masturbation, oral sex, and other alternative forms of sexual stimulation are common and often follow a pattern established in earlier years. Sometimes alternative forms of stimulation such as oral sex, sexually explicit materials, fantasies, sexual devices, self-stimulation, and others are used when the male experiences difficulty in achieving or maintaining erections or during marital separations or loss of a partner (see Brecher et al., 1984; Hegeler & Mortensen, 1977; Starr & Weiner, 1982).

A small percentage of men in the over-60 category may experience a significant decrease in the production of testosterone. Because the symptoms of this condition, such as fatigue, irritability, decreased sexual desire, reduced potency, and poor concentration, often resemble the symptoms displayed by females in menopause, the term, *male menopause* has been popularized. The correct term for this condition is *male climacteric,* and the condition is normally reversed or improved by testosterone replacement therapy.

Male menopause erroneously implies that males experience a normal cessation in their ability to produce children, marked by a readily identifiable biological event. For males, the changes are more subtle. That is, the production of testosterone decreases gradually during middle age and, for most men, levels off at about age 60. Most men do not experience a noticeable decline in testosterone production, but a few experience male climacteric. This wide range of the male's ability to produce testosterone over time suggests that general physical and mental health may be as important as the aging process in the continued development of healthy sexual responses. Although the production of viable sperm may also decrease over time, some males are capable of fathering children well into their 90s or beyond.

Negative cultural messages about sexual behavior by the elderly often take their toll by convincing some older men and women that they are deviant if they desire sexual contact. But studies suggest that most of the over-60 group still find sexual activities desirable and maintain a relatively stable pattern of sexual behavior, with only a slight and gradual decrease in frequency of sexual contact over time. Most studies show that nearly 85% of females and nearly 95% of males are sexually active at age 60 years; about 60% of male and 30% of female 100-year-olds engage in sexual intercourse; about 75% of sexually active elderly people achieve orgasms; and many elderly people also achieve sexual satisfaction through noncoital behavior such as caressing, cuddling, manual stimulation, and oral-genital contact (see Bretschneider & McCoy, 1988; Butler & Lewis, 1976; Kammeyer, Ritzer, & Yetman, 1990; Kinsey et al., 1948, 1953; Reiss, 1988; Schiavi, Schreiner-Engel, Mandeli, Schanzer, & Cohen, 1990; Starr & Weiner, 1982). Masters et al. (1988b) note, "Despite these cultural myths, the psychological need for intimacy, excitement, and pleasure does not disappear in old age, and there is nothing in the biology of aging that automatically shuts down sexual function" (p.180).

It would be unrealistic, on the other hand, to expect that the normal aging process will have no effect on sexual desire and behavior. For example, most sex researchers (see Masters et al., 1988b; Reinisch, 1990) report the following physiological changes in the male sexual response as a function of aging:

Sexual Arousal
Reduced muscle tension

Sex flush decreases and may disappear

Erections

A need for more direct stimulation

Usually takes a longer time to achieve

Somewhat less firm

Subsides more rapidly after orgasm

Testes

Testicles elevate more slowly and only part way into the scrotum

Orgasm and Ejaculation

Less of a physical need to ejaculate during sexual activities

Less intense contractions during orgasm and ejaculation

A reduction in the amount of semen emitted

An increase in the refractory period following ejaculation

In the United States, sexual behavior appears to be restricted to the young and attractive and sex between old people is considered disgusting. At least that is the general belief held by most people in our society and often portrayed by the primary purveyors of the cultural messages (Ade-Ridder, 1985; Reiss, 1988). Few presentations of elderly people engaging in sexual activities are offered. Stop for a moment and allow yourself the opportunity to engage in your favorite sexual fantasy. Regardless of your gender or age, it is doubtful that you quickly conjured up fantasies of elderly men or women having oral sex, engaging in mutual masturbation, or simply copulating.

Sadly, our culture has routinely portrayed elderly sex as some form of aberration of the normal aging process. That is, it is generally assumed that sexual behavior is no longer necessary or desirable when you reach your senior years. This is especially so for women who are beyond childbearing age. Although it is thought that some older males will continue to seek sexual activities, these men are typically viewed by our society as depraved old men who cannot or have never been able to keep their "nasty" sexual impulses under control.

The human organism is a very complex system that grows in complexity as it moves forward in time. Except for simple reflexes, few aspects of human functioning develop completely independently of environmental experiences. The notion that developmental se-

quences and outcomes related to heterosexuality are basically prede-
termined and inevitable because of the prepotent influence of internal genetic and biological directional factors is not supported. Instead, human beings burst on the scene as a well-equipped open
system ready to interact with and learn from the prevailing environment. The neonate begins to receive much stimulation from the
outside world and reacts to that stimulation in many and varied ways
throughout the life span. Moving from birth to maturity, each person
encounters a succession of situations and problems associated with
sexual development that he or she attempts to solve by developing
appropriate skills. These response patterns, regardless of the task, are
the same basic learning mechanisms that the person will call on to
achieve competence in any skill area.

The developing organism is also a system in which some irre-
versible changes occur as a result of the natural growth within the
system and various interactions with the outside world. Although
the developing system has some capacity for self-correction or repair,
many changes are difficult, if not impossible, to reverse. These changes
often produce a modification of the wiring diagram itself, so to speak.
For example, once a child learns language, he or she will never be
returned to a state of never having learned that language. Of course,
the child will be capable of building on that experience and may learn
other languages. Similarly, once a child learns his or her specific
cultural language of sexuality, he or she will have those messages
encoded on the his or her "mother board." And although other sexual
languages may also be learned, the early information coded on the
mother board remains.

As you have seen, the development of sexuality is no exception
to this learning process, except that sexuality, unlike most developmental tasks, receives an inordinate amount of attention and inatten-
tion at the same time. The language of sexuality also varies according
to cultural definitions of gender roles. Thus, any attempt to study the
factors associated with the development of male sexuality must
include an analysis of the cultural variables affecting the language of
sexuality. An examination of the foundations for cultural notions
about male sexuality follows.

# 4

# Sociocultural Variables

## *Messages From the Underground*

$S$ociocultural conditioning begins at first sight of our genitals. At birth, we are assigned a gender identification tag reflecting the specific configuration of external sexual structures awarded to us by our genes and the whims of prenatal hormonal secretions. From that moment on, most of us will receive cultural messages commensurate with those infantile external sexual structures. As Highwater (1990) points out, "Genitalia seal our fate, for at once we are initiated into the separate cultural constructs that are related to the rearing of male or female children" (p. 1).

But what is the foundation for the cultural messages we will receive for the rest of our lives? What do these messages say about human sexuality? Are the messages clear? A search for the answers to these questions will take us on a journey through the evolutionary history of humankind. As humans evolved from more primitive species, sociocultural factors emerged and also evolved. I will begin the trek by exploring the effect of evolution on the development of human sexual behavior.

## ❏ Sex and Evolution

Although many species appear to have developed from the original primordial sexual encounter, millions of years of evolution have produced a number of variations on the basic theme. Charles Darwin (1859/1958) documented many of the variations among living organisms in his controversial work, *On the Origin of Species.* One branch in this evolutionary tree is the humanlike or hominid species from which humans—homo sapiens—developed. Many religious groups reject Darwin's basic hypothesis that all living creatures evolved from the same primordial source, believing instead in divine intervention. Even so, Darwin's theory of evolution remains the foundation for most scientific studies on the development of humans.

According to the Darwinian concept of natural selection or the survival of the fittest, variations that provide an advantage for survival and procreation are passed on to progeny, whereas less favorable variations eventually die out. Thus, survival of the species becomes the driving force behind inherited characteristics. Natural selection assumes a position of biological determinism in the absence of sociocultural variables.

As early hominid groups evolved, certain adaptations or variations took place in some species but not in others. One strain began to develop physical structures that allowed for bipedal locomotion as well as opposable thumbs. Larger and less "primitive" brain structures also occurred. Each of these adaptations allowed early hominid types to adapt to changing environmental conditions in ways not possible for other more primitive species. Through this process, the gradual evolution of the human species occurred.

### ■ Sexual Selection

To explain the development of sexual behavior, Darwin (1958) proposes a binary system called *sexual selection.* One component involves competition for females by males. Through competition, the male with the better developed battle plan, superior physical characteristics, and stamina effects a higher probability of overcoming his challenger and sexually mating with the female, thus ensuring that those successful attributes will be passed along in the gene pool.

The second component of Darwinian sexual selection involves decision making on the part of the female. Success at battle alone does not necessarily ensure the winner of success with the female. The female can still select either, or neither, combatant regardless of the outcome of the battle. Females can choose, therefore, based on factors other than successful competitive characteristics.

Because many of these factors appear to relate to the evolution of elaborate mating rituals and ornamental displays exhibited by the males of most species, Darwin (1859/1958) postulates that the less colorful female is the basic prototype from which the more colorful males developed, over time, due to natural selection. Females were pursued without the aid of bright colors, so it was not necessary for them to develop equally elaborate displays. Darwin's concept here echoes the concepts found in the development of fetal sexual structures. That is, the basic prototype is female; males develop as a function of something being added. On the other hand, Wallace (1878, 1889) criticizes Darwin's notion of active female choice and proposes, instead, that females with elaborate ornamental displays became easy prey and eventually natural selection favored the female with protective rather than designer coloration. In Wallace's scheme, the basic prototype is the brightly colored male rather than the plain colored female.

Cucchiari (1981) describes original protohuman sexual behavior as primarily bisexual. When these groups eventually began to conceptualize males and females as distinct categories, a gender revolution occurred. This revolution was related to the development of a hunter-and-gatherer society that linked females with the role of producing and caring for children, whereas males assumed the role of securing food. From this new gender system came controls over sexuality such as prohibitions on incest and homosexuality, the early foundation for kinship and family social structures.

Fausto-Sterling (1985) contends that debates about the concept of natural selection versus sexual selection and the terms used to describe mating activities and social organizations found in some animal groups represent an interpretation of animal behavior and evolution based on a cultural bias regarding women. For example, she argues that most descriptions of the animal world, including those presented by Darwin and his ilk, reflect culturally conditioned concepts about the nature of women and their place in a male-dominated society rather than objective inquiry. As a counterpoint, Fausto-Sterling refers to Lancaster's objection to the traditional use of "harem" to identify a social organization containing a number of females and one male. Lancaster, instead, refers to this type of organization as "one-male groups as those in which females are virtually self-sufficient, except for fertilization" (quoted in Fausto-Sterling, 1985, p. 181).

Apparently, this tendency to interpret discoveries about animal behavior based on a cultural or even a personal bias did not exclude notions about males. For example, Darwin (1859/1958) believes that human males developed facial and other body hair because this display was attractive to females. Apparently the caveman look was successful and became an integral part of the gene pool. Not surprising, Darwin was an especially hairy man, sporting a thick beard and bushy eyebrows. It is unknown if Darwin's hairy ornamentation afforded him any special favors with women. Perhaps this is another example of one man's cultural fantasy translated into "reality," or one man's reality translated into a cultural fantasy.

Buried deep in the debate about sexual selection is the concept of attractiveness. Geneticists assume that something must have been attractive to protohuman females for them to select one mate from the competition. Attractiveness, therefore, seems to be defined as characteristics that remain in the gene pool. Although this may be the case for lower animals, the social structures developed by humans may have tinkered with genetic certainty. For humans, attractiveness and sexual mating do not rely entirely on physical features or prowess. Concepts about gender attractiveness vary among and within cultures. Messages about attractiveness appear to vary within a society over time, as well.

In most societies, some form of dress code distinguishes gender (Ember & Ember, 1990; Frayser, 1985). For example, traditional Islamic societies require women's bodies to be clothed completely and the face to be veiled. By contrast, contemporary Western societies permit more freedom for both genders, and many types of clothing and other ornamentation are worn by both. Some areas are still considered inappropriate even by Western standards, however. For example, it appears acceptable for females to wear clothing considered traditionally masculine, such as pants, but the wearing of dresses by males is still considered odd by most. Many males, including sports figures, wear earrings or other jewelry traditionally thought to be feminine attire. At one time hair length was a good measure of one's gender, but this too has become a fading indicator.

■  **Walk Like a Man**

The ability to stand erect and walk on two legs also dramatically changed the nature of sexual behavior of our ancestors. One of the most significant contributions was the availability and emergence of frontal entry intercourse. With few exceptions, rear entry copulation is the position of choice by most of the animal kingdom. Although some animals, especially primates, have been observed occasionally to experiment with other positions, including face-to-face positions, frontal sex is more common in humans than in other animals.

Some anthropologists posit that female orgasmic activity evolved as a function of bipedalism. A number of anatomical and physiological devices are found in most lower animals that ensure that the majority of the sperm remains deposited in the female after copulation. Some animal vaginas spasm around the penis, preventing withdrawal for several minutes. The rear entry anatomical structures found in primates also provide a gravitational-proof vessel for semen, as the female remains in a mostly horizontal position, even while leaving her lover.

According to theorists in this area, the upright position poses a significant risk for freshly deposited sperm due to gravitational forces. Theoretically, the loss of a majority of semen decreases the chances of procreation. It is important for the viability of the sperm, therefore, to remain within the vaginal vault until they have had the opportunity to travel upstream in search of ripe ovum. Morris (1969) argues that female orgasmic phenomenon is a physiological device to immobilize females temporarily following copulation. Orgasms produce a sense of release, relaxation, and fatigue, all of which contribute to the likelihood that the female will remain in a restful position. Interestingly, little is mentioned about the purpose of the male's tendency to "roll over and go to sleep" after orgasm and ejaculation.

Others reject Morris's (1969) female-orgasm-as-anesthetic notion and propose other explanations for the development of female orgasms. Sherfey (1972) suggests that female orgasms are linked to the time when primitive groups were matriarchal. She proposes that the female's ability to experience multiple orgasms is indicative of sexual insatiability. Others propose that female orgasm is a way of confusing males about "paternity certainty" or that female orgasms are designed to stimulate males to ensure ejaculation (see Gregersen,

1994). Little has been written from an anthropological standpoint regarding the development of orgasms in males. Instead, the focus has been on the male's anatomical structures, especially the penis.

Evolution also included changes in mating behavior. Most animals mate only during the period of time when the female is biologically receptive. As the female comes into heat (oestrus), she signals her receptivity to mating by physical changes, posturing, or olfactory cues. For example, in some primates the skin around the female genitals changes colors and the area swells. When she presents herself to a male, she does so by exposing her buttocks and genital area in a way that the potential mate can readily observe the sexual cues. Most animals also release sexual odors (pheromones) to signal receptivity.

Because sexual behavior in most animals is related more to procreation than to recreation, breeding seasons are common. Homo sapiens involved into an organism that mates at any time, however. Some say humans shifted from a biologically driven to a socially driven mating pattern. Others quip that sexual mating by humans remains controlled by females and their various hormonal fluctuations. As you will see later in this volume, the debate about biological issues and male versus female control over sexual behavior is far from settled.

The eventual disappearance of oestrus in early hominids significantly affected the development of sexual behavior in our ancestors and ultimately ourselves. Fisher (1983) proposes that females who maintained longer periods of sexual receptivity were favored and pursued by males more than females who displayed less sexual interest. According to this scheme, females who were more receptive sexually received protection and more goods in exchange for sexual contact. Fisher describes these early sexual interactions as the foundation for subsequent human monogamous societies. Clearly, her model depicts males as the pursuer of goods partly to obtain sexual favors from receptive females, a practice still found today in most modern societies. Fisher's portrayal of the sexual interactions between early man and woman appears very much like the beginning of prostitution, but is presented instead as the cornerstone of long-term pair bonding or monogamy. That is, male pursues female and pays for sexual favors. On the other hand, Fisher also proposes that this sexual contract produces not just sexual favors for the man and goods for the female but a long-term commitment.

Another model of human sexuality connects food sharing, rather than division of labor, to the disappearance of oestrus. Lovejoy (1981) proposes that early hominid mothers would not have been capable of rearing their children if their mates did not provide and share food. He further hypothesizes that males were willing partners in this scenario because their mates were available for sexual contact on a more frequent basis than dictated by periodic or seasonal mating.

### ■ Gender Typing

As discussed earlier, a strict biological perspective proposes that gender typing is a function of genetics and hormonal influences on the prenatal brain. This combination is thought to predispose males and females to develop behavior patterns consistent with genetic gender encoding. Although sociobiology also proposes that genes are the foundation for subsequent behavior, the genetic encoding has more to do with the transmission of traits proven successful for survival and the propagation of the species. For example, sociobiology supports the idea that the division of labor found in many primitive groups evolved from successful protohuman types. It is argued that males are better suited for activities such as hunting and physical combat because of superior cognitive abilities and physical features inherited from our ancestors. On the other hand, females have inherited superior traits associated with the care and maintenance of children. The eventual emergence of this division of labor phenomenon in early hominids led to the primitive hunter-and-gatherer social organizational structure.

Sociobiology has been used to explain the basis of nearly all social behavior, including the origin of war and human ethics (Wilson, 1975), the evolution of kinship systems (Fox, 1980), and legal justice systems (Alexander, 1980). Rape, female infanticide, and sex discrimination also appear to have a strong link to evolution, according to the sociobiological viewpoint (see Barash, 1979; Symons, 1979; Tiger, 1970).

### ■ Infant Dependency

Another important variable sets humans apart from the more primitive hominid: a long period of infant dependency. In most primates, offspring develop quite rapidly and achieve a reasonable level of independence within a relatively short period of time. Human infants develop much slower and, as a consequence, remain dependent on caregivers significantly longer.

Most anthropologists point to infant dependency as a major factor leading to the division of labor between the genders. Because female mammals lactate and males do not, the infant is initially more dependent for survival on the mother than the father. This dependency essentially required the mother and child to remain together more than with the male. The male was, therefore, free to pursue other activities, whereas the female's mobility was more restricted. It is assumed that the adult male decided to contribute to the family unit by using his "free" time in productive ways, such as hunting and scavenging for food beyond the immediate base camp. There is also evidence that primitive man may have engaged in a form of warfare during which males would mount raids on the storehouses of nearby tribes. The mother and child remained in or near the base camp. It is also thought that the mother may have engaged in activities near the camp compatible with her limited mobility. These activities seemed to involve foraging for additional foodstuffs such as fruits, vegetables, and edible plant parts. This need to divide labor along gender lines due to infant dependency may have led to a successful hunter-and-gatherer social structure that remained an integral part of human society for thousands of years.

Murdock (1937) found support for this portrayal of early human family and social organization by studying the division of labor practices of more than 200 so-called primitive or nonindustrialized societies. The results produced a bimodal distribution of activities according to gender. Hunting and similar "away-from-camp" activities were found to be primarily the purview of males, whereas "domestic" activities were performed mostly by females. Although Murdock's study appears to support the hunter-and-gatherer notion of human society, the results also show a tremendous diversity in the type of work performed regardless of gender. In fact, it could be argued that the contribution of women-gatherers may have equaled that of males.

Obviously, biology is not the sole determinant of social organization and the development of gender roles. Consider Margaret Mead's (1935/1963) classic studies of primitive tribes living in New Guinea. She found that traditional gender roles were blurred in two groups. A third society consisted of a reversal of expected gender roles, with women in control of the important affairs of the tribe and

performing most of the essential labor functions. Men were considered timid and weaker; they occupied themselves with nonessential
and generally self-absorbed activities. Studies by other anthropologists clearly support the idea that biological factors alone cannot
account for the diversity found among various groups regarding
gender roles (see Draper, 1975; Havemann & Lehtinen, 1990; Herdt,
1987; Meggitt, 1964).

## ❏ Sex and the Natural Order of Things

Western culture is steeped in the notion that the world is parti-
tioned into the natural and the unnatural. This concept is based on
ancient Greek teaching about nature and the natural order of things.
Our Judeo-Christian ancestors were greatly influenced by Greek
philosophy and readily embraced the idea. Simply stated, the natural
order of things relates to actions as possessing an essential purpose.
To engage in an act for the purpose it was intended by nature is
considered natural. It was considered unnatural to engage in an act
for a purpose not intended by nature.

At issue here are two important considerations. The first relates
to the interpretation of events occurring in nature as actually being
the essential purpose for those acts. This interpretation automatically
eliminates consideration of multiple purposes of the same act because there can be, by definition, only one essential purpose. Second
is the assumption that the essential purpose, once preordained as
such by some mythical court of biological potentates, is indeed the
true order of things as established by nature.

Once the natural order of things for sexual behavior was determined, unnatural acts were easily identified and prohibitions were
imposed. For example, the genetic and biological aspects of human
sexuality seem to suggest that the major function of sexual structures
and behavior is to procreate. According to Aristotelian teachings, it
would be easy to argue that the essential purpose of sexual behavior is
to produce children. One could also argue that the essential purpose for
sexual activities in protohumans was to infuse brief moments of pleasure into an otherwise bleak existence. The birth of children may have
occurred simply as a by-product and may even have posed additional
hardships on the parents. Does this mean that having sex for the sole
purpose of producing children would, therefore, be unnatural?

It is unlikely that protohumans understood the connection between sexual behavior and procreation. Perhaps seeking pleasure through sexual contact is the natural order of things and a clever deception to foster behavior that also perpetuates the species. Studies show that the majority of sexual contacts between humans is not linked to the primary purpose of producing children. Can it really be that all these sexual activities are unnatural? Perhaps humans are sexual for numerous reasons not related to procreation. Regardless, much of Judeo-Christian doctrine about sexual matters is based on the belief that procreation, not recreation, is the natural order of things. Cultural messages have evolved accordingly.

Because the natural order philosophy imposes an "either or" view of the world, the messages about sexual activities are quite simple. That is, either the sex act is natural and acceptable or it is unnatural and unacceptable. If one considers that the only natural sexual act is sexual intercourse for the purpose of procreation, everything else is automatically ruled out. This means that nonprocreational sexual activities often observed in lower animals, as well as in humans, are considered unnatural and, therefore, forbidden. The message is clear: Have sex to make babies; do not practice any form of birth control; do not engage in activities such as masturbation, oral copulation, anal intercourse, homosexuality, or any other nonprocreational sexual acts. Copulation with animals is also forbidden unless, of course, you are planning to sire a new breed of progeny.

## ❏ Ancient Attitudes Toward Women

Highwater (1990) believes that the foundation for Judeo-Christian misogyny was laid with the mythic origins of woman. For example, Babylonian mythology offers an account of the creation of the first woman, Lilith, and her negative image. Lilith was created from dust, as was the first man, presumably Adam. Lilith became one of the many wives of Sammael (or Satan) but left her husband to join with Adam. Lilith was a wild and passionate woman who refused to accept her prescribed role as subservient and submissive to Adam. Apparently, she claimed equality based on similar origins: dust. Following a serious domestic dispute, Lilith left Adam. The Lord was not amused and commanded Lilith to return to Adam. When she refused to comply, Lilith was punished by having 100 of her offspring die each day. Lilith was similarly not amused and she vowed vengeance against other children. Soon Lilith earned a reputation as an evil female demon who seduces men and kills newly born children. She is depicted in the Bible as a night monster (e.g., Isaiah 34:14).

The book of Genesis refers to the first woman as Eve, who was created not from dust but from one of Adam's ribs. She was also created from man for man: "Then the Lord God said, 'It is not good for the man to be alone; I will make him a helper suitable for him' " (Genesis 2:18). Unfortunately, the Lord's generous gift did not heed His warnings against eating from the tree of knowledge of good and evil (Genesis 2:17). Instead, Eve succumbed to the enticing messages from a most crafty serpent. Not only did Eve eat from the tree of knowledge of good and evil herself, she gave the forbidden fruit to Adam. Due to Eve's actions, she is generally seen as a temptress whose behavior produced the original sin and subsequent suffering by humankind. Being responsible for being cast out of Paradise is a heavy burden that women have had to bear since creation.

Some early interpretations of the fall of man in the Garden of Eden produced an even more sordid picture. For example, Philo Judaeus, an Alexandrian Jew, and St. Augustine both believed that Eve's actions were the result of sexual desire. Lust was, therefore, born with the expulsion from Paradise. Most early Christians rejected the proposition that the sin of Adam and Eve was sexual. They argued that the true theme of the story is moral freedom and responsibility, not sex. Even so, St. Augustine eventually persuaded leaders of the early Christian church that the original sin was disobedience of the flesh fueled by lust (see Pagels, 1988).

In Ancient Greek mythology, Zeus sent woman, in the guise of Pandora and her infamous box full of misery, as a punishment for man. It is not surprising, then, that ancient Greeks developed a bad attitude about women and excluded them from most privileged activities. For example, females were not seen as intellectual enough to warrant schooling. Only males were allowed the opportunities of learning. Tutors were always male. Females could not own land or participate in the affairs of the state. For the most part, Greek women were confined to their homes except when given leave by their fathers or husbands to attend religious functions or some of the few other special events open to females. Even the great Greek philosopher Aristotle taught that women were naturally inferior to and should be ruled by men.

## ❑ Ancient Attitudes About Marriage

Although the ancient Greeks were monogamous, their misogynistic social organization dictated the conditions and purposes for marriage. In Greek society, marriages did not occur because of some romantic or passionate reason. They were typically arranged by the father, who entered into a contract with the groom. The arrangement often included a dowry provided by the bride's family. Males typically married in their late 20s or early 30s. Their brides were selected from among young girls, usually teenagers. Although premarital chastity and marital fidelity were expected from women, males were expected to be experienced and were free to seek sexual pleasures beyond the marital bed. The marital relationship consisted mostly of the husband providing economic support for his wife and any children born of the union. Wives were expected to yield to their husbands' sexual advances, but husbands typically sought sexual contact with their wives infrequently, preferring instead to partake of the many sexual partners available such as concubines, talented prostitutes, slaves, or adolescent boys. Because marriages were not linked to religious beliefs, the marital contract could be terminated like other business contracts by either partner. If a dowry was part of the marital contract, the divorced husband was required to continue providing economic support for his ex-wife.

The ancient Hebrews also established a society based on the perceived superiority of men and the inferiority of women. Masculinity was so revered by ancient Hebrews that a castrated male was denied entrance to sacred places such as temples. Part of the traditional daily prayer for Jewish males includes thanks to God for not making them women. The daily prayer for Jewish women includes thanks for being created according to God's desire. Ancient Hebrews considered a married woman the property of her husband and she was expected to spend long days working at whatever tasks her husband demanded of her. She could be divorced at will. Women could be stoned to death for adultery, whereas adulterous husbands received lesser penalties associated with the violation of another man's property rights. Although ancient Hebrews emphasized monogamy and sex within the marriage, secondary wives and concubines were allowed.

Monogamy and marriage were introduced to the early Christians by the Graeco-Romans, who had practiced this form of family

organization for centuries. The Judaic custom of polygamy continued for European Jews until banned by their own religious leaders
in 1030 AD as a concession to the majority Christian view, embracing
the sanctity of monogamous marriages.

Although having intercourse for the sole purpose of procreating
was deemed the natural order of things, engaging in this or any form
of sexual activities without the benefit of marriage was forbidden
under traditional Judeo-Christian teachings. Sexual behavior was
deemed acceptable for married heterosexual couples only:

> The only appropriate setting for sex is marriage, which is
> held to be divinely sanctioned. More specifically, the funda-
> mental notion of Judeo-Christian sexual morality is that a
> man should ejaculate only within his wife's vagina. All other
> forms of sexual expression causing a man to ejaculate are
> taboo. (Gregersen, 1994, pp. 8-9)

Contemporary Western culture tends to idealize marriage, linking it to romantic love, but early Judeo-Christian teachings excluded
sensuality and passion from the marriage bed. Love and marriage were
considered incompatible. Romantic love began to develop in Europe
during the Middle Ages. Some see this phenomenon as a rebirth of
passion suppressed for so many years by the dour approach to sexuality
promulgated by Christianity and the Judeo-Christian culture (Highwater, 1990). Birth or rebirth, a number of important changes took place
during the Middle Ages that seem to have had a significant influence
on relationships, love, and sexual matters.

One of these changes had to do with marriage and the role of
women. Prior to the Middle Ages, marriages were little more than a
religious blessing on monogamous relationships for the purpose of
producing children. Many marriages were arranged by family members for persons who had not yet met. Some children were betrothed
during childhood to their future mates, and many marriages were
arranged to preserve family lineages. Wealth, especially in the form
of property, was protected and, in some cases, acquired through
arranged marriages. Although it was generally expected that the
husband would reap the financial benefits of arranged marriages,
women also began to accumulate wealth. For many males, wealthy
women were very attractive. These women produced increased competition from suitors for their favors.

Suddenly, the role of women, at least rich and powerful women, began to change. Instead of being viewed as property and vessels for sperm, women were seen as having other values. This renewed interest in women seems to have spawned a renewed interest in passion as well. Even so, the dominant Judeo-Christian culture, with its predominately sex-negative attitudes, continued to be influential in dictating behavior. Women were still expected to remain chaste, although an adulterous relationship between a wealthy woman and a young knight was often tolerated (Lewisohn, 1958). Even though it was becoming acceptable for women to have passion, it was still forbidden to display sexual excitement openly. Thus, many love affairs were full of passion but empty of sexual activities.

Sophisticated courting practices were also developed during this time. In fact, the Middle Ages has often been called the Age of Chivalry. Literature describing passionate love relationships emerged during this period. Love songs were written and sung by troubadours throughout Europe. Many men were beginning to pursue women in a passionate manner instead of just seeking a release of sexual tension or a mother for their children.

## ❑ Love and Sex

Although romantic love is not found in all cultures, it has its roots in antiquity. In Greek mythology, Eros was a mischievous character who found joy in creating love and passion in people. He accomplished this task by shooting love arrows into the hearts of unsuspecting persons. With arrow in place, the "wounded" person was compelled to fall madly in love with the next person he or she came on. In Roman mythology, Eros is called Cupido. Both variations of this mythical figure embody the concept of erotic or romantic love: Love so deep and intense for another that we feel as though we will die without that person. Within Western society, romantic love is linked to sexual desire and seen by most as the primary reason for marriage (Berscheid, 1988; Hatfield, 1988; Lee, 1988; Roper Organization, 1985). Indeed, the influence of Cupid is familiar to contemporary lovers, especially on Valentine's Day.

Because American society seems to be obsessed with romantic love, it is not surprising that several "scientific" models of love have emerged. One model describes romantic love as a combination of strong physiological arousal (e.g., palpitations, sweating, queasy stomach) connected with thinking or interacting with a love object; a cultural setting that perpetuates the concept of romantic love; and an acceptance that the physiological arousal springs from feelings of love (Berscheid & Walster, 1978; Walster & Walster, 1978). Important to this model is the recognition that romantic love is not a universal phenomenon among humans. For romantic love to occur and be recognized, one must live in a cultural setting that embraces such a concept. The notion that love makes the world go 'round may be little more than a Western fantasy.

A more complex model of love is offered by Sternberg (1988). He proposes a triangular model consisting of three distinct components of love: intimacy (e.g., pleasant feelings associated with being bonded or connected with someone and the reciprocity of emotional support and trust); passion (intense sexual or romantic feelings accompanied by physiological arousal and desire for another person); and decision or commitment (decision refers to deciding that one is, indeed, in love with someone, whereas commitment refers to one's readiness to maintain the relationship over the long term). Different levels of compatibility occur depending on each individual's level of these three components. When partners are similar in their three levels, a good match occurs, whereas incongruence on all three components produces a mismatch.

Another feature of the Sternberg (1988) model is the identification of eight types of love based on the various combinations of the three basic components. The first type of love is nonlove, which is characterized as the absence of all three basic components. Nonlove can be found in casual relationship. Liking is the second type of love and consists of intimacy with another person but the absence of passion and decision or commitment. The third type, infatuation, is familiar to most who have experienced strong romantic and sexual desire (passion) for someone but were unable to generate the other two components. Empty love, the fourth type, is characterized by a decision to love plus a willingness to maintain the relationship without experiencing passion or intimacy. The fifth type is romantic love. This type consists of passion and intimacy but lacks the decision or commitment component. Companionate love, the sixth type, is characterized by a lack of passion but contains intimacy and decision or commitment components. Long-term relationships such as found in some marriages often develop into companionate love. That is, the passion retreats but companionship, friendship, and commitment to the relationship remain. The seventh type is fatuous love. This type consists of a lot of passion and the decision or commitment component. Intimacy is absent. Found with this type are couples who fall madly in love and make quick decisions about committing to the relationship before intimacy develops. Consummate love, the eighth type, is the ideal love relationship, which contains a combination of all three basic components.

Using a love attitude scale, Hendrick and Hendrick (1986) identify six styles of love: romantic love; game-playing love; friendship; logical love; possessive, excited love; and selfless love. Responses to this scale by college students suggest that males tend to develop romantic and game-playing styles, whereas females tend to develop friendship, logical love, and possessive love styles. No gender differences were found with the selfless love style. The findings also suggest that most respondents experience many of the various love styles. Hendrick, Hendrick, and Adler (1988) found a link between romantic and selfless styles of love and a tendency for the couple to remain in the relationship, whereas the game-playing style became one of the major factors in the termination of relationships. Couples who identified themselves as romantically involved also expressed similar type love styles.

## ❏ The Evolution of Western Sexuality

One only needs to examine Greek art and religious figures to realize that Greek males pursued sexual gratification in a variety of ways. Major deities in ancient Greek religion are openly sexual figures, including a female, Aphrodite, the goddess of sexual love. Hermes, the messenger for the other gods, is often depicted with a erect penis. Even Zeus, the chief deity, was known for his sexual appetite that included rape, adultery, and the love of adolescent boys. Greek art objects often depict sexual activities in an unabashed manner. Most of what we have learned about ancient Greek sexuality derives from the study of art objects produced by Greek males.

Central to the ancient Greek's approach to sexuality was the belief that sexual desire was natural, a virtue, and vital to humankind. The pursuit of sexual gratification was also considered natural, virtuous, and important for the establishment of manhood. With few notable exceptions, most sexual activities for males were condoned, if not celebrated, by ancient Greek culture. Let's start with modesty.

The ancient Greeks were not ashamed of their bodies and were tolerant of nudity in their populace and in their art. Although Greek males typically appeared in public wearing traditional Greek clothing, male athletes often competed in the nude without fear of ostracism or legal penalties.

Ancient Greeks tolerated homosexuality, but they developed some interesting rules regarding same-sex sexual activities. Homosexuality was considered appropriate only for males and was to be practiced according to the strict hierarchy of social class that also dictated other sexual relationships. An unmarried male citizen could penetrate anyone below his status, such as free women, concubines, prostitutes, and boys, but he was forbidden to have sexual relationships with females of his own class. Similarly, adult male citizens who allowed themselves to be penetrated were engaging in sexual activities beneath their social class and were generally considered as loathsome creatures.

Because boys, even boys from the citizen class, were not yet considered citizens in their own right, they were often the target for romantic affections of unmarried men. Even though anal intercourse was no doubt practiced in these sexual liaisons, interfemoral intercourse was encouraged instead, especially for boys from the citizen class. Some ancient Greek intellectuals, such as Socrates, suggested chaste homoerotic rather than physical "love" relationships with boys.

Although the ancient Greeks were more open about their disdain for women and the installation of a double standard regarding sexual practices for men and women than currently found in Western culture, similar women-negative and double standard sexual attitudes have found their way into Western thought. The ancient Greeks' philosophy that sexual behavior is natural and an acceptance of homoerotic practices were expelled from Judeo-Christian consciousness, however, much the way Adam and Eve were cast out of Eden.

Like the Greeks, the Romans developed a sexual culture built on a relatively permissive attitude about sexual matters. Prostitution and concubinage were common facets of the Roman and Greek sexual scene, but the Romans were somewhat more reserved in their approach to pederasty. Posner (1992) notes that Roman public bathhouses were the archetypes of homosexual bathhouses subsequently established in many large metropolitan areas such as New York and San Francisco. Posner also argues that Roman sexual permissiveness eventually developed into a more measured approach to sexual matters. For example, Plato's teachings regarding body-soul dualism and sexual asceticism found receptive students. Also, the idea of marriage based on love, mutual respect, companionship, family responsibility, and fidelity began to replace the traditional Greek marriage based on "male sexual desire, financial arrangements, and heirship" (Posner, 1992, p. 45).

Common belief is that corporeality and sexuality are significant aspects of the Judeo-Christian concept of evil. One source for this concept of associating the body with sin appears to be the powerful Orphic religion that thrived in Hellenic times. At the center of this religion was the belief that "the soul was undergoing punishment for ancient sins and that the body was a prison in which the soul had been incarcerated" (Highwater, 1990, p. 24). Immortality could be achieved only by a life of purity and through rituals of purification. Judeo-Christian religious practices are rife with purification rituals, including the practice of sexual abstinence.

St. Paul, against a backdrop of fornicating Romans, proclaimed that practicing celibacy was closer to the Christian ideology of goodness and purity than succumbing to the body's sinful sexual desires. His teachings about celibacy can also be seen as an attempt to purge or purify the soul contaminated by the original corporeal sin of Adam and Eve. St. Paul also allowed that marital sex for procreation was not a sin and celibacy could not be practiced by everyone. In this regard, sexual behavior was deemed acceptable, but only within the confines of a marital relationship. St. Augustine, however, believed that all sexual behavior was evil and wicked, even marital sex. He proclaimed that nonprocreative sexual practices, such as homosexuality and masturbation, were the most sinful of all. St. Augustine believed that lust was responsible for the tragedy in the Garden of Eden. According to St. Augustine, Adam lost control of himself because his body stopped obeying his commands. Adam's sexual parts were the first to rebel. Augustine's interpretation of the role lust played in the tragedy in Paradise appears influenced by his own struggle for control over strong sexual urges (see Pagels, 1988). Augustine, like his pagan father, had a voracious sexual appetite that he habitually attempted to satisfy. In *Confessions*, Augustine chronicles the raging lust of adolescence that never abated and enslaved him as a young adult. It was only with the gradual conversion to Christianity and the final denunciation of all things worldly did St. Augustine break the bonds of sexual slavery. After numerous sexual encounters and two marriages, a 30-something Augustine finally found relief in a monastic life and chastity. It is likely that St. Augustine was the first recovering sexual compulsive canonized. The Roman Catholic Church flourished and eventually dominated Western thought during the Middle Ages. Along with this came St. Augustine's subversive negativism about all things sexual.

Also flourishing during this time was a cult worshipping the Virgin Mary. Mary, the mother of Jesus Christ, became one of the most revered women in history. Through an association with the virginity of Mary, women were thought to have been absolved of sin. Obviously, the cult's teachings were far more woman-positive than those generated from Eve's original sinful and lustful behavior. When the crusaders imported the cult's philosophy from Constantinople back to their homeland, European Christendom was changed forever. The Roman Catholic Church was faced with two conflicting images of woman. This dualism exists today: woman as whore (Eve) and woman as holy (Mary).

In the 16th century, Christian reformers such as Martin Luther and John Calvin split off from the Roman Church. They proposed a somewhat more liberal view of sexuality. Luther believed that marriage was natural and priests should be allowed to raise children. Calvin believed that sexual behavior within a marriage was important for the relationship beyond simple procreation. Although the Protestant Reformation offered a more positive view of sexuality, sexual behavior was still considered acceptable only within the confines of the marital bed. Fornicators and adulterers were punished severely for their sins.

During the reign of England's Queen Victoria, during the 19th century, sex was driven underground by extremely negative attitudes about nearly all forms of sexual expression. Interestingly, Victorian prudish attitudes about sex were based more on "scientific" thinking that sexual activities were dangerous and not conducive to good health than to religious dogma. For example, masturbation was condemned because it was thought to produce all sorts of maladies, not because it was proclaimed unnatural and sinful by theologians. A campaign was waged, therefore, to prevent children from touching or experimenting with their external sexual parts.

Children were warned that masturbation would cause unspeakable medical and social horrors to themselves and possibly to their offspring. Some especially anxious parents laced their medical warnings with a strong dose of religion: "If you play with yourself you will go insane, die early, and burn in hell forever." Although Victorian thinking regarding sex was primarily focused on medical rather than moral concerns, previous theological thought was not abandoned entirely. The marital bed, for example, was still promoted as the only acceptable venue for sexual expression.

Victorian sexologists considered women, for the most part, as sexless. A prominent English physician, William Acton, believed that women were born with a sort of sexual anesthesia. Other medical minds believed sexual intercourse drained men of natural vitality and was, therefore, harmful to a man's health. This belief appears to be the basis for the warning against engaging in sexual intercourse before participating in an important athletic event because ejaculation was thought to sap an athlete's strength and impair his performance. Reverend Sylvester Graham preached against masturbation as a sinful wasting of the seed and warned men against engaging in sexual intercourse more than once per month lest vital juices be dangerously depleted. In the 1830s, Reverend Graham developed a cracker derived from unbolted wheat in an attempt to help control sexual appetites. Dr. Kellogg developed Corn Flakes for the same reason. (Dr. Kellogg also remained celibate throughout most of his life, including the time he was married.)

Victorian beliefs about sexual matters dominated Western thinking well into the 20th century. When Kinsey et al. (1948) published their groundbreaking volume, *Sexual Behavior in the Human Male*, they shocked a nation still talking about sex behind closed doors. When the companion volume, *Sexual Behavior in the Human Female*, was published in 1953, myths about female sexuality were shaken to their Judeo-Christian foundations.

Masters and Johnson went beyond mere surveys by conducting laboratory studies of both men and women during actual sexual stimulation. The most startling part of the data presented in their 1966 book, *Human Sexual Response*, was the finding that males and females appear to have quite similar sexual responses. What happened to the sexual anesthesia found in Victorian women? Did they finally wake up? Most of us are now quite familiar with Masters and Johnson's four phases of the sexual response cycle: excitement, plateau, orgasm, and resolution, although not all men and women fit neatly into their scheme. Masters and Johnson also presented scientific evidence that female sexual excitement is centered more in the clitoris than the vagina. Due to its location at the top of the labia, the clitoris can be stimulated easily manually, but not so easily through vaginal intercourse. For males, this finding meant altering their thinking regarding how they were going to satisfy their partner. Obviously, simply stimulating the vaginal vault through traditional penile thrusting may not be adequate to get the job done. Males were now faced with the fact that their revered penis was not necessary for female sexual excitement.

During the mid-1960s through the mid-1970s, a sexual revolution was attempted. Many of the prohibitions against sexual behavior were ignored as men and women "made love, not war." Although premarital sex was largely frowned on by mainstream society, a more permissive attitude about sexual behavior was being born. Casual sex, alternative life styles, group sex, and sexual experimentation were commonplace among those rebelling against traditional sex-negative cultural messages. In many ways, the sexual revolution allowed males the opportunity to actualize traditional male fantasies, such as unbridled sex without commitment, responsibility, or guilt.

Fast on the heels of the sexual revolution was the feminist movement. Feminists were quick to present a different view of sexuality, especially male sexuality. They correctly railed at the traditional female-negative underpinnings of a male-dominated society. Women demanded equality in all areas, including the sexual arena. Suddenly males were confronted with assertive women seeking sexual satisfaction and intimacy. Many men attempted to dismantle centuries of masculine conditioning and become more sensitive to gender issues. Some men attempted to become more like females in the process. "Let your feminine side show" became a popular theme. This gender blurring had a significant effect on males and how they perceived their sexuality.

As if things are not confusing enough, a new group of activists, comprising mostly females, is proposing that sex is God's gift to humanity and most of us are not getting our share. Erotic writer Susie Bright (1988; Bright & Blank, 1992) and her colleagues, for example, propose a change from the repressive sex-negative attitudes still dominant in our culture, especially for women, to a position of sex positivism. Although her proposal receives support from other so-called pleasure activists, most feminists are not amused. Many feminists view sex positivism as just another way females will be exploited sexually.

## ❏ The Sociocultural Abuse of Sexuality

American culture appears confused regarding sexuality. Overall, it embraces the Judeo-Christian dogma that sexual behavior is sinful except for married heterosexuals. But messages encouraging unsanctioned sexual behavior, especially for heterosexual males, abound. This confusion about sexuality is often reflected in sociocultural messages Bolton et al. (1989) label the *abuse of sexuality*.

The abuse of sexuality model rests on several assumptions. First, sexuality is a constant developmental element from infancy forward. Second, sexuality may be either nurtured or hindered in multiple ways. Third, the hindrances to normal sexual development may reach abusive proportions at any time. As such, the abuse of sexuality model describes a continuum of developmental environments that range from promotion of normalized sexual development in both genders to approaches that are abusive and significantly reduce the probability of normal sexual development. Table 4.1 represents the model.

If one accepts the first assumption that sexuality is nothing more than just another developmental task, then it should be relatively easy to design a social environment to foster, rather than hinder, the development of healthy sexual attitudes and behavior (the ideal environment). Accurate sexual information appropriate to the child's level of curiosity and understanding would be presented within a supportive, understanding, and nurturing family setting. Significant individuals in the child's life would consistently model appropriate expressions of sexuality and feelings. Aggressive and other forms of exploitative sexual expressions would be absent. Because the ideal environment provides a positive approach to the development of sexuality such as used in the development of other human activities—speech, walking upright, and eating with utensils, for example—the results could be very positive. Even though ideals of any kind are seldom actualized, realistic striving for something better usually produces something better. If a child is provided with mostly

**Table 4.1** The Sociocultural Abuse of Sexuality

| Developmental Environment | Degree of Abuse |
|---|---|
| The ideal environment | Nonabusive |
| The predominantly nurturing environment | |
| | |
| The evasive environment | Abuse of developing sexuality |
| The environmental vacuum | |
| The permissive environment | |
| The negative environment | |
| The seductive environment | |
| | |
| The overtly sexual environment | Abuse of developing sexuality and sexual victimization |

SOURCE: Adapted with permission from Bolton et al. (1989).

accurate information about sexuality in a mostly supportive, understanding, and nurturing setting (the predominantly nurturing environment), the probability of developing positive sexual attitudes and healthy expressions of sexuality would seem enhanced.

But most people in Western society do not accept the assumption that sexuality is just another developmental task. Over the centuries, sex has been glorified and vilified, sometimes at the same time. Misinformation and myths about sex, rather than accurate information about the development of sexuality, provide the foundation for attitudes toward sexuality in Western society. Bombarded with all sorts of misinformation and religious proscriptions against most sexual activities, it is not surprising that many families feel compelled to protect their children from exposure to any type of information about sexuality. Other families may be willing to provide information about sexual matters, but the information is typically meager and inaccurate. Thus, the child's natural expressions of curiosity about sexuality are met with no helpful information at all (the environmental vacuum) or unspecific responses based on myths and misinformation (the evasive environment). Children reared in these settings are left to their own immature thoughts and interpretations of sexuality. These children are also especially vulnerable to extrafamilial sources of information about sexuality, such as uninformed peers, media-controlled and commercially driven messages about sexual behavior and gender roles, and sexual materials designed to fill the informational void through titillation and exploitation.

Although some families try to avoid dealing with a child's curiosity about sex by providing misinformation or no information, others actively promulgate religiously driven ideas that most sexual behavior is evil, harmful, and a sign of moral weakness (the negative environment). Misinformation, negative attitudes about sex, and fear tactics predominate. Attempts by children to explore their sexuality through experimentation often result in physical punishment. The all-too-familiar consequence of this aversive approach to sexuality is a pervasive sexual angst consisting of confusion, guilt, ambivalence, and shame; hardly a formula for the development of a positive self-image or healthy adult sexual relationships.

Some individuals renounce sexual repression and adopt, instead, a nonrestrictive and nonpunitive approach to teaching children about sexual matters (the permissive environment). This "let it all hang out" philosophy appears well-meaning and useful on the surface, but it often lacks proper pacing and timing considerations based on the child's developmental level. That is, sexual information and experiences are provided at such a level and frequency that they exceed the child's capacity to process and understand them. A young child can easily become overwhelmed with too much information, even accurate information, and may become confused and frustrated. Some children also become overstimulated with sexual information and experiences beyond their developmental level; troublesome precocious sexual experimentation may follow.

Within some families, a drama of "innocent" seduction occurs (the seductive environment). Children in this type of setting are presented with verbal and behavioral messages about their sexual desirability and a possible sexual interest in the child by an adult family member, usually a parent. Although overt sexual contact does not occur, the child may be exposed to "accidental" partial or full nudity, seductive posing or gestures, and teasing with an underlying sexual motive. Even accurate information about sexual matters is presented in a way to titillate rather than satisfy the child's sexual curiosity. This highly charged environment often confuses the child about sexual feelings, sexual behavior, and appropriate partners.

Transcending simple abuse-of-sexuality settings is the overtly sexual environment. Included here are adult-child sexual activities commonly referred to as *child sexual abuse* (e.g., intercourse, cunnilingus, anilingus, fellatio, genital fondling, digital penetration, simulated intercourse, sexualized kissing or touching, intentional genital exposure, and directed exposure to adult sexual behavior). Exposing a child to educational or pornographic materials for the purpose of sexual titillation and exploitation, as well as encouraging developmentally inappropriate sexual contact between children under the guise of normal sexual experimentation are also considered overt sexual responses. The results of this type of abuse of sexuality are well documented and are discussed later in this volume.

An examination of the abuse-of-sexuality model reveals multiple approaches to addressing the question "What do we do about our child's developing sexuality?" Sadly, most of the approaches are based on fear, misinformation, and myths emanating from deep within the sociocultural underground where sexual behavior has long been exiled.

Examination of the information presented in this chapter suggests that the evolution of Western beliefs about sexuality produced a strange mixture of conflicting ideas and messages. Many concepts are built on "scientific" evidence that males and females naturally evolved into the male-superior and female-inferior sexual creatures that we think we see today. Although many in our society still point to biological factors and evolution as the foundation for a natural separation of gender roles in sexual behavior and the caretaking of children, the evidence from anthropological studies does not support such a clear bifurcation. That is, studies have not found solid support for the traditional notions that women are biologically inferior and stay at home because they are biologically locked into caring for their infants. Also lacking solid support are ideas that males evolved into superior leaders and therefore were justified in assuming control of women. The notion that men are naturally more sexually assertive, whereas women assume the more passive role in sexual matters, may be just another unfounded culturally driven interpretation of early human sexual behavior.

Other Western concepts about human sexual behavior are based primarily on an ancient philosophy associated with the "indesputable" laws of nature or the natural order of things. These concepts were eventually blended with similar religious beliefs to produce strong prohibitions on all sexual behavior except for the purposes of procreation.

Although Western culture tends to glorify love and marriage, an insidious double standard is also tolerated and perpetuated. On the one hand, our society embraces ancient religious doctrine stating that marriage is a holy sacrament requiring both partners to uphold their vows for life. But the roots for the common belief that women must be chaste before marriage and remain faithful to their husbands but men can philander are even deeper than the religious convictions associated with male-female relationships. Also associated with this double standard are the negative attitudes about women found throughout ancient Judeo-Christian teachings. Many of these notions provide rationalizations for "keeping women in their place" and for the sexual maltreatment of women.

So what are the messages broadcast by American society regarding sexual behavior? Unlike societies with a well-established code of conduct regarding mating rituals, our society consists of many different groups and ideas. Although a dominate theme of restriction and repression provides the foundation for most interpretations of acceptable sexual behavior, many variations on this theme can be found. As a result, some messages are clear, straightforward, and very strong. Others are more confusing, rather insidious, but also strong. Many of these messages ignore developmental factors in favor of ancient beliefs about sexual behavior; abuse-of-sexuality sociocultural environments are created as a result. Cultural messages aimed specifically at males are discussed in the next chapter.

# 5

# Sexual Heroes

## *Birth of Superpenis*

Interpretations of cultural expectations are frequently presented through works of art, magazines, novels, and comics, as well as in plays, movies, sports, television programs, and commercials. Counterculture and various subculture groups also use the same venues for presenting their messages. The result can be a confusing mix of information and misinformation regarding what we should believe and how we should behave in society. Males often look to these sources for information and guidance related to sexual matters, especially how to develop into "a real man" sexually. In this regard, portrayals of women are as important as the way men are characterized. Using a historical perspective, I will examine and discuss various popular sources affecting the development of masculinity and sexual attitudes in the all-American male.

❑ **Ancient Symbols and Gods**

The practice of celebrating human genitalia and sexual acts in artworks and other materials has its foundation in antiquity. According to art historian Edward Lucie-Smith (1992), Paleolithic art is representative of early human's drive to understand, survive, and multiply in a very harsh environment. Many of the artworks are thought to be efforts to exert some form of primitive magical influence on the notion being depicted. For example, drawing beasts on the walls of caves may be more than a documentation of the animals; the artwork may have a magical influence on the continued availability of these animals for food and clothing. It was also equally important that human fertility be celebrated and assured. In this regard, Paleolithic artists may have created representations of a primitive understanding of and their belief in the magical basis for the reproductive process. A combination of these two themes may have been responsible for the production of objects with exaggerated sexual features such as breasts and vulvas. Overproportioned female thighs and buttocks are also common in ancient artworks. One of the best known examples of this type of art object is the Venus of Willendorf from the late Aurignacian period.

Although many of the early artworks depicting fertility were primarily representations of female sexual features and other related body parts, some "male Venus" objects exist. Ancient ithyphallic art objects tend to depict males with impressive penises. Perhaps these prehistoric male fertility symbols are the basis for later male penis envy and the myths surrounding the belief that males require a large penis to be attractive to females and successful in sexual mating. Other male body parts appear less important and are not typically exaggerated, as found with most ancient depictions of the female body. These figures can be found throughout most of the world where it is believed ancient humans existed. The Celtic turf figure carved in an English hillside at Cerne Abbas is a good example of ancient male fertility symbols.

Across the millennia, the notion of male fertility was gradually elevated from mere "magical" representations produced by primitive humans to divine status. In most languages, the penis achieved the status of a separate living entity and is referred to as "he" or "him" rather than "it." The ancient Egyptians formally deified the penis and male fertility in the form of the god Min, and a large erect penis typically plays a central role in artworks representing this deity. References to a mighty, potent phallus often appear in ancient Egyptian religious rites: One of the spells contained in the *Book of the Dead* (Faulkner, 1985) reads, in part, "I am Osiris, Lord of persons, alive of breast, strong of hinder-parts, stiff of phallus . . . " (p. 70). Ancient Egyptians also buried women of nobility with the genitals of a freshly slaughtered bull, "ceremoniously placed on her vagina, to ward off evil spirits" (Thorn, 1990, p. 44). And some ancient myths suggest that the creator of man started with the penis.

The ancient Greeks and Romans also established gods of male fertility. The Roman counterpart to the Egyptian god Min is Priapus, and he is often represented with a substantial member, "above which he sometimes holds a drapery full of fruits in allusion to his function as the god of fertility" (Lucie-Smith, 1992, p. 16). The Greek god Hermes is often represented by a free-standing pillar in the shape of a penis or with a penis protruding from a block of stone. In addition to the deification of fertility, the ancient Greeks celebrated fertility and eroticism in a number of ways, including building spectacular phallic altars. Interestingly, eroticism developed in a cult associated with the Greek god of wine, Dionysus. Objects related to this cult were often rich in portrayals of all types of sexual behavior, with large penises playing a central role.

Eroticism was not the exclusive province of the ancient Greeks and Romans. Examples of the celebration of sexuality can also be found in ancient Indian art objects, religious documents, and religious art. According to Hindu doctrine, sexual fulfillment is one of the ways to assure reincarnation at a higher level of existence. It is important, therefore, to achieve a higher spiritual order of sexuality in the present life. To assist in this quest, the ancient Hindus of India produced an illustrated sex manual, the *Kama Sutra* (Burton, 1962), which contains detailed information about sexual techniques, aids, and practices. Although most Western religious leaders label the *Kama Sutra* evil and pornographic, the ancient Hindus viewed sexuality as a religious practice rather than immoral or shameful. In spite of efforts to suppress the *Kama Sutra* following the adoption of more repressive and restrictive attitudes about sexuality in India at about 1000 AD, the manual prevailed. It remains one of the most important ancient documents regarding human sexuality.

Other Eastern cultures also taught the spiritual nature of sexuality. The Taoists (Daoists) of ancient China believed that sex was a form of religious worship that could, if practiced correctly, lead toward immortality. For example, through intercourse, the man could enhance his natural essence, yang, by absorbing his mate's feminine essence, yin. To maximize the energy flow and absorb as much yin as possible, men were encouraged to prolong intercourse for as long as possible and to bring their mates to orgasm. If a man was successful in preventing ejaculation entirely, he would retain his seminal essence and build up yang. On the other hand, the woman could gain the man's yang and avoid losing her yin essence by not having an orgasm. The ancient Taoists were the first to develop sex manuals to assist in learning how to achieve spiritual fulfillment and harmony through skillful sexual behavior. Successful practitioners of the Daoist sex control methods could achieve immortality. As Gregersen (1994) notes,

> The mythical Yellow Emperor, Huang-di, became immortal by having had Daoistically correct sex relations with 1,200 women. A woman, The Queen Mother of the West, was said to have duplicated the immortality of the Yellow Emperor by having gained the yin essence of more than 1,000 women in homosexual unions, and by taking the semen of numberless men who did not know the arts of the bedchamber, and therefore were not able to prevent the loss of their yang. (p. 249)

## ❏ Erotic Art

Many works of art are nothing more than studies of the human nude body, whereas others are designed to be representations of erotic behavior. The latter category is often criticized as being too explicit and, therefore, pornographic. One criterion often used to determine if a work of art should be condemned as pornographic is anatomical depictions of actual, as opposed to symbolic, acts of coitus. Another is depictions of some form of so-called deviant sexual acts such as fellatio, cunnilingus, and anal sex. Many celebrated artists such as Rembrandt, Fuseli, Rodin, and Munch mostly avoided the condemnation of moralists by offering representations of romantic or "normal" love scenes sans anatomical details. Others, such as Picasso, received more criticism because they were much more explicit in their representations of sexual activities.

Representations of so-called deviant sexual acts common to Greek and Roman works of art were much less frequent in European art until about the 19th century, when lesbianism became "the most richly represented of all sexual deviations" (Lucie-Smith, 1991, p. 202). Various interpretations of this phenomenon range from an interest in voyeuristic activities to castration fear and a stronger taboo against male homosexuality. Remember, males produced nearly all the visual arts in the 19th and most of the 20th century.

Another type of art that flourished in Europe was representations of sexual violence. During the 16th century, European artists seemed to be fascinated by libidinous satyrs or other half-human creatures and their forced sexual congress with women (e.g., *A Satyr Assaulting a Woman Defended by Three Cupids*, c. 1542-1545. Etching by Fantuzzi). Depictions of human males as perpetrators of rape of human females were also common from the 16th century on (e.g., *Targuin and Lucretia*, c. 1571. Oil on canvas by Titian). Some representations of females "forcing" males into unwanted sexual activities can also be found (e.g., *Joseph and Potiphar's Wife*, 1634. Rembrandt). Although many of the compositions during this period are symbolic representations of rape, many are more explicit in their renderings of sado-masochism, rape, and other forms of sexual violence.

Sexual violence was not limited to male perpetration. A popular theme was the theft or destruction of a male's virility through female sexuality. Compositions of this type often depict the mutilation of male genitalia (e.g., *Nymph Mutilating a Satyr*, 1543-1544. L.D. after Primaticcio), the severing of heads (e.g., *Judith*, 1537. Lucas Cranach the Elder), and the perpetration of other mayhem by females (e.g., *Jael and Sisera*, 1648-1650. Rembrandt).

More explicit erotic art was popularized in the 19th century and into the 20th century. Many of these works may have been labeled pornographic and suppressed by the predominant Christian establishment, but they were exhibited in more sophisticated and less sexually repressive locales such as Vienna and Paris.

Although males continued to dominate the art scene during the 20th century, feminist art became increasingly more influential during the late 1960s and tended to stress political rather than erotic purposes. Often compositions ridiculed male sexual fantasies (e.g., works by Sylvia Sleigh and Cindy Sherman) or expressed female solidarity (e.g., works by Judy Chicago).

Also during this period, homoerotic art began to emerge. Since the 1970s, compositions using the male nude as well as subtle and explicit depictions of homosexuality have become more prevalent in artworks of all types (e.g., works by George Dureau, Delmas Howe, and David Wojnarowicz). One of the most celebrated and controversial artists of this genre is Robert Mapplethorpe, whose photographic images of sado-masochistic homosexual activities created a firestorm of censorship nearly everywhere his works were exhibited. Although homosexual content can be found in artworks throughout history, especially in art created by ancient Greeks and Romans, the taboo against such depictions remains strong in Judeo-Christian culture, which teaches that such conduct is abnormal and abhorrent (for an excellent review of sexuality in Western art, see Lucie-Smith, 1992).

## ❑ Pornography, Sex, and Violence

The term *pornography* is derived from the Greek, *porne,* a prostitute, and, *graphein,* write. A translation of *pornographos* would be "writing of prostitutes." So, pornography has its origins in the erotic and, presumably, sexually explicit writings of ancient professionals in the field of sexual behavior. The contemporary formal definition of pornography appears to have deleted the prostitute and added other venues: "writings, pictures, etc. intended primarily to arouse sexual desire" (*Webster's New World Dictionary*, 1990, p. 458). Often associated with definitions of pornography is the statement that the work is created for its prurient rather than its artistic value. *Prurient* comes from the Latin word *pruner,* meaning "to itch." The contemporary definition of prurient is "tending to excite lust; lewd" (*Webster's New World Dictionary*, 1990, p. 474). Implicit in these definitions is that material designed to arouse sexual desire is immoral. Otherwise, what would it matter if someone became sexually aroused by being exposed to so-called pornographic material? Isn't sexual arousal a personal event as long as the sexually aroused person does not recruit unwilling participants in his or her state of arousal?

Pornography is also a subjective matter from at least two viewpoints: the creator of the pornography and the consumer of the material. It is impossible to determine with some material if the creator intended to arouse his or her consumer sexually. Some creators of pornographic material may admit that sexual arousal was part of the goals in producing the items, but other nonsexual goals were also strong motivational elements. On the other hand, some materials have strong arousal potential, but the creator denies that prurience was his or her primary purpose for presenting the items. From the consumer's standpoint, pornography, like beauty, may be in the eye of the beholder. That is, some individuals find any depiction of the nude human body as pornographic, whereas others can withstand hours of video portrayals of unbridled sexual escapades without breaking into a sweat.

Attempts have been made to distinguish pornography from erotic art or erotica. The word *erotic* comes from the Greek word *eros*, meaning "love." The contemporary definition of erotic is "of or arousing sexual feelings or desires; amatory," whereas erotica is defined as "erotic books, pictures, etc." (*Webster's New World Dictionary*, 1990, p. 202). Using a content analysis approach, Kronhausen and Kronhausen (1964) conclude that pornographic material contains repetitive seduction themes, pure lust, exploitation and victimization, and violations of conventional standards of sexual behavior. Also, the primary intent of the material is to arouse the consumer sexually. Whereas some of these themes may be present in erotically realistic art, the erotic items also contain depictions of other emotions and behaviors found in intimate relationships. As Goldstein and Kant (1973) write, "Thus the Kronhausens discriminate between pornography and erotically realistic fiction on the basis of the general view of man expressed in the work, not the explicitness with which sexual relations are described" (p. 8). On the other hand, Mosher (1988) defines pornography as any material designed specifically to arouse the consumer sexually through graphic portrayals of sexual behavior.

Pornography is also commonly classified as hard or soft core. Hard-core pornography typically includes material intended to arouse the consumer sexually with graphic presentations of genitalia and sexual acts. Some examples of hard-core pornography are photographs of any type of sexual intercourse with a focus on penetration, written material describing in great detail sexual acts and the arousal of the participants, and X-rated movies and videos with graphic presentations of all sorts of sexual behavior.

Soft-core or soft porn typically includes nudes, but with less of a focus on genitalia and the absence of actual sexual acts. Some examples are magazines such as *Playboy*, which features nude photographs of young women in various poses, typically without the presence of men or sexual activities; and X-rated movies and videos, which contain some nudity (usually female) and the implication or simulation of sexual activities. An increasing number of television programs are considered by some as soft-core pornography due to their focus on "tits and ass," although the actors are not nude. A good example of this type of program is the popular series *Baywatch*, often referred to as "Babewatch," a program about life on the California beaches as seen through the eyes of well-endowed lifeguards. An older series, *Charlie's Angels,* about three beautiful female detectives, was somewhat less bold in showing skin, but not shy about high-lighting each detective's anatomical strengths as these women went about the business of solving crimes. Chase scenes typically produced a whole lot of jiggling plus titillating glimpses of forbidden flesh.

The debate about pornography rages on. Laws attempting to regulate pornographic material have shifted from a definition of pornography to a definition of obscenity. *Obscene* is derived from the Latin *obscenus,* meaning filth. The contemporary definition of obscene is "1. offensive to modesty or decency; lewd 2. repulsive" (*Webster's New World Dictionary,* 1990, p.406). In 1955, Kaplan proposed four categories of obscenity:

Conventional obscenity: Material that is unconventional and attacks conventional attitudes toward and practices of sexuality.

Dionysian obscenity: Material that celebrates excessive sexualism and the release of natural sexual impulses.

Perverse obscenity: Material that portrays sexual behavior as dirty or unnatural.

Pornography of violence: Material that blends the expression of sexual impulses into acts of aggression.

Although the problem of ascertaining the creator's intentions is eliminated by evaluating the material using obscenity criteria, the subjectivity of the consumer remains. What also remains is the determination that most portrayals of sexuality are offensive, lewd, and repulsive.

Regardless of the controversy associated with defining pornography or erotica, most everyone agrees that material with themes of sexuality typically produces interest in and some level of sexual arousal by the consumer, mostly males. The ultimate question remains to be answered, however: Do obscene and pornographic works lead to acts of violence and encourage perverted sexual behavior, or do they actually help to prevent such acts (Goldstein & Kant, 1973)? Confronted with this vexing question, the U.S. Commission on Obscenity and Pornography conducted hearings and reviewed relevant research addressing this issue. In 1970, the commission announced that it was unable to find a definitive link between exposure to pornography and sexual offenses, although some consumers of pornography reported sexual arousal and an increase in the frequency of their usual type of sexual behavior, such as autoerotic practices and sexual activities with a consenting partner (Commission on Obscenity and Pornography, 1970). The commission's recommendation that legislative bodies refrain from efforts to control or criminalize commerce in sexually explicit materials so enraged those who firmly believed that pornography and antisocial sexual acts were linked, regardless of the research findings, that President Nixon ultimately rejected the commission's findings and recommendations.

The controversy was not lost on sex researchers. During the 1970s, various research projects were launched to discover the causal link between pornography and the perpetration of sexual offenses, as proposed by the commission's dissenters. Again, researchers could find an increase in arousal and typical sexual activities following exposure to pornography, but no evidence that pornography precipitated antisocial sexual behavior (see Brown, Amoroso, & Ware, 1976; Byrne, 1977; Hatfield, Sprecher, & Traupman, 1978; Heiby & Becker, 1980; Herrell, 1975; Schmidt, Sigusch, & Schafer, 1973). Even studies of known sexual perpetrators failed to find the elusive link between exposure to pornography and the genesis of sexual maladies, although some perpetrators reported using pornography to augment arousal to deviant fantasies and antisocial sexual behavior. For example, in a well-controlled study of perpetrators of sexual offenses, Goldstein and Kant (1973) found no evidence that exposure to erotic or pornographic material triggers antisocial sexual behavior such as rape and child sexual abuse, although some offenders, especially rapists, appear prone to use scenes from pornographic material in their fantasies.

In the mid-1980s, a new committee, the U.S. Attorney General's Commission on Pornography (the Meese Commission) was formed to reexamine the effect of exposure to pornographic material. Although the Meese Commission found no connection between nonviolent and nondegrading pornographic material such as adult partners engaging in consensual sexual behavior, the commission reported finding a link between sexual violence and violent pornography (U.S. Department of Justice, 1986). The commission also reported that exposure to material with themes of female degradation and subservience increased the acceptability of rape by consumers. Armed with its findings that some form of causal link between pornography, especially violent pornography, and antisocial sexual behavior existed, the Meese Commission issued a large number of recommendations related to restricting the availability of pornography through enacting new legislation or active enforcement of current laws.

As with the report from the first commission to study pornography, the findings from the Meese Commission created quite a stir. Most of those who questioned the Meese Commission's conclusions were critical of the commission's lack of scientific inquiry and objectivity and its overgeneralization of research findings (see Brigman, 1986; Donnerstein, Linz, & Penrod, 1988; Wilcox, 1987). Even so, researchers were now faced with the challenge to take a closer look at the differential effects of nonviolent versus violent pornographic material.

Some studies in this area produced support for the proposition that violence and the degradation of females, rather than just depictions of sexual behavior in pornography, are important in the development of negative attitudes toward women and possible violent sexual offenses. For example, studies conducted by Check (1985) and Check and Guloien (1989) strongly suggest that men exposed to either violent or nonviolent but dehumanizing pornography are more likely to report that they might commit rape, if they are certain they will get away with it, than men who are exposed only to nonviolent, nondegrading sexual pornography. It is also interesting to note that the responses from men exposed to nonviolent and nondegrading sexual scenes, regarding their inclination to commit rape, are similar to responses from men who were not exposed to any form of pornography. Donnerstein, Berkowitz, and Linz (1986) found that college men exposed to violence in pornographic or violence in nonpornographic films are more likely to accept rape myths, a higher willingness to use force for sexual activities, and an increased likelihood of committing rape, if they are reasonably assured of escaping detection and prosecution, than men exposed to nonviolent pornography. Donnerstein (1980) also found that a sample of college men exposed to pornography with violence (rape themes) subsequently show more aggression toward female confederates than males not exposed to violent pornography. Provocation by a female confederate also increases the amount of retaliatory aggression for males exposed to violent pornography. Donnerstien and Berkowitz (1981) found similar results for males who asked to view pornography with scenes of females exhibiting sexual arousal while being dominated and raped by a man. Linz, Donnerstein, and Penrod (1988) examined the effects of viewing X-rated sexually explicit material without violence with viewing nonsexually explicit R-rated violent or R-rated nonviolent material. They found that college males exposed to the violent material subsequently show less sensitivity to women rape victims than subjects who viewed material without violence, with or without sexually explicit sex scenes. It was now time to separate sex from violence, at least in the research laboratories.

Although many studies appeared to support the proposition that it is the depictions of violence rather than explicit sexual behavior that hardens men's attitudes toward women and increases their propensity to engage in aggressive behavior with women, some studies suggest that extended periods of exposure to nonviolent sexually explicit pornographic material may produce similar results. For example, Zillmann and Bryant (1982, 1984) found that male and female subjects exposed to nonviolent but sexually explicit pornography on a repeated and extended schedule subsequently recommend more lenient punishment for a rapist than either control subjects or subjects exposed to the material in a less intense manner. Males also demonstrate more insensitivity toward women following extended exposure to the sexually explicit but nonviolent material. In their analysis of "slasher" films, Cowan and O'Brien (1990) found that sexually permissive women are the targets for violence and are killed more often than women portrayed as virtuous. Results such as these prompted Zillmann and Weaver (1989) to posit a link between portrayals of women as sexually promiscuous and society's tendency to devalue such women. That is, sexually promiscuous women command little respect in our society even though men seek them out for sexual favors. An increase in negative attitudes toward sexually permissive women may trickle down to all women with repeated exposures to such portrayals of women.

Not all studies confirm that exposure to nonviolent pornography increases men's insensitivity to women, especially rape victims, or men's aggressive behavior toward women in a laboratory setting. And some studies have failed to find a link between repeated exposure to nonviolent sexually explicit pornography, and negative attitudes toward women or the acceptance of rape myths (see Linz et al., 1988; Malamuth & Ceniti, 1986; Padgett & Brislin-Slutz, 1987; Padgett, Brislin-Slutz, & Neal, 1989).

So what does the research literature actually tell us about the messages presented to males by pornography? The reviews are mixed. Fejes (1992) concludes that "after a man has viewed violent and/or degrading pornography, callousness toward women becomes an important part of his sense of masculinity" (p. 22). On the other hand, Linz (1989) suggests that exposure to sexually explicit nonviolent material may not necessarily result in an increase in negative attitudes toward women or the acceptance of sexual offenses against women, although demeaning portrayals of women may produce or reinforce some negative attitudes toward women.

In sum, it appears that pornography reflects males' confusion about sexuality and women. Women are placed in two categories: sexual playthings or domestic dollies. Either way they are to be controlled by men and serve as males determine they should. The historical underpinnings for this conservative attitude toward women is discussed in detail elsewhere in this volume. Historically, women are often punished severely for not performing as their male-determined role dictates. One can easily argue that the more conservative the attitude toward women, the higher the likelihood of retribution for not performing as dictated by traditional cultural norms. Although Zillmann (1989) contends that material portraying irresponsible, sexually explicit nonviolent material erodes traditional values regarding marriage and sexual behavior, some studies show that highly sexually aggressive males subscribe to more conservative rather than egalitarian ideas about women when compared to less sexually aggressive men (Koss, Leonard, Beezley, & Oros, 1981, 1985). Scott (1985) also found a positive relationship between the consumption of traditional men's magazines such as *American Rifleman* and *Field and Stream* and rape reports, whereas no such relationship was found between pornography and rape reports.

Males learn a lot of nonsense from pornography. Although research on pornography has focused on the effects of sexually explicit and violent material, much less has been done regarding the effect of these materials on the development of the masculine self-image. The penis and its ejaculatory power are frequently celebrated. Seldom do male porn stars have regular penises. In pornography, men seldom ejaculate inside a woman even after hours of heavy thrusting and sexual ecstasy. No, they typically seem compelled to remove the penis from whatever orifice is stimulating it and display their ejaculatory power. Often, ejaculate appears to emanate from an artillery piece and blasts into the air like a July 4th fireworks display. Nowhere is the artwork better in pornography than during the recording of a male ejaculating in never-ending bursts of semen while the female looks on in wonder. Camera angles are planned carefully so as not to miss a drop of the precious fluid. Slow motion and repeated images give the impression that a real man can come forever. Why, with one shot, a real man could probably populate an entire continent. Ah, the beauty of it all! Beautiful, but dangerously deceptive. Although most males can differentiate between fantasy and reality, many still embrace the myths presented by such powerful portrayals of sexual prowess.

Regardless of the various definitions of pornography or erotica, sexually explicit materials are plentiful, can be found in nearly every culture, and seem to be quite popular. For example, Peat, Marwick, and Partners (1984) found that 38% of a sample of adult Canadians admitted to viewing films with explicit scenes of sexual intercourse. Recent polls conducted in the United States suggest that 25% to 40% of adults have either attended X-rated movies or rented X-rated videos for their private viewing at home. When faced with the choice to impose tighter controls on the availability of pornography or to retain the present level of legal restrictions, 43% of poll respondents in the United States favored tighter restrictions, whereas 48% favored current sanctions (see Press et al., 1986; Roper Organization, 1985). Harris (1988) found that only a minority of people favored the criminalization of sexually explicit material, but approximately 75% of the sample favored legislative efforts to control or ban pornography with violence.

Although pornography is designed primarily for the adult consumer, most males are exposed to some form of pornography by the time they are teenagers. One of the most common types of material available for preadolescents is the "girlie magazine." Bryant and Brown (1989) found that the average age of males' first exposure to *Playboy* was 11 years. (Females' average age was 12 years.) In addition, nearly 90% of a midwestern sample of adults reported preadult exposure to soft-core-type magazines depicting nudity.

In my experience of obtaining sexual histories from hundreds of males in a clinical setting over the past two decades, *Playboy* or similar magazines were mentioned frequently as the male's first exposure to anything sexual, especially the opportunity to view the nude adult female body. Most males, in my experience, either discovered the magazines in their own homes, presumably hidden by their parents, or were offered the opportunity to see naked women by a peer who somehow gained access to this type of magazine. Most males reported being interested in seeing photographs of nude females and sometimes used the material for episodes of masturbation. Almost none identified their exposure to these magazines as propelling them into a compulsion for pornography or inappropriate sexual behavior against others. Many, however, described the development of a preference for the "picture perfect" women portrayed in the magazines and frustration that these women were in short supply.

## ❑ What Sort of Man Reads *Playboy?*

In 1953, a young man working as a promotion copy writer for a popular men's magazine, *Esquire,* asked for and was refused a $5 raise. The young man believed he was worth more than the mere $60 a week he was being paid, so he quit. This young man, Hugh Hefner, also had big dreams. He believed that males would appreciate a more candid view of masculinity and sexuality than was being presently offered:

> I wanted to publish a magazine that both influenced and reflected the socio-sexual changes taking place in America but that was first and foremost—fun. *Playboy* was intended as a response to the repressive anti-sexual, anti-play-and-pleasure aspects of our puritan heritage. (Hefner, 1979b, p. 3)

Hefner borrowed $600 and managed to convince some friends and relatives to invest an additional $6,000 to pursue his dream.

The first issue of his upstart magazine, *Playboy,* was published in December 1953. Marilyn Monroe graced the cover and was the first Sweetheart of the Month. (The rights to publish the now infamous calendar photograph of Marilyn Monroe used for the pictorial were purchased by Hefner for $500.) To everyone's astonishment, the entire 70,000 copies of the first issue of *Playboy* sold out shortly after they reached newsstands. Within a very short time, *Playboy* became one of the world's most popular men's magazines. The *Playboy* empire flourished. The first *Playboy* club opened in Chicago and soon clubs opened in most major cities or resort areas in the world. The *Playboy's Penthouse* television program became very popular soon after its debut in the 1960s. The *Playboy* mansions were built, airplanes and fast cars were purchased, and beautiful young women were everywhere. Hugh Hefner not only accomplished his dream, he was actually living it. His success was so phenomenal that he became a model for thousands of wanna-be playboys. A number of other magazines, such as *Gallery* and *Penthouse,* were subsequently published using the general format or ideas first offered by *Playboy.*

Only recently has Hugh Hefner relinquished his official playboy status by marrying Kimberley Conrad, 1989's Playmate of the Year. Hefner now extols the virtues of married life and the joys of parenting his two young children. Although he remains editor-in-chief of *Playboy* magazine, Hefner has turned over the reins of the parent company, Playboy Enterprises, to his daughter by his first marriage, Christie Hefner.

Because *Playboy* has played a prominent part in many males' sexual lives during the past four decades, its appeal to men deserves a closer look. So what is the appeal? Of course, the first item that comes to mind is the nude photographs of young women. From the beginning, the underlying philosophy guiding the selection and presentation of women in *Playboy* has been to combine "the girl next door" with sexuality. That is, all women who take their clothes off are not whores, sluts, or porno queens. According to the *Playboy* philosophy, nice girls can be sexual and remain nice girls.

But other magazines published nude photographs before and since and few have gained the popularity of *Playboy.* In fact, the early issues of *Playboy* contained only a few photographs of seminude women. Most of the poses allowed for only a peek at exposed or semiexposed breasts; a peek at the pubic area was not allowed. Creative photography produced a somewhat provocative pose without creating a scandal or invoking the wrath of the censors. A good example of this type of presentation can be found in the centerfold photograph of Miss July 1957, a 5' 3" brown-eyed, dark-haired student stewardess. Miss July is found lounging on a couch near a record player. She has shed the top of a see-through negligee but is wearing the companion bottom piece. She is also wearing matching high-heeled bedroom slippers. Although it is quite apparent that the petite young stewardess is blessed with a substantial bosom, a record and her right arm are strategically placed so as to conceal all of her left nipple as well as most of her right nipple. Nonetheless, she is comely and her pose beckons without crass sexuality. This is the only photograph presented of an unclothed Miss July 1957. The pictorial offers three other photographs of her in full uniform while she performs her duties as a stewardess. In the same issue is another pictorial called "Playboy's Yacht Party." In eight pages, the joy of sailing the high seas in a two-masted luxury yacht with a "carefree crew of beauties" is chronicled. Again, the photographs of the four "crew-beauties" reveal only occasional exposed or partially exposed breasts. Mostly, the women are fully clothed, wearing all or part of two-piece bathing suits or changing from street clothes to yacht attire.

An analysis of all the photographs in the July 1957 issue of *Playboy* reveals a total of six partially exposed nipples, no genitalia, and no bare buttocks. If males wanted to see photographs of nude females in the 1950s, the choices seemed to be limited to issues of *National Geographic,* with stories and photographs of "primitive people" who had not yet discovered the breast containment devices so revered by modern societies; magazines documenting the wonderful life in nudist colonies; or hard-core pornographic material.

During the 1960s, *Playboy* expanded its coverage of nude females but maintained its pattern of presenting mostly breasts and little of anything else. For example, an analysis of all the photographs in the March 1968 issue produces a total of 10 fully exposed nipples, 20 partially exposed nipples, two partially bare buttocks, no totally bare buttocks, and no genitalia. This includes a comprehensive pictorial of Jane Fonda and the cast of the $3.5 million erotic film *Barbarella.* (The analysis does not include a six-page pictorial on the art of body painting, however, because it became too difficult to discriminate between the artwork and the body work.)

The sexual revolution began to have some effect on depictions of sex in the 1970s. In an interview for *Gallery* in January 1973, the reputed father of the so-called New Journalism and author of best-selling novels, Gay Talese, responds:

> What is really important in this country, what do I think the big story is? I thought of sex, the changing sexual mores of the 1960s, how life has changed so dramatically, how what had not been permissible in 1960 was permissible in 1970. (quoted in Rosenthal, 1973, p.74)

Gay Talese also points out that *Playboy* is selling fantasy and *Penthouse,* not *Playboy,* was the first to publish photographs of models with pubic hair. Also in this issue is a pictorial featuring "The Gallery

Girl of the Month," which offers several photographs of full frontal nudity complete with pubic hair.

During the late 1960s, *Playboy* teased its readers with an occasional glimpse of partially exposed pubic hair. In the early 1970s, more pubic hair was exposed, although the primary focus of the photographs was not on female genitalia. For example, the January 1972 Playmate of the Month features a full frontal photograph of Miss January posed standing upright against a bookcase. A fireplace with a roaring fire can be seen in the background. Although ample illumination highlights Miss January's breasts, a shadow from a book she is holding in her right hand mutes, but does not hide, her pubic hair. Miss January 1973 was subsequently chosen as Playmate of the Year, 1973. The eight-page pictorial celebrating this event in the June 1973 issue offers a bit more of the Playmate of the Year's pubic hair.

Certainly, portrayals of the female body have changed in *Playboy* over the past four decades. Current readers are exposed to more photographs and more "intimate" skin in general than available in early *Playboy* issues. For example, an analysis of the July 1994 *Playboy* reveals 22 fully exposed nipples, 23 partially exposed nipples, eight shots of partially or fully exposed buttocks, and 15 shots with pubic hair partially or fully exposed. The analysis includes a pictorial of President Reagan's daughter Patti Davis, who authored an erotic fantasy about John Wayne Bobbitt's dismembered penis. Overall, photographs in contemporary issues of *Playboy* contain more provocative poses, such as legs spread apart for an advantageous view of partially concealed or fully exposed genitalia, than earlier issues. And hints at self-stimulation are sometimes present.

As an additional point of interest, the women featured in the July 1957 issue are depicted as engaging in traditional female roles. For example, the Playmate of the Month was a stewardess. In the August 1994 issue, a New York City policewoman was featured on the cover and in one of the pictorials. Although I am not prepared to state that *Playboy* has had a significant change in policy regarding its overall philosophy about women as playmates, featuring a woman in such a traditionally unfeminine role as a police officer is somewhat of a departure. Yet, the girl next door of the nineties could certainly be a police officer. On the other hand, feminists would argue that by presenting a female in a traditionally male-dominated professional role and then reducing her to just another woman who takes her clothes off for men negates the concept that women should be taken seriously and are capable of fulfilling professional positions normally held by men. (The policewoman who posed for that issue of *Playboy* was subsequently dismissed from the force based on allegations that she had made only about three arrests during her 3 years on the force. Apparently revealing herself to *Playboy* readers prompted an investigation that may have revealed even more about her. She reported that she was informed that she was dismissed because her actions constituted a misuse of the police uniform, not because she chose to expose her body in a national magazine.)

Some might argue that the women portrayed in *Playboy* are not at all like the so-called girl next door, at least not like the neighbor girls most men remember. Although most of the women in pictorials, including the Playmate of the Month segments, appear to have modest backgrounds, few men can recall living next door to a Marilyn Monroe, Jayne Mansfield, Kim Novak, Brigitte Bardot, Rachel Welch, Linda Evans, Anita Ekberg, Ursula Andress, Elke Sommer, Catherine Deneuve, or Bo Derek. The beautiful nude women portrayed in *Playboy* may be real, but they more accurately represent and reinforce the American male's fantasy of women than the reality of what the real girl next door is like.

For males who bother to look beyond the nude pictorials, a virtual handbook for achieving success as a man awaits. By reading *Playboy*, a young man can learn to select the proper attire for any occasion, including such inane accessories as money clips, key chains, cigarette lighters, and pipes. Social manners are discussed and expensive toys are presented. Some women also find *Playboy* helpful in learning about men. As one female reader writes, "*Playboy* offers any intelligent woman an almanac of information on the way to her man's heart. . . . Where else can a woman find out what men want, if not from their very own magazine?" (*Playboy*, August 1968, p. 14).

But most important to *Playboy's* success is the "guiding principles and editorial credo" (Hefner, 1979a, p. 81) reflected by all the material selected for publication. In the December 1962 issue, Hefner attempted for the first time to spell out in detail what was presented as "the Playboy Philosophy." It took 25 installments over several issues to complete. The Playboy Philosophy encompasses a wide range of concerns, including, but not limited to, personal freedom (Americans live in a free society and have personal rights); the nature of man (natural and good, not bad and evil); church-state legislation (no justification for organized religion's use of the state to regulate sexual behavior of free citizens); sexuality (sexual behavior is neither the result of a flaw or weakness in the nature of man nor the devil's handiwork); sex and love (sex is an expression of love but sex and love are neither synonymous nor dependent on each other); impersonal sex (personal sex is preferable but no justification to oppose impersonal sex exists unless it is harmful in some way to one of the participants); sex, marriage, and babies (premarital sex does not necessarily increase the chances of establishing a successful marriage but sex should not be restricted to the marriage bed and used solely for the purposes of procreation); homosexuality (heterosexuality is a preference but support tolerance for those with different inclinations; homosexuality is not an emotional aberration); censorship (the human body is a beautiful creation, to devalue it by calling nudity obscene is absurd); depictions of murder and exploitative sex (oppose irresponsible, exploitative, coercive, harmful sexual behavior; sexual behavior should be limited to consenting adults). In addition to material published in *Playboy*, a Playboy Foundation and a Playboy Legal Defense Team were established to support social, legal, and political reforms consistent with the Playboy Philosophy.

Although *Playboy* is selling fantasy sex, it also offers its readers an opportunity to learn more about real sexual behavior as information becomes available from respected authorities in the area. For example, *Playboy* (1968 May) published an interview with William Masters and Virginia Johnson subsequent to the publication of their pioneering book, *Human Sexual Response*. Masters and Johnson give candid responses mostly stripped of the somewhat difficult medicalese found in the 1966 book. Thus, a nonmedical reader could learn, perhaps for the first time, that some very popular myths about sexual behavior are just that—myths. Masters and Johnson make it very clear that penile size does not relate to the male's ability to stimulate a female sexually. Learning that bigger is not necessarily better was certainty a relief for most males with an average or smaller-than-average penis. It was also helpful to know that a circumcised male was no more prone to experience premature ejaculation than an uncircumcised male. But one of the most important bits of information was that sexually responsive individuals, regardless of gender, experience essentially the same cycle of human sexual responsiveness. The reader also learns that women have more of a potential for multiple orgasms than men. Thus, Masters and Johnson are telling millions of *Playboy* readers, who were mostly male, that the size of their penis is essentially unimportant, a woman has the same sexual response cycle as men, and most women are capable of multiple orgasms.

For a decade, the Playboy Foundation contributed more than $300,000 to the Reproductive Biology Research Foundation to support additional research by Masters, Johnson, and their colleagues. A second interview of Masters and Johnson appeared in the November 1979 issue, subsequent to the publication of *Human Sexual Inadequacy* (Masters & Johnson, 1970), *The Pleasure Bond* (Masters & Johnson, 1976), and *Homosexuality in Perspective* (Masters & Johnson, 1979). Again, readers were given the opportunity to learn, in an understandable format, what Masters and Johnson learned about human sexual behavior from more than two decades of laboratory research.

About 15 years later, *Playboy* (March 1994) published an article on adultery written by Masters, Johnson, and Kolodny. The information was based on their research on heterosexual extramarital affairs. Readers learned that extramarital sex in America is neither uncommon nor restricted to married men (26% to 66% of married men, 18% to 69% of married women reported having at least one affair). Readers also discovered that affairs come in a variety of types ranging from situation specific (e.g., one-night stands) to a number of different long-term affairs (e.g., intimacy reduction, cathartic, kinky). Masters and Johnson state that extramarital affairs should not be considered abnormal or inherently destructive, although they do not openly endorse extramarital sexual behavior. For some couples, they advise, sex beyond the marital bed may rejuvenate the marriage, but the risk for a negative outcome is great. Again, *Playboy* provided the opportunity for its male readers to gain factual information from respected authorities about an important sexual issue often shrouded in myth and misinformation. As *Playboy* senior staff writer James P. Petersen (1979) quips:

> I have discovered that there are three kinds of sex articles: "What We Know to Be True," "What We Think We Know to Be True" and "What We Wish Were True." The first kind were written by Masters and Johnson. The second kind are written by people who have read Masters and Johnson. The third kind are written by people who work for *Penthouse*. (pp. 87-88)

*Playboy* conducts its own research on sexual behavior. Periodically, the magazine polls its readers about their sexual attitudes and behavior through informal quizzes or more formal surveys designed by respected researchers. The results are published in subsequent issues and frequently cited in trade as well as scholarly publications. The February 1973 issue offers a quiz on sex fantasies. Readers are given instructions on scoring and interpreting their responses. A wide range of interpretations is available. Men could learn, for example, that the frequency and type of fantasies they have may mean a fascination with exotic human sexuality or a morbid preoccupation with bizarre sexuality. A summary of the results of a Playboy Foundation-funded survey of sex in America was first published in a series of articles in the October, November, and December 1973 issues of *Playboy* (Hunt, 1974). The author of the articles, Morton Hunt, presents information from one of the most comprehensive looks at sexual attitudes and behavior in America since the Kinsey reports. An interested reader could learn that 1970s' women were still not quite as sexually permissive as men but the younger female may be catching up. Although premarital sex without affection was climbing in popularity, the preference for both males and females was sex with a loved one. And an increase in the frequency of and the imaginative aspects of sexual behavior for marital couples was also encouraging for married readers, as well as single readers contemplating marriage. A full report was published by Playboy Press as a book, *Sexual Behavior in the 1970s* (Hunt, 1974). The type of survey typically used by *Playboy* to assess sexuality in the United States and in other countries where the magazine is sold has been criticized by numerous researchers for serious methodological flaws. Some believe that the results from this type of survey are virtually useless (Michael et al., 1994).

In the July 1979 issue of *Playboy*, Morton Hunt authors an article warning that most medical doctors are ill-prepared to diagnose, treat, or give advice about sexual problems. Readers learned that formal training in human sexual behavior increased in many medical schools following the publication of the research by Masters and Johnson, but peaked in 1973. Although some medical schools continue to offer first-rate human sexuality programs, most view the teaching of human sexuality as unimportant or threatening to conservative principles. For the reader, the net result is informative but rather unsettling. To whom do you go for information and advice regarding sexual problems if your most trusted professional—your doctor—does not know beans about sexuality? At least *Playboy* readers were better prepared to discuss the issue of training and expertise with their doctor than those without access to the information.

Although *Playboy* typically devotes several pages to sociosexual issues through various editorials, articles, guest opinions, the Playboy Advisor, and the Playboy Forum, the bulk of the magazine is dedicated to the other side of the statement of purpose: fun. Printed on most covers of *Playboy* is the statement "Entertainment for Men." Peruse most any issue of *Playboy* and you will discover a wide range of presentations, most of which are entertaining is some way. For example, scattered throughout are humorous cartoons; a section called "Playboy's Party Jokes" has been a staple for years; articles on boy's toys—especially flashy automobiles and expensive gadgets—appear on a regular basis; movie and music reviews and presentations of contemporary art are informative as well as entertaining; short stories, written by established authors, are present in nearly all issues; and interviews with celebrities ranging from rock stars to philosophers are appealing to men who think with the large head as well as the small one. Even feminist writer Betty Friedan (1995) informed men in an entertaining manner why they die young. Yes, *Playboy* can be entertaining and the *Playboy* philosophy about male sexuality is perpetuated through most of this entertainment. That is, sexual behavior is normal as long as you are not harming anyone with your actions, so let's all have a little fun!

The message about masculinity and manhood is also clear. Men should strive to be successful, take risks, become powerful, achieve reasonably sophisticated social skills, learn to play, and own a lot of goodies. In other words, be like Hugh Hefner, who took a career risk that produced an empire. You, too, can lounge around the mansion with a bevy of beauties on your arm or in your rotating bed.

*Playboy* and its ilk have been severely criticized for a number of reasons, not the least of which is portraying women as sex objects. But Bernie Zilbergeld (1992) finds the exposure of nude females to young males innocuous:

A number of times, I have watched a group of two, three, or four boys at a bookstore looking at *Playboy* or *Penthouse*. The only word that comes to mind to describe what I saw is *charming*. There's something truly wonderful about it, a lot of what I'd call good energy. I rarely sensed any disparagement of women. (p. 172)

Speaking from the feminist perspective, psychologist Gary Brooks (1995) finds nothing charming about the influence that this type of exposure to fantasy women has on men and women. He writes,

> This male pattern of relating to women's bodies, which I am calling the Centerfold Syndrome, represents one of the most malignant forces in contemporary relationships between men and women. . . . Her airbrushed perfection permeates our visual environment and our consciousness, creating unreal fantasies and expectations, imposing profound distortions on how men relate with women and to women's bodies, and, in turn, how women relate to their physical selves and with men. (pp. 1-2)

According to Brooks, the Centerfold Syndrome ultimately produces men who are unable to develop emotionally intimate relationships with men or women. These men tend to sexualize most relationships with women, especially fantasy centerfold type women. Fantasy and emotional withdrawal rather than reality and emotional intimacy seem to lurk behind the walls of the *Playboy* mansions.

One of my female patients, a physician and survivor of childhood sexual abuse, has this to say about my review of *Playboy* magazines for this book:

> I'm thinking about 40 years of *Playboy*. It must be a stack at least 12 feet high. Four-hundred-eighty issues. I have been in practice 13 years, see 20 patients a day—both breasts except for the occasional woman who has had a mastectomy. Assume 48 weeks a year, and three days a week: $13 \times 3 \times 48 \times 20 \times 2 = 74,880$ breasts. The truth is, they are more the same than different. Pigmented, nobby or inverted, pendulous or almost missing. There are the implants, some hard as rocks, literally, from encapsulation, others soft and almost natural except they don't compress quite the same and there is a scar. I don't think one of them made it to *Playboy*. Female sexuality is as narrowly defined as it was with Victoria: large boobs,

narrow waist, and 120 pounds. Call them mammary glands and keep a look out for lost erections.

So, what kind of man reads *Playboy*? Every man with a fantasy of achieving supermanhood. The myth lives on.

## ❏ Superheroes

Much of what a boy learns about his masculinity and sexuality is found in representations of male heroes. Mostly, male heroes are portrayed as embracing the traditional male values of power, strength, control, aggressiveness, competitiveness, and competence. With these attributes, male heroes will almost surely be successful at whatever task they are attempting to accomplish. Being a winner is the hallmark of masculinity. Traditional female characteristics such as passivity, weakness, emotionality, and helplessness are mostly absent in male heroes but quite apparent in the females superheroes are trying to impress or save. To press the point, many male heroes are portrayed as possessing exaggerated traditional male characteristics and become superheroes.

A rich source for male superheroes is comic books. Since the 1930s and the introduction of the first comic book superhero, Superman (*Action Comics*, 1938), male superheroes of nearly all types have been offered and popularized. Superman was soon joined by Batman and Spider Man, the X-Men, Wolverine, the Punisher, Captain Marvel, Captain America, and many others. And let us not forget Popeye the Sailor Man, who became a superman when he ate his spinach. A recent survey of titles offered by the comic book industry found that nearly 100 superhero titles are published each month and the primary consumers of this type of comic book appears to be boys between the ages of 10 and 15 years (New England Comics Survey, 1990a, 1990b).

Although Superman was considered the most popular comic book superhero for many decades, his popularity began to dwindle during the 1980s. By 1990, Superman's ratings plummeted and he had become one of the least-liked comic book superheroes (NEC Survey, 1990b). In 1992, Superman, at age 52, finally met his match and was killed (*The Death of Superman*, 1992). In June 1993, Superman was born again in a manner reminiscent of the resurrection of Jesus. The reborn Superman had changed and experienced some limitations, however, such as the loss of supernatural sight (*Superman in Action Comics*, 1993a). During this period, other supermen were introduced. Soon, four supermen were buzzing the sky of Metropolis: a partially amnesiatic cyborg with Kryptonian technology; a boy who claimed to be a Superman clone; a man in a armored suit; and the resurrected, but changed, original Superman (*Superman in Action Comics*, 1993b). But by the fall of 1993, all pretenders to the throne of superherodom had been vanquished and Superman was back for good! Superman summarizes his experience as he soars in the sky and performs dangerous acrobatic maneuvers:

> Amazing. What I've experienced in the last few weeks defies description! Doomsday killed me, Mongul and the Cyborg almost destroyed earth . . . and one of my old enemies brought me back to life—and full power! I should feel tired . . . but I don't! All I want to do is fly—and enjoy being alive! I'm rejuvenated in a way I never thought possible! This whole thing has been hard on everybody—and I have no idea what's coming next—but something tells me I'll be able to handle anything better than ever! (*Superman*, 1993)

Superman has been the quintessential male role model for millions of young boys (Pecora, 1992). One can only speculate about the male image proposed for the resurrected Superman. Although subsequent issues of comics portraying the new Superman have him fighting and conquering evildoers in a manner typical of the old Superman, the new Superman has learned to ask for help. For example, Perry White, editor of the *Daily Planet*, reveals that Superman rebuilt Metropolis, which had previously been destroyed by rampaging robots, with the help of other superheroes such as Captain Marvel, J'onn J'onz (the Martian Manhunter), Guy Gardner, a youngster named Impulse, and, yes, two female superheroes, Wonder Woman and Maxima (*The Adventures of Superman*, 1995). Perhaps Superman will let his feminine side show.

The major theme throughout most of the comic books with male superheroes involves conquering some evildoer and saving the world. To accomplish this feat, superheroes often resort to their superpowers. Although bold representations of aggression are standard fare for comic books, representations of sexuality are much more subtle. That is, one sees a lot of "Wham!", "Sock!", "Crunch!", "Pow!", and

"Groan!" but little "Kiss!", "Hug!", "Love!", and "Fuck!" The reader, after all, is still a young boy and he should be exposed to violence, not sex. Later he will have some help in connecting the two.

Although comic book superheroes seldom engage in overt sexual acts in their original format, pirating these figures for pornographic purposes is common. For example, a popular form of erotic art or pornography is the eight-page comic booklet sometimes referred to as the "Tijuana bible" (see Holt, 1971a, 1971b). This format often depicts superheroes engaging in superheroics culminating in supersexual behavior. An excellent example of this type of presentation is an issue (author and source not identified) depicting Popeye rescuing Olive Oyl, his sweetheart, from being raped by Popeye's long-time nemesis, Bluto. After knocking down a door with his huge penis and engaging in a fierce battle, Popeye finally defeats Bluto soundly. Olive Oyl responds to Popeye's heroics and, presumably, his huge penis by becoming overcome with passion. Popeye enters Olive Oyl and as she writhes with sexual ecstasy, his huge penis penetrates her thoroughly and is seen protruding from her mouth. Although anatomically incorrect, this portrayal encompasses a number of male fantasies: strength, defeating a formidable foe, rescuing a damsel in distress, being rewarded for heroics, a large and powerful penis, sexual competence, and erotic sexual positions (simultaneous vaginal intercourse and fellatio). And all this action occurs in a mere eight pages.

## ❏ Sex, Lies, and Advertising

It is a red envelope. Above the address, in white letters, is the message "The Personal, Private Secrets of SUPERMANHOOD!" Below the address, in black letters, is the message "See inside this envelope now!" Peeking out from inside the envelope through a circular window of cellophane is the word "FREE!" More junk mail? Obviously not. The message is IMPORTANT! (maybe SUPERIMPORTANT!) The matter is URGENT! And it is FREE! How can any man who is interested in achieving manhood, let alone supermanhood, resist such a powerful offer? Turn the envelope over to open it and you find this challenge: "Only a Very Select Group of Men Can Handle the Invitation Inside This Envelope." Now you MUST open the envelope. Inside the envelope are several advertising pieces. One

catches your attention right away: "IF YOUR PENIS COULD TALK
. . . IT WOULD SAY. . ." Being hopeful of becoming a real man, you
must listen to your penis, especially if it has secrets to tell. But as you
unfold the paper, you find only a teaser, not the secrets. Yet there is
hope, because the advertising piece promises that some of the secret
messages your penis would give you, if it could talk to you, would
be the following:

- Ten ways to rouse a lazy penis to NEW HEIGHTS!
- This position effectively *lengthens* a short penis.
- Secret of the FOUR-HOUR ERECTION. (And the disadvan-
  tages!)
- How to *make sure* your penis says YES when you want it to.
- Strength training secrets for your PENIS!
- EXPLOSIVE ERECTIONS possible with this extraordinary cream!

But of course, your penis will not reveal these and other equally
important secrets to SUPERMANHOOD directly. It seems that your
penis and most other penises have told their secrets only to the
publisher of a men's newsletter. If you subscribe, you will not only
learn all these secrets but also "169 personal and private secrets of
MALE POTENCY, STAMINA, STRENGTH, AND POWER!" con-
tained in a FREE BOOK just for subscribing. Throughout the advertising pieces are words such as SUPERSEX!, SUPERHEALTH!, SUPER-
STAMINA!, SUPERPOTENCY! and other SUPERSOMETHINGS!
There is nothing subtle about this type of advertising. The company
has done its homework; it knows its target population very well. It
knows that men have been listening to their penises for centuries but
still know very little about sex. It knows that men are always striving
to be Superpenis. Being just a normal sexual human being is not
enough. It also knows that most men fear loss of any kind of power,
but especially sexual power. Another company promises that men
who use its products will increase sexual frequency from once a
month to five times a day. Even octogenarians can develop "towering" erections lasting over 3 hours and foster the development of
multiple orgasms, just like women. And as a bonus, new hair will
grow and clogged arteries will clear.

     Many men no doubt read this type of advertising, become amused,
and toss it away without ordering the products, but the message

about manhood has still been made. More accurately, the myth of masculinity has been further perpetuated. Although Superman may have been killed, the myth of Superpenis is as erect as ever. Even the most liberated males admit to sexual angst and wonder what they will be like after they pass their sexual prime, at about age 18. Males who order products that promise to reveal the secrets of a more active and potent sex life receive instead the same type of blend of snake oil remedies, commonsense advice, superficial health related information, gadgetry, and false hope that have been around for millions of years.

Some informational material that appears to be legitimate also unwittingly perpetuates myths about male sexuality. For example, this subtitle is found in a widely distributed book on men's health:

THE SEX EFFECT
   Is it a good idea to score before the big game? Let's settle
   this question once and for all. (see Lafavore, 1993, p. 149)

Although the use of the term *score* to refer to sexual behavior may seem innocuous to most, it continues to perpetuate the notion that having sex with women is a sporting event, a game. In this regard, it portrays men as competitors who score and, presumably, win and women as losers or the prize to be won.

The purpose of advertising is, of course, to sell products and ideas. To accomplish this goal, the advertising material must capture the potential consumer's attention, communicate a message that is both persuasive and memorable, and then influence the consumer's behavior toward the item being presented (Cohen, 1993). Using this formula, advertising agencies have learned that sexual themes quickly capture attention, can be very persuasive, are visually remembered by consumers, and sales typically increase dramatically. Sex sells, especially for males. Advertisers know that males tend to respond more positively than women toward sexual themes in advertising material (Bello, Pitts, & Etzel, 1983; LaTour, 1990). Sometimes the product itself is transformed into a sexual item for the purpose of increasing sales. For example, *Sports Illustrated* typically underrepresents women athletes in photos and news coverage (Boutilier & SanGiovanni, 1983; Kane, 1988), but "fully exploits the 'tits and ass' motif of soft pornography to produce its annual swimsuit issue, where women models, not women athletes, make the sport scene"

(Sabo & Jansen, 1992, p. 176). According to Sabo and Jansen, *Sports Illustrated's* swimsuit edition sells more issues than any other single magazine issue in the United States. Armed with this information, advertisers often develop advertising material with sexual content to be used in selling all sorts of products to men. Advertisers have also learned to be careful about the sexual presentations, however, because some consumers become more interested in the presentation than the product and fail to attend to the advertising messages (Edgley, 1989; LaChance, Chestnut, & Lubitz, 1978; Severn, Belch, & Belch, 1990). Pretesting advertising material, especially material with sexual content, has become increasingly important and is now fairly standard practice.

Sex often sells even if the sexual theme is not related to the product. Beautiful women are often used to display automobiles and to point out important features of the product. This approach not only gains attention from men, it also uses the principle of association to persuade men that the product will make them more sexually attractive (Hefzallah & Maloney, 1979). Men have been targets for this type of seductive advertising for years. Want to get a man's attention? Show him a beautiful young woman. If you really want his attention, display a seductive young woman alongside a flashy automobile. The man is most likely to associate the woman with the car and think that maybe he could get a woman like that if he had a similar car. He will certainly remember the presentation. And his behavior may be influenced toward purchasing the automobile or another automobile once he has been lured into the dealer's showroom. It is no coincidence that most automobile makers use young female models to pose next to their products at car shows, on calendars, and in many other advertising pieces directed toward the male market.

As a subtitle to an article in a popular automobile magazine, *Car and Driver*, one finds the statement "We reveal a new way to pick up women." The author, Arthur St. Antoine (1991), begins:

> Attention, every Warren Beatty wanna-be! Thanks to a recent discovery by this magazine, now you can throw out your arsenal of Calvin Klein musk-oil lures, subliminal-arousal mood tapes, and Terminator-Brand Prosthetic Pecs! We've uncovered a device—a superb specialty vehicle—that is absolutely guaranteed to pick up women anywhere, anytime! (p. 127)

Although St. Antoine's article is a tongue-in-cheek review of an "amazing" vehicle and not an advertisement, his lead-in certainly captures a reader's attention. His statement is clear: Men, you need only this one product to accomplish all your sexual goals. His subsequent review of the attributes of this vehicle follows a sexual theme throughout, with various comparisons with other vehicles used to capture women. What is this remarkable vehicle? A Toyota 5FGC25 Forklift. To prove his point, the forklift is pictured picking up women. For a forklift, you might expect that the most appropriate choice of women to be picked up would be a herd of female behemoths. Not so. In keeping with the male fantasy of picking up only sexy women, the choice is two model-thin women that any vehicle could have accommodated with ease.

For many males, the automobile has become a symbol of power and sexuality. Although few men can afford exotic and powerful performance cars such as a Ferrari Testarossa, a Lamborgini, or even the new American roadster the Dodge Viper, most men secretly lust for one in a way that they lust for a young beautiful nymphomaniac. And of course possessing such a car will most certainly lead to possessing the woman. (Well, maybe with the help of some English Leather Musk Cologne, Calvin Klein jeans, a Rolex watch, or a Toyota Forklift.)

One of the major users and purveyors of masculine stereotypes is the beer commercial. The predominate type of male portrayed in alcohol advertising exemplifies the essence of traditional masculinity, men who are physically powerful, adventurous, athletic, successful, and sexually competent (Klapp, 1962). Strate (1992) notes that advertising material that attempts to reflect preexisting cultural conceptions of masculinity also reinforces these ideas. Thus, males are drawn to beer commercials because they present ideas that seem familiar and at the same time validate their conception of the cultural stereotype (Postman, 1979; Postman, Nystrom, Strate, & Weingartner, 1987). Not only are adult males influenced by beer commercials, research on alcohol advertisements suggest that most children in the United States are exposed to thousands of beer commercials prior to reaching adulthood and use them as sources to help unravel the mysteries of gender role identification (Wallack, Cassady, & Grube, 1990).

When sex is used in alcohol advertisements, the messages are typically subtle and appear to relate more to seduction than to blatant sexual behavior. In an analysis of Colt 45 commercials featuring Billy Dee Williams, Strate (1992) found that themes associated with alcohol as an aphrodisiac, logos as phallic symbols, alcohol as a confidence builder, and alcohol consumption by women as a sign of and method for easy access to sexual favors predominate.

More recent examples of using subtle sexual messages in alcohol advertisements can be found in the Miller Genuine Draft TV commercials. The backdrop for these commercials is a hot, dry climate with very parched people. Out of nowhere appears a mystery man who performs a remarkable feat: He lowers the temperature and creates snow simply by opening a bottle of Miller Genuine Draft Beer. By the way, the mystery man wears powerful men's clothing such as tight jeans, boots, and outdoor-type shirts. He opens the beer bottle with one flick of his thumb, the way real men do. Although this message alone should convince most consumers that Miller Genuine Draft will do more than an adequate job of slaking any thirst and cool you down, the advertisement inserts another message. With this beer, you also get the beautiful girl. In one commercial, two old men are suffering through the heat sitting on a bench near a dry well. When the mystery man arrives, he somehow manages to extract bottles of Miller Genuine Draft from the well. Once he opens a bottle with the flick of his thumb, the temperature drops, snow falls, and a beautiful woman appears. After throwing her shoes to the side, the beautiful woman disappears into the well to join the mystery man. The older men look on, at first in amazement, but later they exchange looks indicating their understanding and approval of the presumed sexual possibilities. In another Miller Genuine Draft commercial, the mystery man arrives at a dilapidated gas station in the middle of desolated desert area. He takes notice of a particular type of hubcap among several lost hubcaps hanging on one of the station's walls. Suddenly, a vintage Corvette appears speeding along a dusty road. When it stops in front of the gas station, a beautiful young woman exits the Corvette. As she begins to walk toward the mystery man and the older man who appears to operate the business, she says seductively, "I've been looking for that." Hubcap in one hand and a beer in the other, the couple are last seen speeding off in a blizzard. This commercial is more of a Rorschach than some of the other Miller beer commercials. The woman's statement that she has been looking for "that" stimulates all sorts of male fantasies. "That" can be almost anything the male wishes it to be. Of course the lure is the hubcap and the beer, but could she also have been looking for what the mystery man had hidden in his tight jeans? And this is not just any woman. She is a beautiful young woman wearing a tight short dress who drives a vintage Corvette. Alcohol, cars, and sex.

Women are not portrayed as sex objects only for the purpose of selling products to men; often they are depicted in ways that reinforce male gender role expectations. In spite of the feminist movement and some increased awareness of the potential harmful effects of perpetuating gender-role stereotypes, women are still portrayed in traditional roles in advertising material, especially TV commercials (Bretl & Cantor, 1988; Edgley, 1989; Lovdal, 1989). Children exposed to a high frequency of TV viewing tend to embrace the traditional gender-role attitudes being presented. Although some people may applaud the adoption of traditional gender roles by children, others complain that traditional values do not necessarily mean fair play for women who, historically, have been devalued and dominated by males. Many of these traditional attitudes toward women perpetuate the myth of masculinity.

Although most males may pretend that they understand what it means to be a real man, they seem always on a quest to validate this elusive concept. Attempts to validate a man's potential as a sexual god can be found in ancient works of art and fertility symbols. One needs only to stand beneath a towering 25-foot-tall phallic symbol sculpted from stone to get the point. In contemporary times, expressions of male sexuality can be seen through all sorts of sexually explicit materials. But these materials, like ancient fertility symbols, contain exaggerated forms of genitalia and sexual prowess. And, as you have seen in this chapter, males' expressions of sexuality appear only an extension of the equally elusive concept of masculinity. For example, the traditional concept of masculinity states that men are strong, powerful, and aggressive. By contrast, women are seen as weak and submissive. Translated into sexual terms, the ideal sexual male is portrayed as having an insatiable sexual appetite, an unlimited sexual prowess, and a "never take no for a final answer" attitude. To play out this scenario successfully, women are often portrayed as sexual objects and trophies rather than as equal partners. Exaggerations of what is thought to be real masculinity and male sexuality masquerade as the real thing. This portrayal of man as Superpenis gets lots of play and becomes an influential guide for males in search of their own sense of masculinity. As you shall see in the next chapter, much can go wrong with this faulty concept of manhood and male sexuality.

# 6

# Fallen Heroes

## *Superpenis Meets Kryptonite*

$B$y the time a boy reaches manhood, he has considerable investment in his sexuality. Although many things can go wrong while building this sexual portfolio, most males enter manhood with enough assets to function reasonably well in the sexual stock market. That is, most males eventually recognize that much of the sociocultural messages about "blue-chip" sexual investment opportunities actually contain considerable misinformation that could lead to a squandering of resources. In spite of the pitfalls, most men develop a positive self-concept associated with sexuality. Most men do not think women are inferior creatures who should be controlled, beaten, sexually harassed, or raped. Most men do not suffer from clinical sexual dysfunctions. Most men are not addicted to harmful sexual practices. Most men do not molest children.

But like a lot of risky investments, the return may not be nearly as positive as hoped for or expected. For some men, the biological factors, developmental tasks, and sociocultural conditioning fail to provide for or, in many cases, actually deter a male from establishing a strong foundation for healthy sexuality. At a personal level, some males develop problems with sexual functioning. At an interpersonal level, some males occupy themselves with inappropriate sexual behavior such as child sexual abuse, sexual harassment, and rape. At a broader social level, our male-dominated society continues to portray women in negative ways and as sexual objects. Learning what can go wrong with male sexuality can assist all of us in making the corrections necessary to help other males in avoiding these problems. The purpose of this chapter is to examine the various ways males can be deterred in their quest for nonproblematic masculinity and sexuality.

## ❏ Problems With Sexual Functioning

Sexual problems come in a variety of forms. Problems involving difficulties in so-called normal sexual functioning, such as heterosexual intercourse, are commonly referred to by therapists as *sexual dysfunctions*. Sexual problems may occur throughout a person's life (lifelong type) or at some point after a history of adequate functioning (acquired type). Some sexual problems may occur in any sexual situation (generalized type) or under only certain circumstances (situational type; for diagnostic descriptions of sexual dysfunctions, see American Psychiatric Association, 1994). Fortunately, most sexual problems can be resolved with help by well-trained and experienced sexual therapists (see Kaplan, 1987; Masters et al., 1988b; Zilbergeld, 1992).

### ■ Erection Problems

It happens to nearly every man sometime during the life span. Mild-mannered Limp Penis refuses to transform into throbbing hard Superpenis. Perceived as no longer more powerful than a locomotive, most males who experience erection difficulties feel emasculated and ashamed. Even males who have no history of an erectile dysfunction often become panicky when they experience a "failure" for the first time. For most males, the loss of power of any kind can be very threatening, but the loss of sexual power can be overwhelming. Males who seek professional help regarding erection problems often present as anxious, depressed, and unable to understand how "it" could have happened to them. As one young man explained,

I always thought of myself as pretty much a stud. I have had lots of women and nobody has ever complained. I always thought that men who couldn't get it up were wimps or too old for sex. When it happened to me, I went into a panic. I could not understand what was going on, and no matter what I tried I couldn't get an erection. I was humiliated. The next day I couldn't go to work, and I even felt suicidal.

Technically, male erectile dysfunction is a sexual arousal disorder involving a persistent or recurrent inability to achieve or maintain an erection sufficiently firm to allow for the initiation and/or completion of sexual activities. Although this disorder has traditionally been labeled *impotence*, the use of this loss of power terminology sometimes compounds the problem and has been increasingly replaced by the use of less threatening nomenclature.

In spite of most men's fears that one experience of impotency is the death-knell for their sexual life, Masters and Johnson (1970) point out that isolated episodes of not having an erection or losing an erection during sexual activities are common and probably universal. They also explain that solitary or infrequently occurring erection problems do not necessarily mean that a man has a sexual dysfunction. In fact, a total absence of erection is rare except for specific medical conditions. More common is a partial loss of erection as a function of situational factors. These transient episodes are often related to ingesting alcohol or drugs, fatigue, a strained relationship with a partner, physical stress due to an illness, adjusting to a new partner, and other similar situational factors.

Performance anxiety is, by far, the most frequently occurring factor related to temporary, situational erectile difficulties eventually developing into a more persistent problem. Because males are culturally trained to view sex as some form of performance, any failure in this regard produces anxiety. Anxiety, in turn, compounds the problem because anxiety typically reduces the male's ability to respond to sexual stimulation in a normal manner. Some males believe that they can override their occasional bouts with impotency by commanding their penises to "stand up straight and act like a man." This technique seldom, if ever, works and leaves the man with another "failure" on his hands. Therefore, a cycle of anxiety-failure-more anxiety-another failure is born.

Although most clinicians find that performance anxiety is a major factor in erectile dysfunctions, analogue studies conducted in laboratory settings produced mixed results. For example, Barlow,

Sakheim, and Beck (1983) found that subjects who were told they would likely receive an electrical shock if they did not achieve an adequate level of sexual arousal while watching a film with explicit sexual scenes produced a higher level of arousal, as measured by a penile strain gauge, than a group in a noncontingent shock situation and a no-shock control group. In a follow-up study, men with a history of sexual dysfunctions responded to contingent and noncontingent shock threat conditions with less sexual arousal than men without a reported history of sexual dysfunctions (Beck & Barlow, 1984). These findings suggest that performance anxiety may have more of a negative effect on already sexually dysfunctional men than on men who appear to be sexually functional. Other studies also suggest that anxiety-inducing erotic films increase sexual arousal in sexually functional men, while producing lower levels of sexual arousal in sexually dysfunctional men (see Beck, 1988).

Although anxiety appears to be an important factor in sexual dysfunctions, cognitive variables may also play a central role. Barlow (1986) proposes that sexually functional men establish a cognitive feedback loop consisting of an accurate representation of the cues. This includes erectile responses, positive affect, a perception of control, and an increasingly efficient focus on the erotic stimuli, in spite of autonomic arousal related to anxiety. On the other hand, sexually dysfunctional men tend to establish a negative feedback loop consisting of an inaccurate representation of cues, expectations, and erections. Negative affect, a perceived lack of control, and an increasingly efficient focus on nonerotic issues, such as the perceived negative consequences of not being able to perform sexually, follow. Although Barlow's model appears to be at odds with the clinical literature, with its focus on anxiety as the major culprit in sexual dysfunctions, cognitive distortions such as those described by Barlow are often a focus of treatment by most experienced sexual therapists. In my experience in working with men with sexual dysfunctions, nearly all report worry about performance, concern over the consequences of not performing adequately, and negative affect associated with a perceived lack of performance.

Barlow's (1986) model differentiates between the cognitive processes of sexually functional and dysfunctional men, but it does not address the issue of why some men, with no history of being sexually dysfunctional, suddenly succumb to irrational fears and anxiety following an isolated episode with an erectile problem, whereas other so-called sexually functional men take this transitory problem in stride and do not engage in the destructive cycle leading to the possibility of a more serious sexual dysfunction. The answer may lie in individual differences and each man's vulnerability to perceptions of weakness. That is, many men may never experience a sexual disorder because they have strong appropriate self-concepts as well as positive and realistic views of their sexuality. A transitory problem will more than likely be handled without much ado. Other men may go for years without any overt hint of sexual problems but may be harboring poor self-concepts and a overall poor perception of their sexuality as it relates to their masculinity. Clinically, this type of man, although not yet technically a sexually dysfunctional, may eventually respond to transitory sexual difficulties, as do Barlow's dysfunctionals, due to his vulnerability to performance variables. In this regard, these men may be seen as "latent" sexual dysfunctionals; men without the necessary emotional resources to cope with the almost inevitable transitory sexual miscue. A limp penis waiting to happen. As one man said,

> I never thought I was much of a lover, even though I tried to be. And I always thought that it was just a matter of time until I would start to have problems getting it up. When I did have a problem, I didn't feel good about it or myself, but I was not surprised.

## ■ Premature Ejaculation

Although Superpenis may remain more powerful than a locomotive, sometimes his sexual response is faster than a speeding bullet. Kinsey et al. (1948) propose that a man's ability to become aroused quickly and ejaculate rapidly is a superior biological response; however, few sex researchers have embraced this rather glorified view of a man's ejaculatory prowess. Males with ejaculatory control problems seldom brag about how fast they can come. Most report embarrassment, emotional distress, and interpersonal difficulties. Premature ejaculation is apparently common and may affect as many as a third of all men (Derogatis, 1980; Spector & Carey, 1990).

A precise definition of premature ejaculation remains elusive, although most researchers and clinicians agree that this sexual disorder consists of a persistent or recurrent inability of the man to delay orgasm and ejaculation during minimal sexual stimulation or before his sexual partner wishes it to occur. Masters and Johnson (1970) define a premature ejaculator as a man who is unable to delay ejaculation for a sufficient length of time during intercourse to satisfy a sexually responsive partner 50% of the time.

Some men ejaculate within a few seconds of vaginal penetration, whereas others may ejaculate during foreplay or on first penile-vaginal contact. Still others may delay ejaculation several minutes, but the time period is not sufficient to satisfy their partners. Some males complain that they are premature because they are unable to satisfy their partners even after prolonged coital thrusting (e.g., 60 minutes) before ejaculating. The sexual partners' expectations may be a bit unrealistic in these cases. Men who identify premature ejaculation as a problem for them or for their partners frequently report anxiety, depression, and a serious concern about their masculinity. Many men report something like this:

> I have always been fast, but I thought I would eventually learn to control myself. I have tried everything but nothing works. Even though I want to have sex, I feel so bad about not being able to satisfy a woman that I don't even try anymore.

A premature ejaculator who engages in home remedies such as attempting to distract himself during sexual activities (e.g., thinking of a basketball game or solving mathematical problems) runs the risk of initiating an erectile disorder as well. That is, if the premature ejaculator is successful in distracting himself from the sexual activity, his arousal level may plummet and his penis may deflate. Men who experience both an erectile dysfunction and premature ejaculation sometimes develop more serious emotional and interpersonal relationship problems.

### ■ Inhibited Male Orgasm (Male Orgasmic Disorder)

Although many males fantasize about delaying ejaculation until their partners have experienced more sexual excitement than they can bear, many coitally inorgasmic males suffer emotional distress and interpersonal relationship difficulties similar to males with premature ejaculation problems. Most males who experience inhibited orgasms report that sexual intercourse becomes more of a chore than a pleasure once the initial sexual arousal wanes. Few take comfort in living out other men's fantasies of being Mr. Stud who can maintain an erection and ejaculatory control for hours or until his partner begs for mercy. Masters et al. (1988b) report that for some couples, the staying power brought on by ejaculatory incompetence can be a source of great sexual pleasure until the partner discovers that the man is unable to ejaculate intravaginally. The female partner may then begin to worry about her attractiveness and her ability to arouse the man sexually. One of the few men who I have seen in therapy with this problem said:

> At first my wife thought it was great that I had such staying power. Then, later, she began to wonder why she could not satisfy me. I tried to explain that it wasn't her, but I don't think she believed me. She even thought I was having an affair with someone more attractive. I wasn't.

This condition, sometimes referred to as *ejaculatory incompetence*, is relatively uncommon and rarely situational. That is, the problem persists during coitus regardless of the male's partner. Many coitally inorgasmic males are able to reach orgasm and ejaculate during other forms of sexual stimulation, however, such as oral sex or masturbation. Retarded ejaculation is more common than total ejaculatory incompetence and is characterized by a long delay before finally reaching orgasm and ejaculation during coitus, even with prolonged periods of penile thrusting.

### ■ Inhibited Sexual Desire

Contrary to popular belief, not all men are eager or willing participants in sexual behavior. Increasingly, men are showing a lack of interest in sex that was thought to be a sexual desire disorder seen primarily in females. For example, in the mid-1970s, women accounted for approximately 70% of these cases. But by the 1980s, men accounted for 60% of clients seeking therapy for lack of sexual desire. At present, it is unclear if this increase in a lack of interest in sex by males simply reflects an increase in this disorder in the general population or if other factors may be at work. At any rate, disorders of sexual desire have recently become the most frequently cited reasons by couples seeking help from sex therapists (for a review, see Spector & Carey, 1990).

In my practice over the past two decades, I have also seen an increase in the number of men who seek therapy for this problem, either by self-referral or by being coerced into therapy by a frustrated and angry partner. Either way, the male typically describes losing his desire for sex with his partner along with a decrease in interest for nearly all other forms of sexual activities previously found desirable. Some comment, "It just doesn't seem worth the bother anymore. I'll do it if I have to." Others state, "I still love her and find her attractive, but I just don't feel horny like I used too. I'm not even interested in looking at other women." Still others report never having experienced much of a sexual drive, "I never have been very interested in sex. I don't see what the big deal is about sex. I'm much more interested in other things like running or playing racquetball."

Inhibited sexual desire disorder (now called *hypoactive sexual desire disorder*) is a persistent or recurrent deficiency (or absence) of sexual fantasies and desire for sexual activity that produces marked distress or interpersonal difficulties and is not better accounted for by other disorders except another sexual dysfunction. Men with this disorder can be sexually aroused, achieve erection, and even reach orgasm, but other sexual dysfunctions may also be present. Although various factors such as substance abuse, hormonal deficiencies, severe chronic illness, medications, and the normal aging process may contribute to a decrease in interest in sex, the majority of cases of inhibited sexual desire appear to be psychosocial in origin. At the top of the list are factors such as partner dissatisfaction, relationship problems, depression, emotional stress, prior sexual trauma, poor self-esteem, and interpersonal hostility (see Kaplan, 1979; Leiblum & Rosen, 1988; Masters et al., 1988b; Schreiner-Engle & Schiavi, 1986).

### ■ Sexual Aversion Disorder

Some people develop an irrational fear or phobia about all things sexual that leads to high anxiety and an active avoidance of sexual situations. Although sexual aversions are less common than a simple lack of desire, especially in males, the symptoms can be severe and debilitating. Men with sexual aversions describe an intense fear or dread accompanied by physiological symptoms often seen in panic states such as nausea, diarrhea, profound sweating, difficulty in regulating breathing, and a pounding heart. Not surprisingly, sexual aversion in men is frequently accompanied by erectile problems.

Males with sexual aversions often have a history of being exposed to severely negative parental sex attitudes; sexual trauma, such as child sexual abuse or adult rape; and a pattern of being pressured into sexual activities by a long-term partner. Some males with sexual aversions may also show various forms of gender identity confusion (see Kaplan, 1979; Masters et al., 1988b).

## ❏ Sexual Misconduct

In 1975, feminist writer Susan Brownmiller noted, "Man's discovery that his genitalia could serve as a weapon to generate fear must rank as one of the most important discoveries of pre-historic times" (pp. 14-15). Although Brownmiller's statement is seen by some as an overstatement, most agree that the inappropriate use of sex by males has been extremely harmful to their victims, to society, and to the men themselves.

### ■ Stranger Rape

The legal definition of rape varies from state to state. Most clinicians agree that rape is a form of sexual coercion by which a person is forced into some type of sexual behavior, usually involving penetration. Securing accurate estimates of the number of women who have been victimized by sexual assault has been difficult because researchers have used various methods and definitions of rape. It is also believed that the majority of rapes go unreported. Current estimates suggest that 15% to 25% of women in the United States will be raped during their life span. Although specific figures are unavailable, most researchers, clinicians, and legal authorities agree that the vast majority of rape cases involve a female victim and at least one male perpetrator (see Calhoun & Atkeson, 1991; Department of Justice, 1990; Koss & Harvey, 1991; Michael et al., 1994).

Are men who rape different from men who do not? For years, sexual researchers have been trying to understand the dynamics of rape and to categorize men who rape. Most studies of rapists are conducted with men who are arrested and subsequently incarcerated

(Harney & Muehlenhard, (1991). Because it is estimated that only about 4% of men who rape are caught, convicted, and imprisoned, the information gleaned from studies of incarcerated rapists may not be representative of the general population of men who rape and go undetected. And most typologies are based on stranger rape and not on acquaintance, date, or marital rape cases (Russell, 1984).

Gebhard, Gagnon, Pomeroy, and Christenson (1965) suggest six categories of men who rape:

• *Assaultive:* This category includes men who usually have a history of violence and harbor strong, hostile feelings toward women. The violence may substitute for sexual behavior. Erectile impotence is found more frequently in this than in other categories of rapists. Favorite targets are strangers.

• *Amoral delinquents:* This category comprises men who may not necessarily harbor strong hostile feelings toward women but who view women simply as sexual objects whose role is to provide sexual pleasure for men. These men may rape women they know, as well as strangers.

• *Drunken:* As the term implies, drunken rapists may act out while intoxicated. The inappropriate behavior may range from clumsy forms of seduction to openly hostile physical attacks.

• *Explosive:* The major distinguishing factor for these men is the absence of prior indications of aggressive behavior. Often others are quite surprised at the suddenness of the sexual assault. Some evidence of psychosis may be present in this type of rapist.

• *Double standard:* This type of rapist views women as either good and deserving of respect or bad and not deserving of any kind of consideration. They are similar to the amoral type but usually do not resort to force until their repeated efforts at persuasion fail.

• *Other:* This category contains various combinations of the types above, as well as rapists who are diagnosed as psychotic or mentally defective.

In 1978, Richard Rada presented a topology with five categories of rapists:

• *Psychotic:* This type of rapist is not in touch with his actions at the time of the rape except for being overwhelmed by rage and anger.

• *Situational stress:* Rapists in this category typically do not have a history of violent behavior or sexual deviations. The sexual assault is usually precipitated by some form of personal and temporary stress factors.

• *Masculine identity conflict:* This type of rapist experiences real or imagined deficiencies in his masculinity identity. To compensate, he exaggerates the traditional male role by exhibiting overly aggressive and sexual behavior. He often plans his attacks and expresses little or no empathy for the women he assaults.

• *Sadistic:* As the term implies, sadistic rapists focus on forcing their victims to engage in various humiliating and degrading activities beyond sexual intercourse.

• *Sociopathic:* This type of rapist has a history of antisocial behavior. Rape is considered as only one component, but not the central aspect, of his aggressive criminal activities.

Scully and Marolla (1983) offer a typology based on two factors: men who admit to raping women and men who rape women but deny their actions were rape. Admitters usually recognize that their behavior was inappropriate but state that it was triggered by situational factors and was not in keeping with their typical demeanor. Deniers harbor hostile attitudes toward women and believe that males are entitled to sexual behavior with women without incurring any sanctions for forcing females to comply with the male's sexual demands.

Of all the typologies offered, the one presented by Groth (1979) seems to have been most widely accepted. At the foundation of all rape, according to Groth, are three components: anger, power, and sadism.

• *Anger:* This type of rapist uses sexual assaults to express anger and usually uses more force than necessary to achieve sexual compliance. Many of these men do not get sexually excited or experience sexual gratification. Some may even experience erectile difficulties.

• *Power:* These rapists typically have strong underlying feelings of inadequacy. They use sexual assault as a means of expressing strength and authority and to validate their masculinity. The goal of rape is to gain mastery over the victim and to possess her sexually. Because power, not anger, is the driving force with this type of rape, the power rapist may use only the amount of force necessary to accomplish complete control over the victim. Power rapists often do not acknowledge that they used force to achieve their goals. Instead, they convince themselves that their victims were willing and satisfied participants in the sexual scenario. Some power rapists even attempt to establish a social relationship with their victims subsequent to the sexual assault. Many power rapists also report little personal sexual gratification from rape because the sexual activities seldom match their fantasies about mastery and control.

• *Sadistic:* The primary goal of the sadistic rapist is to achieve sexual gratification by tormenting and inflicting pain on his victim. The sadistic rapist derives intense sexual pleasure from his victim's anguish and suffering. Psychologically, a fusion of sexuality and aggression occurs, resulting in the eroticization of violent behavior. Sometimes sadistic rapists culminate their acts of sadism by viciously killing their victims. Strangers who seem to represent something the sadistic rapist feels compelled to harm or destroy are frequent targets.

Researchers have not yet reached a consensus regarding the specific categorization of men who rape. The problem appears to rest in seemingly contradictory research findings regarding rapist characteristics. For example, some rapists appear to lack heterosocial skills and avoid social contact with females, whereas others do not show a higher level of social skills deficits than nonrapists of the same socioeconomic ranking. Some studies of men who rape suggest that rapists may not show greater sexual arousal to scenes depicting forced versus consenting sexual contact with females, whereas others have found that rapists may become more sexually aroused by scenes that portray rape than do nonrapists. As a group, men who rape appear to vary widely in their intelligence levels, family backgrounds, psychological characteristics, mental health, and criminal histories (see Barbaree & Marshall, 1991; Baxter, Barbaree, & Marshall, 1986; Hall, 1989; Langevin, 1985; Overholser & Beck, 1986; Prentky & Knight, 1991; Renzetti & Curran, 1989; Segal & Marshall, 1985; Wolfe & Baker, 1980).

Although some researchers and theorists point to sexual factors as possible motivational components in the majority of rapes (e.g., Barbaree & Marshall, 1991; Hall & Hirschman, 1991; Symons, 1979), most everyone agrees that rape involves more than just a male's biological desire for and attempts to have sexual intercourse with a female. For example, most convicted rapists, in one study, reported experiencing erectile difficulties, premature ejaculation, or ejaculatory incompetence during the sexual assault (Groth & Burgess, 1977). These findings suggest that something beyond simple sexual desire appears to be at play here.

Russell (1975, 1984) argues that rape is a "natural" consequence of at least two major socialization processes most cultures impose on men: the *masculinity mystique* and the *virility mystique*. The first defines masculinity in terms of aggression, power, force, dominance, competitiveness, and similar concepts associated with strength and superiority. Males who feel inferior in this regard or who, for other reasons, exaggerate these notions of masculinity could easily play out the perceived male role by acting out against women. The vitality mystique conditions males to separate their sexuality from affectional needs or concerns. In this regard, males are trained to be sexual animals constantly on the prowl for sexual prey. Males are also told they should be prepared to perform regardless of circumstances or their own feelings. Women, therefore, are merely sexual objects to be exploited in the service of the male's need to uphold the cultural expectations regarding his manhood and virility. When the masculine mystique and the virility mystique are played out together, a fusion of aggression and sex can be the unfortunate outcome.

Men in our society are mostly conditioned to embrace positive attitudes about and pursue aggressive and competitive behaviors, while simultaneously learning to reject attributes often associated with the feminine role such as empathy, tenderness, and caring. Possible restraints to sexually aggressive behavior are thereby removed through the socialization of males to be aggressive and sexually dominate (Albin, 1977; Burt, 1980; Lisak, 1991). For example, a study of Chinese nonoffender college males found that variations in aggressive drive (a tendency to think, feel, and behave in an aggressive, hostile manner) was the only successful predictor of sexual aggression against women (Tang, Critelli, & Porter, 1993). When Tang and her colleagues compared their results with the findings of a similar study of American nonoffender males (Porter, Critelli, &

Tang, 1992), they found that the level of sex drive was unrelated to nonoffender sexual aggression. Both American and Chinese males with high sex guilt reported using less coercive methods in their episodes of sexual aggression, however. These findings suggest that motivation for sexual aggression may depend more on cultural levels of general aggressiveness, sex guilt, and aggression desirability than on levels of sex drive. Thus, rape may involve an act of sexual violence associated with a distorted view of gender roles, including aggressiveness, and a male's need to control, dominate, and harm women (see Briere & Malamuth, 1983; Groth & Birnbaum, 1978; Koss & Leonard, 1984; Malamuth, Check, & Briere, 1986).

Unfortunately, the foundation for the forcible taking of women may be embedded in Western culture's history of patriarchy and misogyny. Women have traditionally been viewed as inferior to men, property of fathers or husbands, and sexual objects without rights of refusal. During wars, women and female children of the enemy have been and continue to be frequent targets for sexual assaults by invading forces. To rape, pillage, and plunder is considered acceptable behavior by many military personnel.

Historically, women who were raped faced additional trauma through public ostracism, physical punishment, mutilation, and in some cases death. Although some progress has been made in treating the rape victim as a true victim rather than as a coconspirator in her own victimization, female rape victims still face issues of responsibility and stigmatization not usually assigned to victims of other personal tragedies. For example, there is a tendency in the general public to blame or hold the rape victim responsible, in some manner, for the sexual assault, with males more likely than females to assume that the victim provoked the attack or was, at least, partially responsible for the incident (see Calhoun, Selby, & Warring, 1976; Cann, Calhoun, & Selby, 1979; Deitz & Byrnes, 1981; Feild, 1978; Fulero & Delara, 1976; Janoff-Bulman, Timko, & Carli, 1985; Jenkins & Dambrot, 1987; Kanekar & Kolsawalla, 1980; Kanekar & Nazareth, 1988; Seligman, Brickman, & Koulack, 1977; Thornton, Robbins, & Johnson, 1981; Tieger, 1981).

The justification for the punishment of or the attribution of blame to rape victims may lie in the various myths that persist regarding a woman's secret desire to be "taken by a man," her ability to resist a sexual assault, or her use of rape allegations to protect her reputation (Burt, 1980). Another popular belief is that only "bad girls" or "seductive" women get raped. These and similar cultural myths and stereotypes are frequently reinforced by the images of females portrayed in novels, movies, television, and other forms of popular materials (Berkowitz, 1984; Donnerstein et al., 1986; Linz, Donnerstein, & Adams, 1989; Linz, Donnerstein, Bross, & Chapin, 1986; Linz et al., 1988; Stock, 1991).

Recent studies in the area of gender differences in attributions of blame for rape have found that not only do males tend to blame the victim more than females, they do so even if the victim is male (McCaul, Veltum, Boyechko, & Crawford, 1990; Weisz & Earls, 1995; Whatley & Riggio, 1992, 1993). These findings suggest that factors other than cultural myths about women and sexuality may be responsible for the victim blaming by males. Even so, many males believe cultural myths about women and may act accordingly. For these males, it may be an easy step from sexual stereotyping to sexual assault (see Check & Malamuth, 1983; Lisak & Roth, 1990; Malamuth, 1981, 1989; Muehlenhard & Falcon, 1990).

Although researchers have not been able to delineate specific profiles for men who rape, Harney and Muehlenhard (1991) found several common characteristics reported in studies of self-identified sexually aggressive men. These men tend to embrace traditional ideas about gender roles; are generally hostile toward women and condone violence and rape against them; are sexually experienced and engage in sexual behavior as a means to express or maintain social dominance; are generally irresponsible and lack a social conscience; and have and are responsive to peer groups that may pressure them into sexual activities, some of which may be deviant.

Some studies of men who sexually assault women reveal that many were sexually abused by females as children. Freeman-Longo's (1986) retrospective study of male rapists found that 40% of his sample described childhood sexual abuse experiences perpetrated by females. Similarly, Groth (1979) found that 66% of a sample of incarcerated rapists had been sexually abused by females in childhood, whereas Petrovich and Templer (1984) found that 59% of their sample of rapists reported female perpetrators. And Briere and Smiljanich (1993) discovered that 80% of their sample of sexually abused men who admitted to committing sexually aggressive acts against women had been sexually abused during childhood by females. Although a number of factors, including the cultural variables described above, may propel some males into subsequent sexual aggression against women, sexual victimization by females must also be considered an important factor (Mendel, 1995).

### ■ Acquaintance and Date Rape

Most people believe that rapes are committed by strangers. The truth is that the majority of rape victims are forced into sexual behavior by men they know; acquaintance rapes are less likely to be reported to law enforcement than stranger rapes (see Koss, 1985, 1988; Koss & Harvey, 1991; Russell, 1984). For example, from a recent sample of women living in the United States who reported that they had been "forced to do something sexual that they did not want to do by a man," the majority reported being in love with the perpetrator (46%), knowing the perpetrator well (22%), or that the perpetrator was an acquaintance (19%), whereas only 4% described their perpetrators as strangers (Michael et al., 1994).

Some studies suggest that men who force sex on their dates may have more sexual partners and higher sexual expectations than less sexually aggressive males. Date rapists also tend not to believe that forced sex on a date is rape (see Jenkins & Dambrot, 1987; Kanin, 1985; Koss & Dinero, 1989; Malamuth, 1986; Malamuth, Sockloskie, Koss, & Tanaka, 1991; Muehlenhard & Linton, 1987). The results of one study suggest that date rapists may be somewhat more sensitive to crying and reasoning by their victims than stranger rapists. For example, in a study to assist in developing effective strategies for avoiding acquaintance rape, Levine-MacCombie and Koss (1986) found that active rape avoidance strategies (e.g., screaming for help, running away, physical resistance) found effective in attempted stranger rapes were also effective in avoiding rape by acquaintances. Although cognitive strategies (e.g., reasoning, pleading, turning cold, quarreling, or crying) were much less effective than active strategies overall, crying and reasoning were more effective in avoiding an acquaintance rape than a stranger rape.

Many feminist researchers believe that culturally transmitted heterosexual sexual scripts support violence in dating relationships by casting the male as the sexual aggressor and women as sexual objects whose right of refusal is either not genuine or is genuine but must be overcome (see Koss et al., 1994). Support for this notion is found in studies in which preteens, adolescents, and young adults express similar beliefs that it is acceptable for a male to force sex on a woman if they have been dating for more than about 6 months (Goodchilds & Zellman, 1984; Goodchilds, Zellman, Johnson, & Giarrusso, 1988; Muehlenhard, Friedman, & Thomas, 1985; "Teens Express Themselves," 1988).

My experience with young males who were referred to therapy for sexual misconduct in dating situations and with males in therapy for other sexual problems reveals a general attitude by men that women are expected to withhold sexual favors at first, but after a series of dates men expect women to "put out." Females who continue to date but refuse sexual overtures are often labeled *prick teasers*. In these situations, some men feel justified in being more aggressive in their approach for sexual activities. As one young man said, "She had been around and knew the rules. She knew what to expect but was just being hard to get. I spent a lot of money on her and felt like she was just leading me on. It was time for her to give in so I pressed the issue."

Culturally driven notions about genders may provide scripts that guide sexual behavior, but some of these harmful ideas and attitudes may be altered if addressed directly. In an attempt to examine university students' perceptions of acquaintance rape and to discover methods for positively affecting those perceptions, Harrison, Downes, and Williams (1991) found that college men showed greater tendencies than women to blame the victims of date rape. Men also showed a low level of understanding of women's perceptions of rape issues, a higher level of factual misconceptions, and a failure to examine their own values regarding sexual aggression against women. The study also showed that men's attitudes about women and sexual violence can improve with a directed program approach. That is, men exposed to rape awareness intervention treatment strategies improved their accuracy of perception of factual information about sexual aggression, as well as decreased their level of victim blaming.

### ■ Marital Rape

Until about the 1980s, laws protecting husbands from criminal prosecution for sexually assaulting their wives were commonplace. Most of the older and many of the current laws in the United States reflect the common belief that rape occurs only when a man forces himself on a stranger, certainly not his wife. This is a form of marital exclusion rooted in English common laws stating that a woman forever gives her consent to sexual behavior with her husband once she enters into the marriage. Thus, a man is granted sexual access to his wife regardless of her subsequent desires because it remains her "duty" to serve her husband sexually. If a wife resists her husband's sexual advances, she is effectively violating the marriage contract. Many traditionally oriented men believe that the "manly" thing to do is to "take" their wives anyway. This belief system about marital sex led Finkelhor and Yllö (1985) to call the marriage license, "the license to rape." In some states, a husband may be prosecuted for marital rape if his assault was excessively violent. Other states may not prosecute males for raping their wives but will attempt to prosecute them on other charges, such as physical assault, thereby avoiding the problem with the marital exclusion for rape.

Although actual frequency rates for marital rape are difficult to obtain, it is generally believed that between 10% and 15% of wives are raped by their husbands or ex-husbands (Michael et al., 1994; Russell, 1982). Linking sex and violence on the domestic scene, marital rape seems to occur at a higher rate in relationships in which other forms of nonsexual assault are also present (Frieze, 1983; Shields & Hanneke, 1983; Walker, 1984).

### ■ Sexual Harassment

Some men in positions of power have been using sexual harassment to gain sexual favors from women for centuries. But this conduct was largely ignored or denied by a male-dominated society until Farley (1978) and MacKinnon (1979) exposed the practice for what it really was: another type of sexual exploitation of women by men. Even so, "there are no official statistics or national surveys; its existence is ignored in studies of both sexual victimization and workplace behavior, and women's stories of their experiences are routinely disbelieved" (Koss et al., 1994, p. 111). One of the major obstacles to achieving acceptance of sexual harassment as a serious social problem is the failure to reach consensus on a definition. Although some forms of sexual harassment are very clear and are easy to identify, such as men requiring females to engage in sexual behavior to keep their jobs or be promoted, other sexual actions are less clearly misconduct. For example, is inviting a female workmate or subordinate to join you for dinner sexual harassment? How about all those female pinups posted throughout the workplace? Should men refrain from swapping "dirty" stories in the presence of female workmates? Should a professor date his students?

Various attempts at defining sexual harassment have used key terms such as *unsolicited and unwanted sexual requirements in the workplace, violation of authority relations, unequal power, gender stratification, male sexual prerogative, unwanted nongenital touching of any kind, verbal behavior with sexual content, sexual leering, sexist remarks, seductive behavior*, and *displays of offensive sexual material*. In 1980, the Equal Employment Opportunity Commission (EEOC) composed a legal definition of sexual harassment incorporating many of these concepts. Six years later, the U.S. Supreme Court held that sexual harassment was a form of sex discrimination under Title VII of the Civil Rights Act of 1964. In 1993, the EEOC expanded its definition of sexual harassment by including gender-related conduct that was not specifically sexual in nature but nonetheless denigrated or showed hostility based on gender. Thus, two classes of behavior were declared illegal:

> (a) any attempts to extort sexual cooperation by means of threats (either subtle or explicit) of job-related consequences (*quid pro quo harassment*), and (b) any sex-related verbal or physical conduct that is unwelcome and offensive (*hostile environment*). (Koss et al., 1994, p. 115)

Although governmental sanctions against sexual harassment apply equally to both genders, it is clear that they were formulated primarily to put males on notice that this form of sexual exploitation of women will no longer be tolerated.

Reliable prevalence rates for sexual harassment have been difficult to obtain, but existing data suggest approximately 50% of working women experience sexual harassment of some kind in the workplace. It is believed that only 2% to 5% of sexual harassment victims seek legal help or file a formal complaint. Most confront the harasser directly, ignore the harasser, or change the employment situation through a position transfer or by quitting the job. Most studies show that approximately 20% to 55% of women in the workforce experience some form of sexual harassment, however, such as unwelcome sexual remarks; suggestive looks; insulting comments, looks, and gestures; expectations to socialize as a requirement for employment;

direct pressure for dates or sexual favors; expectations to participate in sexual activities as a requirement for employment or advancement; and actual or attempted rape (see Fitzgerald, 1993; Fitzgerald & Shullman, 1993; Fitzgerald et al., 1988; Livingston, 1982; Loy & Stewart, 1984).

The estimates of the frequency of sexual harassment of women university students range from approximately 10% to 65%. Although direct pressure for sexual activities and sexual assault are reported, the vast majority of the sexual harassment of female college students involves unwelcome sexual comments, sexist comments (gender harassment), suggestive looks, unwanted sexual attention, and unwelcome light touching. Some female college students switch colleges or courses to avoid persistent sexual harassment from lecherous professors (see Benson & Thomson, 1982; Dziech & Weiner, 1984; Fitzgerald, 1992; Fitzgerald et al., 1988; Maihoff & Forrest, 1983; Rubin & Borgers, 1990; Wilson & Kraus, 1983). But sexual harassment on campus is not limited to professors attempting to exploit students. Some female professors report being the target of sexual harassment by male students in the form of obscene phone calls, unwelcome and undue attention, sexist remarks, and unwelcome sexual comments. On rare occasions, direct sexual advances or sexual assaults occur (Grauerholz & Koralewski, 1991).

Like efforts to establish a specific profile of men who rape, attempts to identify harasser-specific characteristics have not yet been successful. Male harassers appear indistinguishable from the typical nonharassing male worker or college professor (Gutek, 1985). Pryor (1987), using the Likelihood of Sexual Harassment Scale (LSH), did find that men who are authoritarian, lack empathy, and hold adversarial sexual beliefs or traditional attitudes about gender roles reported that they were more likely to engage in some form of sexual exploitation of attractive women over whom they had some control or power than men low in these characteristics. In addition, men who scored high on the LSH were more likely to exhibit harassing behavior if exposed to episodes of harassment of females by a male confederate (see Pryor, LaVite, & Stoller, 1993). The results of these and other preliminary studies of sexual harassers are similar to studies showing that many men who engage in or admit that they might engage in sexually aggressive behavior with females often hold more conservative than egalitarian beliefs about women and gender roles (see Brooks & Perot, 1991; Malovich & Stake, 1990).

■ **Sexual Exploitation of Patients**

Most forms of sexual harassment occur in a setting containing an unequal power or status relationship between the man and the woman. This power and status differential is sometimes exploited by professionals such as physicians and therapists, in spite of strong ethical proscriptions against sexual intimacies with patients. Studies show that approximately 7% to 12% of male therapists and 2% to 3% of female therapists admit to engaging in some form of inappropriate sexual behavior with their patients (Pope, 1989; Pope & Bouhoutsos, 1986). Because underreporting is common in these cases, Simon (1989) proposes that 15% to 25% of all types of clinicians may initiate sexual activities with their patients. In fact, therapists' sexual attraction to patients is not rare. Pope, Keith-Spiegel, and Tabachnick (1986) found that 87% of a sample of clinicians admitted to being sexually attracted to some patients. Most of the sample also expressed feelings of guilt, anxiety, or confusion associated with that attraction.

Although some have claimed that sexual intimacies with patients are inconsequential or even beneficial to the patient (e.g., McCartney, 1966; Romeo, 1978; Shepard, 1971), most reputable researchers and clinicians in this area have argued strongly that sexualized dual relationships with patients produce negative consequences that are both serious and possibly enduring (e.g., Brown, 1988; Feldman-Summers & Jones, 1984; Gabbard & Pope, 1989; Pope, 1989; Sonne, Meyer, Borys, & Marshall, 1985). Pope (1988, 1990a) contends that engaging in sexual intimacies with patients is similar to perpetrating rape and incest.

Although most mental health professionals believe that therapists who engage in sexual intimacies with patients are poorly trained and least involved in professional affairs, research does not support this stereotype. Pope (1990a, 1990b) posits that high educational accomplishments, professional status, and personal psychotherapy are positively associated with tendencies to abuse patients sexually. For example, psychiatrists who sexually abuse patients are more likely to have completed accredited residency programs and to have participated in personal psychotherapy than nonoffenders (Gartrell, Herman, Olarte, Feldstein, & Localio, 1989); offending social workers are more likely to have completed additional requirements for advanced certification than nonperpetrators (Gechtman, 1989); and well-trained, knowledgeable, and seemingly successful psychologists show a higher rate of engaging in sexual intimacies with patients than colleagues with less impressive credentials (Pope & Bajt, 1988).

### ■ The Sexual Abuse of Children

Although most men do not molest children, the majority of child sexual abusers are male. In spite of the disproportionate amount of media attention given to the more sensational, out-of-home, dirty-old-man-lurking-in-the-shadows-type cases, the sexual assault of children by strangers of either gender is considered rare (Conte & Schuerman, 1987). Most children are sexually abused by a family member or other males in trusting relationships with the family or child such as clergy, teachers, counselors, or coaches.

Over the years, a number of factors have been posited to explain why men sexually abuse children. Included are incestuous family dynamics in which roles are switched between a child and an inadequate and possibly collusive mother or wife (see Brandt & Tisza, 1977; Justice & Justice, 1979), as well as placing the responsibility on attractive child victims who exhibited seductive behavior that the offender could not resist (Bender & Blau, 1937; Bender & Grugett, 1952).

Incorporating both psychological and sociological concepts related to child sexual abuse, Finkelhor (1984) presents one of the first comprehensive analyses of the sexual maltreatment of children. His paradigm, the Four-Preconditions Model of Sexual Abuse, proposes that each of the following conditions must be met before sexual abuse can occur:

1. A potential offender needs to have some motivation to abuse a child sexually.
2. The potential offender has to overcome internal inhibitions against acting on that motivation.
3. The potential offender has to overcome external impediments to committing sexual abuse.
4. The potential offender or some other factor has to undermine or overcome a child's possible resistance to the sexual abuse. (Finkelhor, 1984, p. 54)

More recently, Faller (1990) proposed only two prerequisites for sexual abuse: "(1) sexual arousal to children and (2) the willingness to act upon the arousal" (p. 55). But she also describes several factors and circumstances that contribute to but do not cause the sexual abuse of children:

Childhood experiences of the offender (e.g., personal sexual victimization, socialization of inappropriate use of sexuality)

Cultural factors (e.g., norms that sanction or support concepts of male dominance and paternal control, as well as the stereotypic role of males as sexual aggressors)

Vulnerable role relationships (e.g., stepfather, mother's boyfriends, foster fathers, professional roles with extended periods of unsupervised contact with children)

Partner characteristics (e.g., withholding of sex, infidelity, verbal and physical abuse, desertion)

Environmental factors (e.g., easy access to children such as crowded living conditions and unsupervised caretaking on a regular basis; insults to the perpetrator such as loss of a job, financial problems, accidents, illnesses)

Child factors (e.g., access to vulnerable children such as children with a history of sexual abuse, neglected or deprived children, compliant children, mentally retarded children)

Fantasy (e.g., sexual fantasies about children, use of child pornography)

I find that some males have persistent or recurrent sexually arousing fantasies, sexual urges, or behaviors involving sexual activities with prepubescent children. Clinically, this is a type of paraphilia diagnosed as *pedophilia* (American Psychiatric Association, 1994). Pedophiliac males generally report a preference for children only, but some are sexually attracted to adults as well. Although some pedophiles never act on their urges to engage children in sexual behavior, many follow their compulsions repeatedly. Some studies found that incarcerated pedophiles commit significantly more sexual offenses against children than the few for which they were convicted (Ames & Houston, 1990). A study of convicted child sexual offenders who were guaranteed confidentiality revealed that 232 child molesters had attempted more than 55,000 acts of child molestation and were successful nearly 39,000 times (Abel, Mittelman, & Becker, 1985). Similarly, Freeman-Longo and Wall (1986) found that 53 perpetrators had committed between 25,000 and 26,000 sexual offenses against children. Pedophiles who prefer female children may average more than 60 girl victims in their lifetimes (Abel, Becker, Murphy, & Flanagan, 1981). Although some pedophiles show a gender preference, many will choose a child based on convenience and availability, regardless of the child's gender (Groth & Birnbaum, 1978).

Studies on the etiology of pedophilia have produced varied and diverse findings that suggest that the development of pedophilia is not based on any single determinant. Factors appearing in some cases of pedophilia are sexually deviant families, especially pedophiliac first-degree relatives (Gaffney, Laurie, & Berlin, 1984); a history of childhood sexual victimization experiences (e.g., deYoung, 1982; Finkelhor, 1986; Russell, 1984); idealization of childhood (Lanyon, 1986); psychoticism, introversion, and neuroticism (Wilson & Cox, 1983); and possible endocrinological abnormalities (Gaffney & Berlin, 1984). There is little agreement on how pedophilia develops, but most researchers agree that the majority of pedophiles appear to be shy and isolated men who lack social skills; are threatened by intimate relationships with adults, especially females; and who turn to children for sexual gratification (Ames & Houston, 1990; Overholser & Beck, 1986; Tollison & Adams, 1979; Wilson & Cox, 1983).

Most pedophiles I have treated describe a sexual attraction to children that began early and never abated. As one pedophile explained:

> I always knew that I was different. During puberty, while most of my male friends were moving from child sexual play to a real sexual interest in adolescent girls or women, I remained attracted to young children or older children who were not yet sexually developed. If given the chance, I would always choose to be with kids. Once they started to show pubic hair or real boobs, I began to lose interest. I have had sex with adult women and men, but it is difficult to do and not at all satisfying.

A man does not have to be a pedophile to engage children in sexual activities. In fact, it is believed that most men who molest children are not clinical pedophiles at all, even though they exhibit some form of sexual attraction to children. Many of these men molest their own children, other blood relatives, or stepchildren. These men are often referred to as *incest perpetrators* (see Horton, Johnson, Roundy, & Williams, 1990). Some researchers argue that many so-called incest perpetrators also molest children outside the family and some even admit to raping adult females (Abel, Becker, Cunningham-Rathner, Mittleman, & Rouleau, 1988). Although sexual arousal patterns as measured by penile plethysmography appear similar for incest offenders and for extrafamilial offenders (Abel et al., 1981), extrafamilial offenders appear to have a higher level of cognitive distortions related to justifying their sexual behavior with children than incest offenders (Hayashino, Wurtele, & Klebe, 1995). Some incest perpetrators use their role as a parent to institute a form of socialization called the *grooming process* to prepare children to participate in sexual activities (see Christiansen & Blake, 1990). Variations of the grooming process are sometimes seen with nonparental perpetrators who have developed trust relationships with children.

Some pedophiles find their way into marriages with women who have children. Often, these men are seeking children in a trust relationship so they can eventually use this trust to gain access to the children sexually (Salter, 1988). Other men may be pedophiles who marry, have children of their own, and subsequently molest them. Although this type of sexual behavior is technically incestuous, the motivational factors are clearly pedophilic. In fact, Lynn Sanford (1980) prefers to call incest offenders *lazy pedophiles.* On the other hand, Anna Salter (1988) states, "while many incest offenders are closet pedophiles, incest offenders exist who are not" (p. 51).

Historically, researchers and clinicians have proposed a number of child sex offender typologies with a broad range of descriptors. Early efforts suggest two types of perpetrators based on either a stable erotic attraction to children or the use of a child as a surrogate for an adult partner, whereas others refer to multiple perversions due to the polymorphous perverse nature of man. Still others attempt to type sex offenders based on such etiological factors as mental or emotional disorders, misogyny, stress, symbiosis, and masculinity problems (for a review, see Bolton et al., 1989).

Based mostly on their own clinical and research efforts with incarcerated sexual offenders, Groth, Hobson, and Gary (1982) propose that sex offenders should be categorized into two types: fixated and regressed. The fixated type includes men with a primary sexual preference for children, usually boys, and who seem to identify sociosexually as a child rather than as an adult. Fixated men typically report that their sexual interest in children is long-standing, usually dating back to at least adolescence. Regressed offenders include men whose primary sexual orientation is age appropriate and their sexual behavior with children is seen as a departure from their typical sexual pattern. The inappropriate sexual acts committed by regressed offenders with children are usually ego-dystonic, episodic, and precipitated by situational factors such as stress. Primary targets are female children, who may be seen as adult substitutes.

This typology was quickly embraced by professionals trying to make sense of a complex and confusing subject. Soon, suspected pedophiles or out-of-home molesters were referred to as *fixated offenders* and the in-home or so-called incest perpetrator was seen as a *regressed offender*. Conte (1990) points out, however, that no empirical evidence exists supporting this type of classification of child sexual offenders. In fact, research has found little difference in the pattern of sexual preference shown by the two types (Abel et al., 1981). Many offenders not only have characteristics of both types, they may even warrant multiple paraphiliac diagnoses (Able et al., 1988). Although some aspects of this dual classification were and remain helpful in the overall understanding of men who molest children, the terms *fixated* and *regressed* are seldom used today by knowledgeable mental health and forensic professionals to classify sexual perpetrators.

Thus, the clear categorization of men who sexually abuse children proves a most formidable task. Conte (1985, 1990) effectively circumvents the problems inherent in attempting to assign child sexual perpetrators to specific types by proposing a more individualized approach. He recommends an individual assessment of the offender, regardless of previous or presumed classifications, along the following dimensions:

> denial, sexual arousal, sexual fantasies, cognitive distortions (e.g., it's OK for an adult to rub a child's genitals to make her more sexually responsive when she grows up), social skills deficits, and other mental health problems (e.g., drug abuse, depression). (1990, p. 23)

Support for this type of conceptualization can be found in studies showing that men who molest children display a number of historical and personal characteristics related to the concepts proposed by Conte. For example, a history of isolation was found to contribute to social skills deficits, cognitive distortions, and other mental health problems in a clinical sample of adult male perpetrators of child sexual abuse (Gilgun & Conner, 1990); confirmation of the proposition that some perpetrators lack essential social skills has been documented in comparative studies ( e.g., Ballard et al., 1990); an inability to confide in others as a child and adolescent regarding emotional problems and personal victimization experiences was found more in convicted child molesters than with nonfelons (Gilgun & Conner, 1990); and cognitive distortions developed during a dysfunctional early family life often provide the foundation for sexually addictive behavior, including sexual behavior with children (Carnes, 1990).

In spite of strong sanctions against sexual behavior with children, some men still find children, even their own, sexually attractive. But how aberrant is sexual arousal to children? Few individuals will admit openly that they have had sexual thoughts about or urges toward children. Even fewer will admit to acting on their sexual thoughts and feelings related to sexual contact with children, unless caught in the act. Although we will probably never know how common sexual arousal to children is with adults, some hint of the frequency is found with a study conducted by Briere and Runtz (1989). In this study, college males were asked to respond anonymously to a survey about sexual behavior. Their responses indicated that 21% had been sexually attracted to some young children, whereas 9% reported sexual fantasies about children and 5% masturbated to the fantasies. About 7% admitted that they might have sexual contact with a child if they were certain they could avoid detection and punishment. It is certainly too early to generalize these findings to the general population of men in the United States, but the figures suggest that sexual attraction to children may not be as uncommon as commonly believed.

Fortunately, not all sexual arousal to children is acted out. For those who do not control themselves, a number of therapeutic approaches are available to help ameliorate the problem (see Horton et al., 1990; Knopp, 1984; Laws, 1989; Maletzky, 1991; O'Connell, Leberg, & Donaldson, 1990; Patton, 1991; Salter, 1988).

As stated at the beginning of this chapter, most men do not display any of the sexual problems described here. Because problems with sexual responses do not surface with every male, it seems unlikely that the genes and juices associated with the development of male sexuality are significantly responsible for sexual dysfunctions and sexual misconduct. Rather, the overall design appears oriented more toward a gradual increase in the awareness of one's sexual potential as a human being and the ultimate diverse expressions of that potential. Problems seem to emerge after males are bombarded with a wide range of messages and misinformation about sexuality and how sexual behavior fits with the cultural notions of spirituality and masculinity. Males are told they must strive for supermanhood and supersexuality or be considered less than a man. Men are also told that sex with a spouse for the purposes of procreating is the only acceptable expression of sex. Men who buy into these conflicting cultural notions adopt unrealistic and confusing expectations as the standard to which they constantly compare themselves. It is not surprising, therefore, that many of these men become frustrated, anxious, and depressed; form negative self-images; and experience problems in their sexuality. Other men act out culturally written sexual scripts about women—scripts that portray women as inferior or as sexual objects—and sincerely believe that they are justified for doing so. Still others are thwarted from learning to express their sexuality in generally acceptable ways and find themselves looking elsewhere. Sometimes, their gaze falls on totally inappropriate targets such as children and vulnerable adults.

Although it appears that the pervasive cultural messages about sexuality provide the foundation for most of the sexual problems experienced by males, unaffected males are also exposed to sociocultural Kryptonite but do not experience sexual dysfunctions or exhibit sexual misconduct. Why? No one knows for sure why some men absorb all the toxicity, some absorb only a moderate amount, and others escape relatively unscathed. The answer probably lies in the level of exposure allowed by the male child's primary caregivers and each male's potential for detecting toxic messages and shielding himself from them. The key to preventing problems with sexuality appears to be lowering the level of toxicity overall and increasing each child's potential for detection and protection. Although this approach may never lead to supersexuality in the traditional sense, it could allow males a better opportunity to realize their natural potential as sexual human beings and reduce the probability for personal sexual problems and harmful sexual misconduct. And it could address many of the factors associated with the next topic, the sexual maltreatment of males.

# 7

# Not for Women Only

## *Personal Sexual Victimization*

T ypically, males are considered perpetrators, not victims, of sexual maltreatment. This view is consistent with sociocultural prescriptions that real men are strong, powerful, and aggressive. There is no room in the myth of masculinity for weaknesses or victimization experiences, especially sexual victimization. But reality speaks volumes.

## ❑ Rape

Because most male rape victims do not report their assaults to law enforcement agencies and are reluctant to discuss their experiences, securing accurate figures regarding prevalence rates has been difficult. The bastion of male rape is the criminal justice system. Stephen Donaldson (1993) estimates that 294,000 males incarcerated in adult jails, adult prisons, and juvenile centers are raped annually. Victims tend to be young, nonviolent, first offenders who are vulnerable to being overpowered by more violent and powerful inmates. Many victims in holding tanks at city and county jails are raped by several prisoners daily until the victim is released. Some victims have reported that they were "thrown in" with violent offenders by law enforcement officers who then "looked away" while the assaults took place. It is not unusual for a victim of gang rape in the prison system to pair off eventually with one inmate who serves as a protector from the other prisoners while the victim serves his benefactor with sex. But males do not have to be incarcerated to be raped. Male rape occurs all too frequently in the general population as well as under the guise of hazing and initiation rites in military institutions and college fraternities. Some studies suggest that 6% to 10% of unincarcerated rape victims in the United States are men (McMullen, 1990).

Although some men are raped by women, male rape by females is considered rare. Most male rape victims are raped by other men and often sustain more physical injuries than female rape victims. Males are also more likely to be attacked by multiple assailants than females. It has been noted by some clinicians that the amount of force used, including the use of weapons, typically increases as the age of the male rape victim increases. That is, adult males usually face more lethal weapons and aggression than their younger, and perhaps weaker, counterparts (see Calderwood, 1987; Forman, 1982; Kaufman, DiVasto, Jackson, Voorhees, & Christy, 1980; Warshaw, 1988).

Contrary to popular belief, most males who rape men are heterosexuals, not homosexuals. When homosexuals are targeted for rape, the assailants are typically heterosexual men engaging in a violent form of gay bashing. Although prevalence rates for date rape among gay men are not available, reports from clinicians suggest this form of coercive sexual behavior is not rare (Funk, 1990). Forced sex on males appears to contain similar motivational factors such as degradation, domination, power, control, retaliation, and sadism often associated with the rape of women.

Male rape victims typically display a cluster of traumatic symptoms quite similar to that observed in female rape victims, including fear, anxiety, anger, depression, suicidal ideation, lowered self-esteem, and sexual dysfunctions (Calhoun & Atkeson, 1991; Funk, 1993; Koss & Harvey, 1991; Mezey & King, 1989). Heterosexual males raped by males often experience a sexual identity crisis following the assault. Many of these males worry about why they were singled out and become concerned that something about their appearance and behavior may have been seen by their assailants as effeminate or gay. Some believe that the sexual assault robbed them of their heterosexual identity. Others may feel that they are no longer "a man" because they failed to live up to the masculine credo "Always be strong, powerful, and protect yourself." Many male rape victims struggle with all these plus other cognitive distortions related to the role their sense of masculinity played in the sexual assault.

Funk (1990) and Prokopis (1990) note that homosexual male rape victims who are secure in their sexuality do not usually experience an identity crisis as do their male heterosexual counterparts. It is thought that secure homosexuals assign the responsibility for the rape appropriately to the assailants and not inappropriately to some "defect" in their masculinity or sexuality. On the other hand, some homosexual males who experience shame and guilt about their sexuality may feel that the rape was in some way a "justified" punishment for their own "aberrant" sexual behavior. Of particular concern for nearly all homosexual male rape victims is that their report about the sexual assault will not be taken seriously or they will not be believed because they are gay.

As with female rape victims, males often show very high distress levels within the first 3 weeks of the assault. Although some improvement may be seen within a 3- or 4-month period, most symptoms persist at high levels for at least 1 and often for several years. Some male rape victims seem never to recover completely. In a study of female rape victims, Girelli, Resick, Marhoefer-Dvorak, and Hutter (1986) found that the severity of symptoms and length of time to recovery are linked more to the victim's level of subjective distress during the assault than to other factors. For males who almost always see sexual assault as life threatening, the level of subjective distress tends to be quite high and, therefore, quite severe. This pattern has been observed frequently in the male rape victims I have treated. Consider the following case:

> Spike enlisted in the U.S. Marines but performed poorly during boot camp due to his small size and severe learning disability. He was frequently singled out by his superior officers for verbal harassment, extra disciplinary actions, and physical punishment. One night he was overpowered, physically beaten, and sexually assaulted by three superior officers who also brandished a gun and threaten to kill Spike if he did not comply with their demands. He was warned not to tell anyone about the assault lest he be killed. In spite of repeated verbal threats and physical attacks, Spike reported the sexual assault to the

proper military authorities, who took no action against his assailants. Spike was eventually given an early discharge.

Spike did not enter therapy until several years later. His clinical presentation included the cluster normally seen with the diagnosis of Post-Traumatic Stress Disorder (PTSD), including recurrent and intrusive recollections of the assault, nightmares associated with the assault, sudden flashbacks, hypervigilance, fear, anxiety, and outbursts of anger. He also reported increased distress when exposed to situations that resembled some aspects of the physical and sexual assaults, as well as mostly unsuccessful efforts to avoid thoughts or feelings about the rape. Since his discharge from the military, Spike had experienced difficulties in heterosocial relationships and had frequent episodes of impotency secondary to stress and anxiety. He was unable to tolerate certain sexual activities and positions that triggered flashbacks and severe anxiety. He also reported arrests for criminal activities, other interpersonal relationship problems, and vocational instability.

After several years of therapy, Spike continues to experience PTSD and rape trauma symptoms, but to a lesser degree than on initial presentation. Fortunately, he has recovered sufficiently to reduce the frequency of sexual dysfunctions, establish a stable marital relationship, and complete training for a satisfying career choice. Therapy continues.

Other than private practitioners, resources for male rape victims are sparse. Most rape crisis centers are designed for and staffed by women, not men. In fact, few medical and mental health practitioners are emotionally or professionally prepared to respond therapeutically to male victims of sexual assault. After all, it is a common belief that women get raped, not men, at least not real men. In most states, it is legally impossible to be raped as a man because rape is defined in terms of male perpetration and female victimization.

Most of the male rape victims I have treated reported that health care professionals responded with disbelief, were insensitive, or were harsh in their treatment of them. For example, one male victim of a severe physical assault and attempted rape was told to "quit acting like a baby" when he actively resisted a male emergency room physician's ill-advised attempts to remove the patient's pants for the purposes of the examination. Later, in therapy with a male mental health professional, he was told to "quit worrying about it and be thankful you weren't killed." And we wonder why most male rape victims refuse to disclose.

## ❏ Childhood Sexual Abuse

Like rape, childhood sexual abuse is generally thought of in terms of male perpetration and female victimization. And, also like rape, most cases of childhood sexual abuse, especially the sexual abuse of males, go unreported. Research shows that male children are much less inclined to reveal episodes of sexual victimization than female children. When males do disclose childhood sexual abuse experiences, they typically wait until many years following the period of time when they were abused (for reviews, see Bolton et al., 1989; Mendel, 1995; Perry, 1993).

Male socialization experiences appear to be the major factor in developing a strong inhibition to revealing information about events suggestive of personal weaknesses (Dimock, 1988; Finkelhor, 1984, 1986; Hunter, 1993; Lew, 1988; Morris, 1993; Nasjleti, 1980; Struve, 1990; Vander Mey, 1988). Traditional concepts of masculinity include neither acceptance of nor disclosure about victimization experiences. Stereotypic ideas about the masculine role provide little to no room for incorporating victimization (Harrison & Morris, 1996). Early in the socialization process, boys are told about and frequently exposed to stereotypic ideas that a real man will fight to the death when his manhood is challenged. Males who disclose defeat or victimization experiences run the considerable risk of being viewed by other males as weak and emasculated. To disclose is also a sign of weakness because "big boys don't cry." Males are supposed to handle adversity by "taking it like a man."

Boys are also conditioned to believe that all sexual behavior with females, except blood relatives, is desirable and all sexual behavior with males is bad. If a young boy is sexually victimized by a female, he is less likely to label the experience as abusive, even though his feelings tell him otherwise. Early sexual experiences with older females are often reinterpreted by males to fit traditional concepts of masculine sexuality. It has been my experience that many male survivors of sexual abuse by females are not only reluctant to disclose this information but often fail to see those experiences as either abusive or related to their emotional and behavioral problems. For example, after several sessions of rather unproductive work, a male survivor first disclosed his sexual abuse experiences by a female with something like this, "Well, I don't know if this has anything at all to do with anything that's going on with me but . . ." He then described extensive childhood sexual victimization experiences by an adult female over a several-year period. At first he portrayed himself as a young boy who got "lucky" and was introduced to sexual behavior well before his peers. When his feelings took over, he described quite a different young boy: One who was frightened, confused, anxious, ashamed, and angry. He was unable to discuss his experiences with anyone until that day in therapy, many years later.

When a young boy is sexually abused by a male, two societal taboos are broken: adult-child sexual contact and same-gender sexual activities. Sexually abused boys who are growing up heterosexual often become confused about their sexuality and worry that the sexual contact with a man either signifies that they are gay or that they will become gay. Gonsiorek (1993) notes that young boys growing up gay may become especially vulnerable to sexual victimization by older males due to the boy's preexisting tendency toward homosexuality. What young boy victims of sexual abuse do not understand, of course, is that child sexual abuse has very little to do with sexual orientation or gender preference. It has much more to do with the fact that they are children. Some perpetrators of child sexual abuse may prefer one gender or the other, but most will select a child simply due to availability and convenience, regardless of gender.

A review of the literature pertaining to the prevalence of childhood sexual abuse among males in the United States reveals a wide range of findings depending on methods used, definitions of sexual abuse, and the population sampled. For example, studies of males in the general population suggest a prevalence rate from 8% to 13%; among male college students the range seems to be from about 5% to 33%; and clinical studies reveal a possible range of 9% to 50%. Overall, childhood sexual abuse prevalence studies suggest a rate from about 3% to 50% for male children compared to a range from about 6% to 60% for females. Most clinicians in the field of child sexual abuse now think that 25% to 40% of male children and 30% to 50% of female children experience some form of inappropriate sexual intrusion in their lives before reaching the age of 18 (for reviews, see Bolton et al., 1989; Mendel, 1995; Morris, 1995).

Researchers generally agree that the majority of sexual offenses against boys are committed by older boys or adult males. Historically, the suggested or accepted prevalence rate for female perpetration has been 20% or less of cases involving sexually abused boys. More recently, studies suggest that female perpetration is much higher than generally believed. Fromuth and Burkhart (1987, 1989) found that 72% of one and 78% of another sample of male college students with sexual abuse histories identified females as their perpetrators. Similarly, Seidner and Calhoun (1984) found that 82% of a sample of college men reported that older females were involved in their childhood sexual activities. Of a sample of college males who disclosed personal childhood sexual abuse histories, 28% reported being abused by a female only, whereas 11% reported both male and female perpetrators (Lisak, 1993); a study of Child Protective Services cases revealed that male victims were sexually abused by females only in 34% of the cases and by both male and female perpetrators in 41% of the cases (Ramsey-Klawsnik, 1990a, 1990b); and among a sample of male sexual abuse survivors in higher education, 43% reported being victimized by a female only and 4% by both (Risin & Koss, 1987). In incest cases, Olson (1990) found that the mother was the perpetrator in about 61% of his sample of male victims of incest.

Allen (1990) argues that the incidence of female sexual perpetration has been underrecognized due to three main barriers: overestimation of the strength of the incest taboo, overextension of feminist explanations of child sexual abuse, and overgeneralization of the observation that child sexual abuse by females is rare. Other researchers and clinicians have presented related explanations for the underidentification of female perpetration. These include disbelief, denial of the capacity for female sexual aggression, and rejection of behaviors not in keeping with the accepted societal image of femininity (Banning, 1989; Kasl, 1990; Maccoby & Jacklin, 1974; Masters, Johnson, & Kolodny, 1985; Mathews, Matthews, & Speltz, 1990). Others argue that the type of sexual abuse perpetrated by females is more likely to be covert, such as fondling, seductive, or exhibitionistic behavior, rather than the more overt acts of penetration and violence often perpetrated by males, and therefore less likely to come to the attention of authorities (Kasl, 1990).

Although most agree that more female children are sexually victimized than male children, the negative effect of childhood sexual abuse is not for females only. Kempe and Kempe (1984) note that sexually abused boys may experience more traumatic effects and do worse than sexually abused girls.

Using Browne and Finkelhor's (1986) model of initial effects (within a 2-year period of the sexual abuse) and long-term effects (beyond 2 years and even into adulthood), Urquiza and Capra (1990) studied the effect of sexual abuse on males as reported in the research literature. The initial effects for males appear to be behavioral disturbances and aggression, emotional reactions and self-perceptions, physical consequences and somatic complaints, and sexuality problems. Included as long-term effects are depression and somatic disturbances, effects on self-esteem and self-concept, interpersonal relationship problems, influence on sexuality, and addictive behaviors.

Based on their clinical experiences with sexually abused males plus an extensive review of the literature, Bolton et al. (1989) propose six categories of negative effect:

Emotional distress (e.g., depression, suicidal ideation, guilt, low self-esteem, anger, fear, sleep disturbances, dissociation, obsessive compulsiveness, addictions, and psychoticism)

Behavior problems (e.g., aggressive, antisocial, and undercontrolled externalizing behaviors; tendency toward sexualizing behavior; substance abuse)

Sexual problems (e.g., exaggerated interest in sexual activities, sexual dysfunctions, general dissatisfaction with sexual experiences)

Cyclical victimization (e.g., tendency for some, but not the majority, of male sexual abuse victims to perpetuate sexual offenses)

Sexual orientation conflicts (e.g., confusion about sexuality and sexual orientation, homophobia)

Prostitution (e.g., engage in "hustling" on the streets, being exploited by others through sex rings or participation in the production of pornographic material featuring children)

Clearly, childhood sexual abuse can affect nearly all aspects of a male victim's life and may require gender-sensitive treatment strategies to remediate (see Bolton et al., 1989; Friedrich, 1995; Gonsiorek, Bera, & LeTourneau, 1994; Harrison & Morris, 1996; Hunter, 1990; Lew, 1988; Mendel, 1995; Morris, 1995; Porter, 1986).

## ❏ Circumcision

As the glans penis develops in utero, it is covered with and attached to a protective layer of skin. The process of separation between the glans and this skin, which will eventually become the foreskin or prepuce, begins at approximately the 17th week of the gestation period. At birth, the penis is not yet fully developed and the separation process has just barely begun. If unhindered, separation is normally completed by age 3 to 5, producing a healthy, fully retractable foreskin. This covering of loose skin is attached to the penile shaft just behind the glans. It moves freely over the glans penis and allows for and covers the lengthened shaft during erection. The foreskin or prepuce may also contain a greater concentration of complex nerve endings than the glans itself (Taylor, 1991). So what should we do with this sensitive, well-designed, clever little tag of skin? The consensus among many religious groups and medical authorities has been, "It must go. Cut it off!"

Circumcision, the surgical removal of the prepuce, has its roots in antiquity. An ancient Egyptian relief, dated approximately 2800 BC, appears to depict ritualized male circumcision. Male circumcision is also described in the Old Testament as part of the covenant between Yahweh and the people of Abraham (Genesis 17:10-14; 18:23-27). The covenant states "every male among you who is 8 days old shall be circumcised throughout your generations" (Genesis 17:12). Abraham, already an elderly man when the covenant was established, "was 99 years old when he was circumcised in the flesh of his foreskin" (Genesis 17:24). Historically, Moslems have also performed ritual circumcisions on males in accordance with the Abrahamic covenant; however, this religious group also embraces female circumcision, a form of genital mutilation that may include the removal of the clitoris (clitoridectomy).

Although Jesus, a Jew, was circumcised, the practice of circumcision has little or no religious foundation among Christians. In fact, some New Testament scriptures seem to abrogate the ritual: "Behold I, Paul, say to you that if you receive circumcision, Christ will be of no benefit to you. And I testify again to every man who receives circumcision, that he is under obligation to keep the whole Law" (Galatians 5:2, 3); "For in Christ Jesus neither circumcision nor uncircumcision means anything, but faith working through love" (Galatians 5:6; for additional information, see Ephesians 2:11, 15; Colossians 3:11; Acts 15:1-29; 1 Corinthians 7:18, 19).

During the 19th century, masturbation was cited as one of the major causes of a number of physical diseases and mental disorders. Some physicians believed that circumcision was an effective medical procedure to stop masturbation and, therefore, all the attendant maladies. Remondino (1891/1974) suggests circumcision to prevent or cure just about anything from alcoholism to curvature of the spine. Once the scientific and medical community conceded that masturbation was not a legitimate etiological factor in the development of diseases, the emphasis on circumcision as a preventative or curative measure gradually declined. Quickly, however, other medical and health reasons were proposed to perpetuate the practice of male circumcision. For example, in the 1920s, circumcision was touted as a prevention for venereal diseases; in the 1930s, foreskins were thought to cause penile cancer; and in the 1950s, foreskins were thought to be linked to cervical cancer (for a review, see Milos & Macris, 1992). As a result, the practice of circumcision in the United States increased steadily until the early 1970s, when the rate reached 90% of all newborn males (Lindsey, 1988).

After decades of debate, the medical community eventually began to respond to the paucity of evidence supporting the purported health benefits of routine neonatal circumcision. For example, Abou-David (1967) found no differences in the rate of cervical cancer in wives of Lebanese Moslems who practiced circumcision and Lebanese wives of Christian men who were uncircumcised. The findings of Abou-David do not support earlier studies that suggest that Jewish women have a somewhat lower rate of cervical cancer than Christian women (see Terris, Wilson, & Nelson, 1973). And penile cancer, a rare disease found mostly in elderly men, seems to occur at about the same rate in circumcised as uncircumcised men (see Milos & Macris, 1992). By 1971, the American Academy of Pediatrics (AAP) took the official position that no medical evidence existed to support routine circumcision of newborns and recommended against the practice. In 1983, the American College of Obstetricians and Gynecologists assumed a similar position regarding routine circumcision. In 1984, the AAP went a step further and described medical problems that may occur as a result of circumcision (American Academy of Pediatrics, 1984). This information was deleted in a subsequent revision, however. From 1970 to the mid-1980s, the incidence of circumcision in the United States decreased from 90% to 59% of newborn males (Lindsey, 1988). Even though the rate of routine circumcision has declined significantly, the United States remains the only country in the world that continues to practice routine medical infant circumcision on a majority of its males (NOHARMM, 1992; Wallerstein, 1980).

The medical benefits of routine male circumcision continue to be debated. Some researchers maintain that penile cancer, although rare, is found somewhat more frequently in uncircumcised men (e.g., Harahap & Siregar, 1988; Warner & Strashin, 1981), whereas others argue that the results are a function of methodological flaws in the research design or data analyses (see Milos & Macris, 1992). Still others suggest that the rate of penile cancer in the United States is similar to rates found in countries such as Denmark and Japan, where neonatal circumcision is not a routine procedure (Waterhouse, Shanmugaramam, Muir, & Powell, 1982). Even Benjamin Spock, the renown baby doctor, now recommends against circumcision and questions the wisdom of circumcising 1 million baby boys annually to reduce the already low rate of 150 deaths a year in the United States from penile cancer (Spock & Rothenberg, 1992).

During World War I, circumcision was proposed as a prevention of venereal diseases. It was not. Now some are suggesting that circumcision may decrease the risk of infection with the human immunodeficiency virus (HIV; see Cameron, Simonsen, & D'Costa, 1989; Simonsen, Cameron, & Gakinya, 1989). Although these studies conclude that uncircumcised men in Kenya exposed to HIV during heterosexual intercourse seemed to be more susceptible to infection than circumcised men, the findings are not conclusive and appear compounded by additional factors, such as mucosal or cutaneous ulcers, and may not generalize to other populations (Poland, 1990). Touchette (1991) suspects that some cells in the foreskin may be especially susceptible to HIV, but more research is needed before this notion is verified. At present, no evidence suggests that routine circumcision will ever be as effective in preventing HIV/AIDS as reducing the number of sexual contacts and by the proper use of condoms.

Other than the possibility that urinary-tract infection in infancy may occur at a somewhat lower rate among circumcised boys, most concerns about general penile hygiene have been settled. That is, with proper cleansing by a caretaker while the child is young and by the boy himself as he grows older, uncircumcised males do not appear to be at a significantly higher risk for infections or other maladies associated with poor genital hygiene than circumcised boys.

In some cases, an abnormal condition (phimosis) occurs that renders the foreskin so tight that it cannot be retracted from the glans. The AAP (American Academy of Pediatrics, 1975) warns, however, that phimosis is not a valid diagnosis in newborns because the normal separation between the glans and the preputial layer of the penis has not yet developed. True medical phimosis may be difficult to diagnose in young boys through the preteen years because natural full retractibility may simply be delayed and not due to an abnormal condition. In cases where true phimosis exists or premature forced retraction has caused damage to the foreskin, rendering retraction difficult or impossible, circumcision may be the treatment of choice.

Circumcision, if performed by an experienced practitioner, is generally considered a low risk for complications. Yet hemorrhage, infection, and even death have been reported. In Atlanta, one young boy lost his penis and another was so badly mutilated that subsequent sexual reassignment surgery was deemed necessary to correct a seriously bungled circumcision (see Milos & Macris, 1992).

It has been assumed, also, that circumcision is a relatively painless procedure for the newborn. Although this may have been the case when mothers were routinely anesthetized during childbirth, the increasing popularity of natural childbirth over the past couple of decades or so has left many newborns without the secondary benefits of their mother's pain blockers. Studies on the effects of circumcision suggest that baby boys do experience pain during the surgical procedure. Porter (1986) found that newborn cries intensified significantly during routine procedures used in circumcision such as the crushing, clamping, and slicing of the baby's foreskin. An increase in physiologic and behavioral changes associated with pain and trauma, as well as prolonged stress effects, also have been documented (see Anand & Hickey, 1987). Interestingly, some researchers suggest that the male-female difference in the behavior of neonates may be due to the effect of circumcision on males, a variable not considered in most studies investigating gender differences in young children (see Williamson, 1984).

What about the effect of circumcision on a male's sexual behavior? A common belief is that circumcised men experience a loss of sensation from the glans penis and, therefore, experience more sexual problems than uncircumcised men. Another common belief is that circumcised men actually experience an increase in sensation from the glans penis and, therefore, experience more sexual problems than uncircumcised men. Either belief points to more sexual problems for circumcised males when compared to their uncircumcised counterparts. Personal preferences not withstanding, no reliable evidence is reported supporting the notions that neonatal circumcision subsequently decreases or enhances sexual functioning at sexual maturity. For example, Masters and Johnson (1966) found no significant differences between circumcised and uncircumcised men regarding various forms of penile stimulation. In my clinical practice over the past 25 years, I have received no complaints from either circumcised or noncircumcised men regarding the sensitivity of their glans penis.

Overall, some clinicians are suggesting that infant circumcision is a significant traumatic event that may produce long-term psychological damage in many males, including a poor self-image and sexual adjustment. At present, a growing number of these men are speaking out about the negative effect of their childhood circumcision on their physical, emotional, and sexual well-being. Many also contend that subjecting unconsenting minors to an unwarranted medical procedure such as circumcision is tantamount to child abuse and a serious violation of basic human rights to an intact body (see NOHARMM, 1992). Some men are attempting to restore their lost foreskin through a number of procedures, including surgical reconstruction.

Like females, males can become victims of misconduct by others and harmful sociocultural notions about gender roles. Unlike females, males typically do not disclose victimization experiences, especially sexual maltreatment. And, until recently, circumcision was viewed by most males as a "normal" practice to conform to religious beliefs or medical pronouncements. Besides, as an infant you have to take what is given to you. So, most males faced with being labeled a victim—not strong, not manly—assume the age-old male role of stoicism and suffer in silence. Sometimes the silence is broken, not by disclosure of the abuse, but by the anguished and seemingly disconnected cries of the sufferer himself. Sometimes the silence is broken by the sympathetic crys of those who suffer with him but know not why. Secrecy allows sexual abuses to continue and prevents healing. Although the road to recovery begins with first disclosure, this route is too often barricaded with strong cultural admonitions that big boys don't cry. The task facing both the male victim of sexual abuse and society as a whole is to understand how most of the culturally driven scripts for achieving and securing manhood become accomplices to the sexual victimization of males by reducing the availability of disclosure and healing experiences. It is time to disregard traditional gender roles and understand that sexual abuse, in whatever form, is not for women only.

# 8

# Last Dance

## *Dancing the Dangerous Dance With Disease*

$S$exual behavior, any kind of sexual behavior, is much more of a risk today than ever in the past. Sexually active individuals continue to be faced with the threat of usually treatable sexually transmitted diseases (STDs) such as gonorrhea, genital warts, chlamydia, and syphilis; but presently incurable diseases such as genital herpes and HIV/AIDS have reached epidemic proportions. For example, Michael et al. (1994) found that one in six Americans reported having had a sexually transmitted disease.

Although the information contained in this chapter may be technical and unpleasant, any book on male heterosexuality would be incomplete without a presentation on STDs. Why? Most heterosexual males know not only little about sex in general but they tend to know even less about the dangers lurking under the sexual bed. Sure, most males have heard about and know something about herpes, gonorrhea, and syphilis. In fact, some older males will tell you that contracting the clap (gonorrhea) used to be considered somewhat of a rite of passage for younger men; clap confirmed that a young man had actually engaged in sexual intercourse. A young man could join the ranks of sexually experienced men by saying something like, "Yeah, we had sex and she gave me the clap. But the Doc gave me a shot of penicillin in the ass and I'm OK." And most males know AIDS will kill, but many still believe that heterosexual men seldom contract HIV. Mostly, males know very little about STDs and many fail to put forth the effort to increase their knowledge.

Anything that affects male heterosexuality is important for males to learn. STDs affect male heterosexuality in a number of significant ways. The cultural messages regarding masculinity and sexuality also affect males' approach to this very sensitive area. But knowledge is power. Accurate information about STDs provides males with more choices regarding their sexual behavior. If males are going to dance the dance of sex, they need to know who their dance partner really is before signing the dance card.

## ❏ Acquired Immunodeficiency Syndrome (AIDS)

AIDS is a cluster of symptoms believed to be caused by several types of retroviruses called human immunodeficiency viruses (HIV). Presently, the most prevalent forms identified as causing AIDS are HIV-1 and HIV-2. Once the virus enters the body, it seeks out and identifies a certain class of white blood cells called lymphocytes or T-Helper cells. This special lymphocyte normally plays a key role in recognizing pathogens (e.g., bacteria, viruses, fungi, and other threats to the body) and then calling other lymphocytes into action against the menace. After attaching itself to the T-Helper cell, the virus penetrates the cell's membrane and injects the virus's own genetic material into the cell's nucleus. The DNA from the virus then combines with the cell's genetic material. This process transforms the T-Helper cell from a combatant against into a manufacturing plant for the virus. Each time the infected cell divides, the virus is replicated and additional infected cells are produced. The infected T-Helper cell is destroyed once it reproduces the virus.

Although HIV directly attacks, invades, and eventually disables the body's natural defenses against diseases, HIV is a killer only by proxy; it merely provides the circumstances for other diseases to proliferate and take their toll. With a seriously weakened immune system, the person is much more susceptible to opportunistic and potentially life-threatening illnesses. For example, many AIDS patients die from a rare form of pneumonia, pneumocystis carinii pneumonia; a rare form of cancer, Kaposi's sarcoma; and other types of infections from which most people, without some form of immune deficiency, recover. The HIV/AIDS virus may also attack the central nervous system, causing a progressive deterioration of mental and motor functioning. This neurological syndrome is known as AIDS dementia complex (ADC). Patients with ADC show a tendency to deteriorate more rapidly than those without this complex.

Once infected with HIV, a person may experience flulike symptoms for a short period of time, then become relatively free of symptoms for a period of months to several years. During this asymptomatic period, HIV-infected persons become carriers and can infect others with HIV in spite of showing no symptoms themselves. Eventually, most HIV-infected persons begin to experience the now all-too-familiar symptoms of AIDS. Approximately 50% of HIV-infected persons display full-scale AIDS symptoms within 5 years of infection, whereas 75% have diagnosable AIDS within 7 years. The median number of years from HIV infection to a diagnosable case of AIDS is approximately 10.5 years. The average length of survival for patients with full-scale AIDS is estimated to be about 1 year, with only about 3.4% of diagnosable AIDS patients surviving 5 years. Virtually no one recovers from full-scale AIDS, although antiviral drugs such as Zidovudine (AZT) and Dideoxyinosine (DDI) may help in slowing the progression of the disease. Medical researchers are hopeful that their efforts in studying HIV will eventually produce a safe and effective vaccine, but none is available presently (for reviews, see Masters, Johnson, & Kolodny, 1988a; Nevid, 1993).

Although a virus similar to HIV is found in a West African monkey, the origins of HIV and AIDS remain unclear. Theories explaining the transmission of the virus from other primates to humans range from stories about people being bitten by infected monkeys to experiments designed to determine if malaria parasites in primates would infect humans. During the malaria experiments, from the 1920s through the 1950s, humans may have been inadvertently "inoculated" with blood from monkeys and chimpanzees containing early strains of immunodeficiency viruses. It is also speculated that the strain of immunodeficiency viruses found in simians may have mutated to the forms now found in humans.

Most agree that the first documented case of AIDS in the United States occurred in 1968, but it was 1981 before the effects of AIDS were reported in medical journals and by the Centers for Disease

Control (CDC). Because the symptoms seemed to appear only in homosexual males, AIDS was originally called, gay-related immune deficiency. This highly prejudicial label was changed to acquired immune deficiency syndrome in 1982 once it was learned that AIDS was not restricted to gay men but was also diagnosed in a nongay population of hemophiliacs and Haitian immigrants. The first cases of AIDS in heterosexuals were reported in 1983. The HIV thought to cause AIDS was isolated by Dr. Luc Montagnier in 1983 and by Dr. Robert Gallo in 1984.

During the decade since the first AIDS cases in the United States were documented, the number of cases soared from a handful to more than 200,000. AIDS quickly became the second leading cause of death for American men in the 25- to 44-year-old age group (Centers for Disease Control, 1991a). Preliminary analyses of data collected by the CDC for 1993 indicated that AIDS had not only surpassed accidents as the number one killer of American men in this age group but it was the fourth leading cause of death and rising rapidly for American women. The National Center for Health Statistics estimated that by 1993, about 550,000 Americans were infected with HIV, about half of whom were white males; the rest were primarily black, and about 25% of the HIV-infected people were female (for a review, see Michael et al., 1994). Clearly, HIV/AIDS is not just a gay plague brought down by an angry deity on homosexuals for engaging in "unnatural" sexual acts, as some religious zealots would have us believe. HIV has proven to be color blind, gender blind, and sexual-preference blind. In fact, AIDS appears to be increasing more rapidly among American women (29% increase) than among men (18% increase) (Chu, Buehler, & Berkelman, 1990). Worldwide, women account for nearly one third of the AIDS cases (Kent, 1991). And heterosexual sex is now the most rapidly increasing mode of HIV transmission (National Commission on AIDS, 1993).

Bodily fluids such as blood, semen, and vaginal secretions from persons infected with HIV harbor the AIDS-causing virus. The exchange of contaminated bodily fluids from one partner to another during sexual activity is the primary form of transmission of HIV. Homosexual or heterosexual anal intercourse carries the greatest risk of transmission. Although the rate of transmission appears lower for vaginal than anal intercourse, Masters et al. (1988a) estimate that the risk for infection through vaginal intercourse is higher for women (1 in 400) than for men (1 in 600). The higher concentration of HIV in the semen of infected men as compared to the somewhat lower concentration found in the cervical and vaginal secretions of infected women may account for the differential transmission rate.

Although some studies have failed to find a link between oral-genital sex and HIV transmission, other studies are beginning to suggest that oral sex with an infected partner, regardless of gender, may pose more of a risk of transmission than previously believed. Normal wear and tear of the mucous membrane lining of the mouth could produce lesions and an easy access for HIV-infected semen or vaginal secretions (Masters et al., 1988a).

How about kissing? Because HIV has been isolated, at least at a low level, in the saliva of infected persons, the possibility of transmission through kissing must be considered. The popular view is that HIV is not transmitted through kissing (see Richardson, 1988). But some researchers express concern that more passionate, saliva-inducing, mucosa-assaultive kisses, such as the popular tongue probing "French" kiss, may increase the probability of saliva-borne HIV finding its way into some minor break in the protective lining of the lips and oral cavity (Hein, DiGeronimo, et al., 1989; Masters et al., 1988a).

Although HIV is primarily transmitted through sexual activities, it is also readily transmitted by sharing drug paraphernalia, such as hypodermic needles, with a person infected with HIV. The CDC (1991b) estimates that nearly one quarter of AIDS cases in the United States are injectable-drug users. It is thought that many of these individuals may transmit HIV both through sharing their infected needles and by sexual contact. Injectable-drug-using prostitutes and their clients are at increased risk for being infected with HIV/AIDS.

Sadly, HIV may also be transmitted from an infected mother to her fetus during pregnancy, through the birth process itself, or by breast feeding the baby (Glasner & Kaslow, 1990). Studies suggest that 1,500 to 2,000 newborn children in the United States are infected with HIV annually (Centers for Disease Control, 1990a). Fetuses of HIV-infected mothers face a one-in-three probability of being born with HIV (Centers for Disease Control, 1992).

In a study comparing nonmonogamous heterosexual men and women with heterosexual men and women in long-term monogamous relationships, Masters et al. (1988a) found a relationship between the number of sexual partners and the prevalence of HIV infection. Only 0.25% of monogamous men and women were found to be infected with HIV, whereas 7% of women and 5% of men who averaged up to 11 sexual partners annually had evidence of HIV infection. The prevalence of HIV was higher for nonmonogamous women (14%) and men (12%) who reported more than an average of 12 sexual partners annually. Nonmonogamous persons were also more likely to have engaged in anal intercourse and at a higher frequency than the monogamous group.

Heterosexuals who are very active sexually with numerous partners are at an increased risk for contracting and spreading HIV than heterosexual men and women who establish long-term monogamous sexual relationships. To reduce this risk, sexually active men and women must begin to change their attitudes about risky sexual behavior, such as anal intercourse and unprotected sex of any kind, as well as reducing the number of sexual partners. Michael et al. (1994) found that some people are beginning to take the personal risk of contracting HIV/AIDS seriously. For example, 27% of Michael et al.'s sample of more than 3,000 adults said they had been tested for HIV, with most of those tested reporting numerous sexual partners since age 18 and within the past year. Thirty percent of the sample reported changing their sexual behavior, with the higher-risk group (younger and with numerous sexual partners) more likely to have changed their conduct than those in monogamous relationships.

## ❑ Common Sexually Transmitted Diseases

### ■ Herpes

The two most common types of herpes are oral herpes and genital herpes. Both are caused by variants of the Herpes simplex virus: Herpes simplex virus type 1 (oral) and type 2 (genital). Oral herpes (HSV-1) consists of fever blisters or cold sores on the lips and in the mouth. HSV-1 can also cause similar type cold sores on the genitals if transmitted from an infected area (usually by oral-genital contact or by hand) (Braude, Davis, & Fierer, 1986).

Genital herpes (HSV-2) consists of relatively shallow but usually painful lesions or sores on the genitals, anus, buttocks, or thighs. HSV-2 can also be transmitted to the mouth, lips, and throat through oral-genital contact. About 6 to 8 days after initial infection with HSV-2, reddish, painful bumps (papules) appear. The papules transform into groups of small blisters that eventually fill with pus and burst, leaving painful lesions. The infected person is the most contagious during the active sores stage. The lesions then begin to form a crust or scab and may heal within a 1- to 3-week period. Internal infections such as in the urethra, vagina, cervix area, or rectum may require another week or so to heal than the more common external sores. Other symptoms may also accompany an outbreak of genital herpes. Some patients complain of headaches, muscle aches, fever, swollen lymph glands, and general malaise. Once the symptoms of genital herpes disappear, HIV-2 typically goes into a dormant stage that may last a few weeks, several months, many years, or a lifetime. Although the infected person is the least contagious during the dormant stage, HSV-2 has not disappeared. It has found a resting place in nerve cells near the base of the spine and simply waits to be spurred back into action.

Medical research has not been able to explain why some people infected with HSV-2 experience recurrent outbreaks whereas others do not. Some researchers report that HSV-2 becomes reactivated in approximately 30% to 70% of cases. Recurrences may be related to a wide range of factors such as emotional stress, fatigue, exposure to sun, hormonal fluctuations, depressed mental states, extreme climate changes, and other infections. Some patients report that recurrences may occur on a monthly basis. Others report that outbreaks occur on a less frequent basis, such as once a year or once every 5 years. Many patients report that the severity of the symptoms decreases after the initial outbreak. And some patients even find that the frequency of the repeat attacks reduces over time (see Kemeny, Cohen, Zegans, & Conant, 1989; Longo & Clum, 1989; Masters et al., 1988b; Straus, 1985).

Genital herpes is generally transmitted by sexual activities such as vaginal intercourse, anal intercourse, rubbing the genitals together, oral-genital contact, or oral-anal contact. It can also be spread by kissing and by touching genitals with fingers or hands contaminated with the herpes virus (e.g., touching genitals after touching an infected area). Infected people must also be careful not to spread the herpes virus to other vulnerable parts of the body such as the eyes. Ocular herpes can be quite serious and may cause blindness.

Although the risk for transmission of genital herpes is thought to be higher during the active lesions stage, transmission may also occur during a prodromal stage that occurs with some infected persons before blisters actually appear. Early warning symptoms may include burning or pain with urination or defecation; itching or tingling in the affected area; or tenderness, aching, or pain in the groin area, the buttocks, or lower extremities. Unfortunately, asymptomatic transmission also appears to occur in some cases. That is, sexual contact with an infected partner who shows no prodromal or active herpetic symptoms may result in contracting genital herpes (see Dawkins, 1990; Mertz, 1990.)

Sex with a partner infected with genital herpes poses a considered risk for contracting the disease. A man's chances of contracting genital herpes from a single encounter with an infected woman is approximately 50%, whereas the risk for a woman contracting the disease from an infected man is 80% to 90% (Straus, 1985). Although no one knows for sure how many people in the United States are infected with genital herpes, the estimates range from 25 to 30 million.

Presently no cure for genital herpes is available, although an antiviral drug, acyclovir (Zoviraz), in ointment form, has been shown to relieve pain and speed the healing process when applied directly to external infected areas. Oral administration of acyclovir, in pill form, may be effective in relieving the symptoms of internal lesions, as well as reducing the frequency and duration of repeated outbreaks.

Faced with a lifetime of possible recurrent painful sores, the risk of transmitting the disease to others, and the social stigma of having an incurable sexually transmitted disease, herpes sufferers often feel isolated, angry, depressed, damaged, and anxious (Levy, Dignan, & Shirreffs, 1987). Some abstain from sexual activities, whereas others seek out partners who are also infected with genital herpes. Most, however, learn to accept their situation and make the adjustments necessary to reduce the risks of infecting others while establishing a normalized lifestyle.

## ■ Gonorrhea

In the old Testament (Leviticus 15), Moses speaks to Aaron about cleansing unhealthiness due to a man's discharge. Most historians believe that Moses was describing gonorrhea and the risk of becoming "unclean" through contact with an infected person or by touching the objects the unclean person had "infected." Notations about a disease thought to be gonorrhea can also be found in the writings of some ancient Greek philosophers and physicians. Hippocrates taught that the penile discharge typical for gonorrhea was an involuntary loss of semen or other fluids due either to engaging in too much sexual activity or by an overly passionate worship of the goddess of love, Aphrodite. In the second century AD, Galen, a Greek physician, named the "love" disease, *gonorrhea* (from *gonos*, semen, plus *rheein*, to flow). When the bacterium responsible for the disease was isolated in 1379 by Albert Neisser, the microorganism was named *Neisseria gonorrhea*. Gonorrhea is also commonly known as "the clap" and sometimes as "the drip."

Gonorrhea remains one of the most common types of sexually transmitted diseases in the United States, even though its growth seemed to slow during the 1940s and 1950s, when penicillin was found to be an effective treatment. The CDC (1990b) reports a decline in the rate of gonorrheal infection, except for African Americans, during the period of 1980 to 1988. Even so, nearly 750,000 new cases of gonorrhea are reported each year, with young people between the ages of 20 and 24 accounting for the majority of new cases (Centers for Disease Control, 1989a). In addition, a penicillin-resistant form of gonorrhea has been on the increase since 1976, although it can be treated successfully with other antibiotics (Masters et al., 1988b).

The primary method by which gonorrhea is transmitted is by any form of sexual activity with an infected person, such as vaginal intercourse, oral-genital contact, anal intercourse, oral-anal contact, and sometimes kissing. Although gonorrhea is a highly contagious bacterial infection for either gender, the risk of contracting the disease appears higher for women. A man who has sexual intercourse on one occasion with an infected woman stands a 20% to 25% chance of being infected, whereas the risk for a woman with a one-time exposure to an infected man is about 50% (Platt, Rice, & McCormack, 1983). Increased exposure to an infected person, regardless of gender, increases the risk of contracting the disease.

Men who have contracted gonorrhea typically develop symptoms within 2 to 10 days after exposure, although the symptoms may first appear after several weeks. The first symptom is a clear discharge from the penis that changes to a yellowish, rather thick, and puslike discharge within about 24 to 48 hours of the first discharge. Painful and frequent urination are also symptoms of the infection. If left untreated, the symptoms of gonorrhea typically subside within a few weeks or so. The gonococcus bacterium will continue to spread, however, and may infect the prostate, seminal vesicles, and epididymis. In some cases, untreated gonorrhea has caused sterility in men. Fortunately, most men seek early treatment and are cured through the use of antibiotics.

Less than half of the women infected with gonorrhea display any visible symptoms. For this reason, women may not seek early medical intervention and, therefore, are at a higher risk for more serious complications, such as pelvic inflammatory disease. Also, asymptomatic women may unwittingly transmit the disease to sexual partners because they are unaware of their own infection. Women with gonorrheal symptoms typically experience a vaginal discharge, irritation of external genitals, burning sensation while urinating, and irregular menstrual bleeding.

## ■ Syphilis

Although researchers have been unable to identify the origins of syphilis clearly, one common belief is that Christopher Columbus and his crew brought it back to Spain from their first voyage in the "New World." Apparently Columbus was suffering from syphilis when he died in 1506. Syphilis reached epidemic proportions as it traveled quickly throughout Europe and into other continents. Another theory is that syphilis was already present in some parts of Europe when Columbus returned. Its spread could have been due to the movements of military personnel across Europe and the ever-present prostitutes around military encampments. Some researchers believe that Columbus may have contracted syphilis from romantic trysts with European rather than Native American women because no strong evidence linking Native Americans and syphilis has been found.

Regardless of the origins of the disease, the name *syphilis* comes from a story written by Girolamo Fracastoro in 1530 about a young shepherd boy, Syphilis, who contracted the disease after making the mistake of insulting Apollo. The bacterium, *Treponema pallidum,* that causes syphilis was isolated in 1905 by a German scientist, Fritz Schaudinn. Sometimes the bacterium is referred to as a spirochete. Both names refer to the bacterium's threadlike spiral shape.

Like gonorrhea, the incidence of syphilis decreased in the United States after penicillin was found to be effective against the disease.

Yet in the mid-1980s, reported cases of syphilis increased dramatically. For example, from 1985 to 1990, the number of reported cases in the United States increased from approximately 28,000 to about 50,000 cases annually (see Centers for Disease Control, 1991b; Melvin, 1990; Rolfs & Nakashima, 1990). The rising incidence of syphilis is often attributed to the risky and irresponsible sexual behavior exhibited by a rapidly growing population of cocaine users, especially crack cocaine users, many of whom engage in prostitution to support their drug addiction (see Farley, Hadler, & Gunn, 1990; Rolfs, Goldberg, & Sharrar, 1990).

Syphilis is most commonly spread through some form of sexual behavior with someone infected with the bacterium. Syphilis can also be transmitted by touching the open lesions caused by the disease. Reinisch (1990) estimates that the probability of contracting syphilis from one sexual encounter with an infected partner is one in three.

Syphilis typically progresses through four distinct stages. The earliest sign (first stage) of the disease is the appearance of a hard, oval, ulcerlike lesion called a *chancre* (pronounced "shanker") about 2 to 4 weeks after initial exposure. The chancre typically appears at any site where the spirochete entered the skin. In most cases, the sore is painless and heals within 4 to 6 weeks.

If effective treatment is not administered, symptoms of secondary syphilis appear about 1 week to 6 months after the first-stage chancre sore heals. Secondary symptoms often resemble many other maladies and may include fever, headaches, pains in the joints, loss of appetite, sore throat, hair loss, and a pale rash on the palms of hands and soles of feet. The symptoms of secondary syphilis may occur intermittently for about 3 to 6 months, then disappear.

The absence of all symptoms, without treatment, usually indicates that the disease is going into the latent stage. During this stage, the spirochetes are busy multiplying and burrowing into various tissues, bones, blood vessels, and the central nervous system (brain and spinal card). The majority of people with untreated syphilis remain in the latent stage for a number of years and perhaps the rest of their lives.

In some cases, the disease progresses to the tertiary stage, or late syphilis. During this stage, life-threatening infections of the liver, skin, muscle tissues, digestive organs, and the cardiovascular system may occur. If the infection attacks the central nervous system (neurosyphilis), paralysis, mental illness, and death may occur.

Syphilis can be treated with penicillin in any stage, but larger doses and a longer treatment period are normally required for the latent and tertiary stages. The infected person is highly contagious during the primary stage and for a few weeks into the secondary stage.

## ■ Chlamydia

Many men have never heard of chlamydia, and most who have erroneously believe it is a disease that affects only women. Only about one in three men and women infected with chlamydia develop symptoms. Most people are unaware of chlamydial infections even though these infections are the most common bacterial sexually transmitted diseases in the United States. It is estimated that approximately 4 million cases of some form of chlamydial infection may occur each year. Teenagers and college students appear to be at a higher risk of infection than the general population (see Goldsmith, 1986; Reinisch, 1990; Toomey & Barnes, 1990).

The bacterium *Chlamydia trachomatis* is responsible for several different types of sexually transmitted infections. About 50% of nongonococcal urethritis found in men are chlamydial urethritis (inflammation of the urethra) and about half of the new cases of acute epididymitis (infection of the epididymis) are also the handiwork of chlamydia bacterium. In women, chlamydial infections show up as nongonococal urethritis (usually called the *urethral syndrome,* or sometimes just chlamydia), cervicitis (infection of the cervix), endometritis (infection of the endometrium), and pelvic inflammatory disease (a major cause of female infertility).

The primary form of transmission of chlamydia is vaginal or anal intercourse, although Handsfield (1988) reports that chlamydial infections of the throat may occur through oral-genital contact with an infected person. When symptoms of chlamydial infections appear, they seem to be a milder form of symptoms typical of gonorrhea. Men with chlamydia urethritis may produce a thin white discharge from the penis and some pain and discomfort during urination; gonorrhea produces a thick yellow-green discharge, as well as severe burning and pain during urination. Infections caused by the chlamydial bacterium often occur in conjunction with other sexually transmitted diseases, most notably gonorrhea (Centers for Disease Control, 1989b).

Chlamydial infections normally respond to treatment with antibiotics such as doxycycline, tetracycline, or erythromycin, but not penicillin. Partners should also be treated even if they have no symptoms (Martin, 1990). Asymptomatic men need to realize that it is not just their sexual partner who has the problem. They are also at risk to develop symptoms, to reinfect the partner, or to infect others.

### ■ Genital Warts

A widespread, but a little-known sexually transmitted disease, genital warts (*condylomata acuminata*) is caused by the human papilloma virus. It is estimated that about 20% to 30% of sexually active people in the United States are infected. Teenagers and young adults between the ages of 20 and 24 and women who became sexually active before the age of 18 years and have had many sex partners are at a higher risk to contract the disease than the general population (Reinisch, 1990).

In men, genital warts usually appear somewhere on the penis, on the scrotum, or within the urethra. Genital warts typically form somewhere on the vulva, in the vagina, or on the cervix in women. Other than warts that form in the urethra, which may cause a painful discharge and some bleeding, infected persons usually show few symptoms of infection other than the warts themselves. Genital warts have been linked to cases of penile and cervical cancer, however (Rando, 1988).

Genital warts may appear a few weeks to several years after the person has been exposed to the virus. Similar to common plantar warts, genital warts often resemble small cauliflowers. They can be removed through medical procedures such as freezing the warts with liquid nitrogen (cryotherapy), the application of podophyllin, or laser surgery. Although the genital warts themselves can be removed, the offending virus remains in the body, leading to possible recurrences.

### ■ Viral Hepatitis

Hepatitis, an infection of the liver, can be caused by several different types of viruses and is spread mostly by nonsexual means, such as contact with infected fecal matter, eating poorly prepared shellfish taken from contaminated waters, or through contact with contaminated blood. The four major types, hepatitis A (formerly called infectious hepatitis), hepatitis B (previously called serum hepatitis), hepatitis C (formerly known as non-A and non-B hepatitis), and hepatitis D (sometimes called delta hepatitis) may also be transmitted through sexual activities, usually involving oral-anal contact or anal intercourse (Centers for Disease Control, 1989b; Masters et al., 1988b).

Most people infected with viral hepatitis are asymptomatic and may spread the disease unwittingly. When symptoms occur, they usually include poor appetite, vomiting, abdominal pain, indigestion, diarrhea, and jaundice (yellowish appearance of the skin and eyes). Bowel movements tend to be whitish and urine appears brownish. More serious medical problems such as chronic liver disease, cirrhosis of the liver, and cancer of the liver may also occur. Although no cure for viral hepatitis has been found, a vaccine that provides protection against hepatitis B and hepatitis D is available and is recommended by the American Academy of Pediatrics as part of routine baby immunization procedures.

## ■ Ectoparasites

In addition to the many sexually transmitted diseases caused by some type of virus or bacterium, humans are plagued by ancient parasitic organisms known as ecotoparasites. As their classification implies, these pesky critters attach themselves to the outside of the body. Two of these parasites, commonly known as crabs and scabies, are particularly fond of areas of the body covered by hair, especially pubic hair. Each is generally transmitted through sexual contact or by generous contact with clothing, bedding, towels, or other fabrics that have been used by an infested person and are not adequately sanitized.

Pubic lice (*Pthirus pubis*) are biting parasites that resemble crabs when viewed under a microscope. Adult lice can be seen with the naked eye. They typically attach themselves to pubic hair and then settle down to a feast of blood, compliments of their host. The primary symptom is intense itching in the area of the infestation. Scratching may produce a rash susceptible to bacterial infections. Although pubic lice are short-lived, they may produce hundreds of offspring before they die. Effective treatment is available through prescription medications or by nonprescription drugs containing pyrethrins or piperonal butoxide.

A tiny mite is responsible for a common type of parasitic infestation known as *Sarcoptes scabiei,* or scabies. Like crabs, these mites favor the genital area and attach themselves to the base of pubic hair.

They then burrow into the skin to feast and lay eggs, causing intense itching and discomfort to their host. Other symptoms include welts or sores on the skin, as well as reddish lines produced by the burrowing. This parasitic mite has a life cycle of approximately 30 days. Prescription medications effective in treating pubic lice also appear to be successful in the treatment of scabies.

## ❏ Less Common Sexually Transmitted Diseases

Several sexually transmitted diseases are either less common in general or found more commonly in countries other than the United States and Canada but are beginning to find their way into North America.

### ■ Molluscum Contagiosum

This pinkish-orange, painless lesion with a pearly top is caused by a pox virus. Lesions normally appear about 3 to 6 weeks after exposure to the virus. The infection usually causes no serious complications and typically heals spontaneously within 6 months. Lesions can also be medically removed by freezing them with liquid nitrogen or frozen carbon dioxide.

### ■ Chancroid

The bacterium *Hemophilus ducrey*, more commonly found in Eastern nations and in the tropics, causes chancroid. Sometimes referred to as "soft chancroid" because the rim of the chancre is soft, the lesions typically appear on the genitals, perineum (skin between the genitals and the anus), or anus. A cluster of bumps or pimples usually appears within a week of exposure to the bacterium. Within a few days, the lesions rupture, producing open sores or ulcers. Although men usually describe the sores as painful, women often do not experience the pain and may not know that they are infected. The disease can usually be treated effectively with antibiotics.

### ■ Lymphogranuloma Venereum

Lymphogranuloma Venereum (LGV) remains rare in the United States, even though some veterans of the Vietnam war came home infected with it. LGV appears to be common in Asia, Africa, and South America. Several strains of the Chlamydia trachomatis bacterium cause LGV. The first symptom, a small pimplelike sore on the genitals or in the urethra, occurs 3 to 12 weeks following exposure. Often the lesion goes unnoticed because there is little pain unless the sore is in the urethra. Spontaneous healing is rapid. Within several months following the emergence of the primary lesion, most infected men, but only about 20% to 30% of infected women, experience painful swelling of lymph nodes in the groin. Flulike symptoms may also occur, as well as symptoms of rectal infection. Some women experience abdominal and back pain. Late complications of LGV may include elephantiasis (large swelling) of the legs and genitals, growths in the genitals, or rectal scarring. Antibiotics appear to be effective in the treatment of LGV.

### ■ Granuloma Inguinale

This disease is also rare in the United States, but more common in tropical regions. Similar to chancroid, granuloma inguinale is caused by the bacterium *Calymmatobacterium granulomatous*. The primary symptoms are painless red bumps in the groin area that eventually become ulcerlike and spread. Serious complications such as holes in the rectum or bladder, scarring of the skin, and destruction of internal organs may occur if the disease is not treated. Antibiotics have been shown to be effective against this disease.

### ■ Shigellosis

The *Shigella* bacterium causes shigellosis. Normally transmitted by contact with infected fecal material through oral-anal sex, the primary symptom is inflammation of the large intestine. Effective treatment is available through antibiotics.

## ❑ Other Troublesome Infections

Organisms that cause common vaginal inflammation or infections may be transmitted to males and then on to other females. For example, *Trichomonas vaginalis* is a parasitic protozoan ordinarily found in small quantities in the vagina. In large numbers, they cause trichomoniasis, commonly called *trich*. In women, the symptoms are burning and itching of the vagina, accompanied by a foul-smelling whitish to yellowish-green discharge. Some women are asymptomatic. Nearly 8 million cases of trichomoniasis in the United States are reported annually (Martens & Faro, 1989). The organism is also found in approximately 30% to 40% of male partners of infected women. In men, *Trichomonas vaginalis* can cause nongonococcal urethritis (NGU). Symptoms in men usually range from none to a slight discharge from the penis and some mild pain or irritation while urinating. The most effective treatment occurs when both partners are treated simultaneously with the prescription drug Flagyl.

The bacterium *Gardnerella vaginalis* is the culprit in most cases of bacterial vaginosis (often called *nonspecific vaginitis*). Although infected women are often asymptomatic, the most common symptom is an unpleasant smelling, rather thin, vaginal discharge. Most men show no symptoms, even though the bacterium can be found in the infected man's urethra. Due to the high probability of men and women not being aware of the infection, both may unwittingly pass the bacterium on to sexual partners. The prescription drug Flagyl appears reasonably effective in the treatment of females, but may be of limited or no benefit for males (Centers for Disease Control, 1989b).

Another bacterium, *Hemophilus vaginalis,* causes a foul-smelling, brownish-white to grayish vaginal discharge accompanied by itching and burning. Although the infected male may have the bacteria in his urethra, he will typically show few if any symptoms. Treatment with some antibiotics has been shown to be effective if both partners are treated simultaneously.

Although most men have at least heard of vaginal yeast infections, few are aware that they, too, can be infected and may subsequently transmit the disease to others or back to the original infected partner. A yeastlike fungus, *Candida albicans,* is found normally in the vagina and typically causes few or no problems. If something alters the natural balance of the vaginal environment, such as diabetes, pregnancy, the use of oral contraceptives, antibiotics, or the wearing of nylon or synthetic underwear, an overgrowth of the microorganism can occur. The result is the fungus or yeast infection, candidiasis (also known as monilial vaginitis or moniliasis thrush). Reinisch (1990) estimates that about 75% of women experience at least one yeast infection during their reproductive years. Symptoms usually include a thick, white, cottage-cheese-looking, vaginal discharge accompanied by inflammation and intense itching.

Candidiasis in males usually appears as NGU with itching and burning while urinating. Some reddening of the penis may also occur. Yeast infections can also mask the presence of syphilis or gonorrhea. Various prescription and nonprescription medications have been shown to be effective treatment agents.

The probability of contracting some form of sexually transmitted disease increases significantly by participating in activities that research has identified as high risk. At the top of the list is engaging in unprotected sex with any sexual partner. Next is having sex with a large number of partners or having sex with someone you know has had sex with a large number of partners. For those who still don't grasp this concept, think of it as trying to win the lottery. The more tickets (partners) you have, the greater your chances of winning the prize (contracting a disease). At present, the odds of being exposed to a sexually transmitted disease are much better than winning the lottery. Another especially high-risk sexual behavior is anal intercourse, a common way to encounter the HIV/AIDS virus.

Although it is clear that there is no such thing as safe sex, safer sex is possible. But men must be willing to consider options that may seem unfamiliar or even counter to their ideas of male sexuality. Men must first educate themselves about the many facets of sexual behavior, including the risks and responsibilities associated with sexual behavior. Although sexual acts typically require little brain power, considerable thought should be exercised to reduce the chances of turning a moment of sexual ecstasy into a lifetime of sorrow.

Two key elements of safer sex are avoiding high-risk sexual contact, such as unprotected anal-genital sex, and avoiding sexual contact with prostitutes. Taking the time to gather information about a potential sexual partner's past sexual behavior, medical history, and use of drugs is time well spent. If unsure of any prospective sexual partner's veracity in these matters, look for another partner. The routine use of latex condoms, in conjunction with spermicides, can be an effective line of defense against most STDs. Personal inspections for symptoms of disease and routine medical examinations can be helpful in increasing early detection and prevention. Men must be responsible, inform sexual partners of any disease they may have, and take all necessary precautions not to transmit the disease to anyone else. Establishing a monogamous relationship with an uninfected partner provides excellent protection. And, of course, there is sexual abstinence. Men must learn to dance a different dance.

# 9

# The New Warrior

## *Sex at the Beat of a Drum?*

Traditional concepts of men, masculinity, and patriarchy are rooted deep in the history of the United States. Some of our earliest ancestors, the Puritans, created a social order based, in part, on religious beliefs that men were superior to women. Men should, therefore, be placed in a position of authority over women. God's gender was identified as male and used as additional evidence of the superiority of men. During the 17th and 18th centuries, males governed the affairs of church and state, as well as establishing a place within the family as head. Rotundo (1993) points out that colonial families, with their farms, shops, and mercantile firms, served as the fundamental unit of society and "the head of the household was the embodiment of all its members" (p. 12). Although this rule of the family by the male was certainly patriarchy, most historians do not view this custom as tyranny. Rather, it was seen as a man's duty to rule in a way that provided benefits for all family members, even though the man wielded the social authority. According to Rotundo, the ideal man in colonial times was "pleasant, mild-mannered, and devoted to the good of the community. He performed his duties faithfully, governed his passions rationally, submitted to his fate and to his place in society, and treated his dependents with firm but affectionate wisdom" (pp. 13-14).

## ❑ The Seeds of Discontent

Changes in economic and sociocultural factors during the 19th century began to alter the male's role in the family and the definition of masculinity. Of primary importance was the Industrial Revolution, which radically changed the way men provided for and interacted with their families. Many family-owned and -operated business ventures gave way to industrialized commercial enterprises. Although patriarchy remained the cultural and philosophical foundation for American families, men were gradually required to spend more time away from their families toiling in the industrial workplace. Men were still expected to support their families, but the domestic scene became more feminized in their absence. In particular, sons who may have accompanied their fathers to the family business or worked alongside their fathers in the fields now had to rely more on their mothers, who remained at home, for mentoring than on their mostly absent fathers.

Also during this time, males were beginning to struggle against what they perceived as an increasingly feminized society. A shift in cultural values regarding the male body and manly passions emerged as one way to compensate for this threat to manhood. During the latter half of the 19th and the first part of the 20th century, physical fitness, competitive sports, and body building became a near obsession for many American males. It was believed by many that a strong muscular body was also a sign of a strong manly character. One of the best examples of this focus on body building was the real-life transformation of a skinny and weak kid from Brooklyn, Angelo Siciliano, into a powerfully muscled national hero, Charles Atlas, during the 1920s. Charles Atlas stressed the sex appeal of the smooth-muscled, proportioned look rather than the exaggerated and narcissist bulging-muscled look desired by other body builders. Ads claiming to transform weaklings into bully killers through a process Charles Atlas called "dynamic tension" were extremely successful and are considered classics in the industry. To accompany the new male body, male traits such as ambition, lust, aggression, selfishness, and greed were again being viewed as positive characteristics to be exploited rather than "dangerous sources of evil that threatened both soul and society" (Rotundo, 1993, p. 227).

This blending of cultural influences provided the template for early-20th century man. By most accounts, he believed he was still in charge of his family, even though the family operated without him most of the time. He was expected to provide for his family by working long hours at a job he probably disliked. He was to be physically healthy and strong. He could, when necessary, call on his primitive or animal instincts to slay dragons and get ahead. Sexually, men were still expected to be more aggressive than women. Other than the women's suffrage movement, few successful challenges to traditional sociocultural ideas about gender roles occurred during most of the first half of the 20th century.

During World War II, young men were sent off to foreign lands to confront and defeat the powerful military machines launched by Germany and Japan. Traditional ideas about masculinity dictated that it was a man's duty to slay all dragons that threatened family and the American way of life. Most young American men eagerly took up the challenge. Many American women moved into industrial jobs either vacated by American men or created specifically to produce war goods. This arrangement proved to be a successful combination. It also left its mark on traditional American families. While American men fought overseas, American women remained at home, where they became instrumental in providing the material necessary for winning the war. But when Johnnie came marching home, Rosie the Riveter remained in the industrial workplace. America's postwar economy eventually adjusted to and ultimately demanded a two-person income to support a family. Many men found no honor in being deposed from their traditional position as the family's primary bread winner and head of the household. Men were also confronted with having to deal with an increasing number of women in a traditionally male-dominated environment, the workplace. And married women were becoming absent mothers due to a 20th-century "economic revolution," much as men became absent fathers due to the Industrial Revolution in the 19th century.

In spite of a glorious victory over the world's evil forces in the 1940s, the traditional American male was to face an even more formidable foe in the 1950s and 1960s—the emergence of the independent American female. By the early 1960s, women such as Betty Friedan (1963) were beginning to speak out against the culturally constructed roles imposed on women by a male-dominated society. A powerful wave of feminism passed swiftly over the country. Profeminists launched a frontal attack on the sociocultural, political, and psychological ideologies of both men and women in America.

Patriarchy was redefined as a dirty word. Men became "male chau-
vinist pigs." And many women abandoned their traditional passive
sexual role for a more assertive one.

By the 1970s, most men were reeling from the powerful salvos
discharged at them by the feminists. Men were confused. The old
manual on how to be a man did not have a chapter on how to deal
with ideas of gender equality as posed by those embracing the
profeminists' radically new ideology. The need for a new manual
was great.

One of the first authors to offer a guidebook for male survival in
the 1970s was psychologist Herb Goldberg. In *The Hazards of Being
Male*, Goldberg (1976) deftly describes how the myth of masculine
privilege and power has misled men to believe that traditional masculinity is healthy masculinity. He offers suggestions on how men
can liberate themselves from the "harness" of painful and self-
destructive predefined masculine roles. He describes a free male, in
part, as someone who "will celebrate all of the many dimensions of
himself, his strength and his weakness, his achievements and his
failures, his sensuality, his affectionate and loyal response to women
and men" (p. 184). Although Goldberg anticipated that his book
would be welcomed by men battered by the feminist initiative, he
found that the majority of his readers, and those who attended
workshops based on his book, were women seeking information
about men. Later, in *The New Male*, Goldberg (1979) characterizes
men as "macho warriors" who are:

> self-contained, active, emotionally controlled, striving for
> dominance and out to stave off and slay the economic drag-
> ons. . . . His manliness is in his erection, his ability to win, to
> provide, to be strong, unafraid, rational, certain and autono-
> mous. (p. 99)

Goldberg also provides valuable suggestions to assist men in freeing
themselves from a pattern of self-destructive stereotypic ideas and
behavior associated with traditional masculinity. Eventually, both
books became popular with men as well as women.

Other men, such as Joseph Pleck and Jack Sawyer, were also
responsive to messages broadcast by profeminists and they began
questioning themselves about manhood and what it meant to be a
man. As they engaged in a retrospective examination of boyhood

experiences, Pleck and Sawyer found themselves at odds with many of the ideas about manhood they had apparently embraced unconsciously through the socialization process. They also discovered that several other men had similar retrospective experiences and had written personal accounts about or analyses of the masculine role for various publications. A collection of many of these writings, plus three articles on the subject written by women, appears in *Men and Masculinity* (Pleck & Sawyer, 1974), one of the first books to address masculinity in this manner. The articles provide a candid and often unsettling look at masculinity and its negative effect on boys who are just learning it (e.g., abandon or suppress all feelings except anger); men who are still trying to achieve it (e.g., real men achieve and never stop achieving); men who are fathers (e.g., I must achieve and provide for my family financially); gays who are men (e.g., real men don't have sex with real men); women who are trying to survive it (e.g., I want intimacy, he wants sex); and a society dominated by it (e.g., patriarchy is alive and well). The obvious conclusion is that something is amiss and few men are prepared to understand what is wrong, let alone do anything about it. To help, the authors propose a form of male liberation that will free men "of the sex-role stereotypes that limit their ability to be human" (1974, p. 170).

In *The Myth of Masculinity*, Pleck (1981) criticizes the commonly held belief that men have an inherent need to develop a gender role identity based on traditional ideas of the masculine role. This concept, known as the "gender role identity paradigm," is based on the notion that a relatively stable masculine essence exists and a male's need to achieve a masculine identity is met only to the extent that he assimilates the traditional ideas about and norms regulating the male gender role. Historically, avoiding femininity; restricting emotionality; seeking achievement and status; and striving for self-reliance, aggression, homophobia, and nonrelational attitudes toward sexuality are commonly considered the essence of male role norms (see Levant et al., 1992).

Because Pleck (1981) finds very little support from research studies for the gender role identity paradigm, he proposes, instead, the "gender role strain paradigm." This concept is based on the notion that gender identity is not inherent and stable but socially constructed and subject to change. As such, gender roles are defined by prevailing stereotypes and norms communicated to children by the various socialization agents in the child's social milieu. Being socially constructed, gender roles often are contradictory and inconsistent. Pleck's paradigm proposes that most people violate gender roles, even in the face of strong condemnation and other negative consequences; males are more severely punished for violating gender roles than females; and some people tend to overconform to gender roles, fearing any type of infraction. Also, some gender role expectations, such as male aggression and hypersexuality, can be sources of severe problems for both society and the individual.

In 1985, journalist Perry Garfinkel chronicled American men's experiences with their fathers, brothers, grandfathers, male friends, and other male mentors. The stories told by hundreds of men strongly suggest that male socialization experiences are quite similar and typically reinforce traditional concepts about manhood. Men also revealed their disappointment in their role models, especially paternal role models, who did not prepare them for the demands of a changing society. Many of these men felt adrift in uncharted waters. But at least men were beginning to share some of their feelings with each other. Even so, a long legacy of grooming boys into "real men" does not give way easily. As the *New York Times* psychology columnist Daniel Goleman warns:

> These are perilous times to be a man in America. There are forces afoot that have changed men's senses of themselves, blurring what once seemed clear-cut modes and models of manhood. John Wayne is dead, and we have not yet picked his stand-in. (Garfinkel, 1985, p. xi)

Another decade has passed and many men are still in crisis. Men have seen the time-honored code of masculinity eroded to the point of near collapse. Males are now expected to express themselves and perform in ways often counter to their self-image as a man and beyond their skills (Levant, 1992). Not only is John Wayne dead but so is the original Superman. In the absence of models to help guide the way along a seemingly treacherous new trail to manhood, many men are turning to movements that seem to promise a resurgence of traditional masculinity.

## ❑ Enter the Wild Man

In 1990, poet Robert Bly published *Iron John*. His compelling story about rediscovering true masculinity by getting in touch with the "Wild Man" hidden deep within each man was readily embraced by millions of men struggling to find their masculine self. *Iron John* became a national bestseller for several months and remains one of the best-selling books within the so-called mythopoetic men's movement. Suddenly, Bly was hailed as the leader of a new men's movement, even though "it was never my intention, with *Iron John*, to be a leader of a men's movement. And I don't much like the term, mythopoetic, either" (Bly, 1994).

In *Iron John*, Bly (1990) presents a history of the Wild Man in religion, literature, and folk life. Throughout history, this hairy man appears in many forms. The ancients saw him variously as the releaser of animals, master of creatures, lord of animals, or master of the hunt. Little is known about the Wild Man's sexuality until he was eventually transformed into the Indian god, Shiva, sometime during the Bronze Age and the Neolithic period. According to Bly, "the Dravidian culture of southern India, which was prior to the Hindu culture, gave the name Pashupati to the Master of Animals and gave the name Parvati to his companion, the Lady of the Mountains" (p. 240). Apparently, the result of this union was Shivaism, which merged with the earlier animism, and became the energy source for subsequent religions. According to Bly, this is a significant transformation of the Wild Man:

> Shiva is a blossoming or development of the Wild Man, immensely articulate, Shiva keeps the wild aspect—his followers go naked and do not cut their hair—but also has an ascetic aspect, a husbandly side, and the enraged or Bhairava side. (p. 241)

The Wild Man takes a wife.

The Lord of Animals, or the Wild Man, continued his existence throughout the Mediterranean as various deities such as Thessaly, Zeus, and Dionysus. Although Bly correctly describes the tremendous influence the ancient Mediterranean cultures had on subsequent societies, including our own, Zeus's reputation as a rapist is curiously omitted (see Brod, 1985; Caputi & MacKenzie, 1992). If the Wild Man blossomed in India and became a loving husband, he appears to have regressed in Greece and became an exploiter of women. Kimmel and Kaufman (1994) warn aspiring Wild Men, "loading up on 'Zeus juice' may make compelling myth, but it makes for bad gender politics" (p. 275).

In ancient Europe, the Wild Man appears variously as Herne the Hunter, and Cernunnos, Lord of the Animals, Guardian of the Fountain. Although Cernunnos was known to have a female companion, Bly (1990) does not mention his sex life. The Wild Man in medieval Europe seems to have been a lusty fellow, however. Bly describes numerous works of art, as well as folk plays and pageants, that depict many aspects of the Wild Man (and Wild Woman), including sexual behavior and consequences: "Sometimes the figures are praised for their spontaneity and sexual energy but more often punished or exiled or killed for them" (p. 247).

To conclude the history of the Wild Man, Bly (1990) describes the threat the Wild Man, especially the Wild Man's sexuality, has posed to Christianity and Western culture. Clearly, the Judeo-Christian emphasis on controlling evil sexual impulses allows no room for a hairy, virile Wild Man whose sexuality is expressed spontaneously. Bly writes:

> Powerful sociological and religious forces have acted in the West to favor the trimmed, the sleek, the cerebral, the non-instinctive, and the bald. . . . The same forces have doomed male sexuality to the banal and the profane and the hideously practical. . . . Young men in contemporary culture conclude quickly that their sexual instinct is troublesome, intrusive, weird, and hostile to spirit. . . . When the Church and the culture as a whole dropped the gods who spoke for the divine element in male sexual energy—Pan, Dionysus, Hermes, the Wild Man—into oblivion, we as men lost a great deal. (pp. 248-249)

It is not clear if resurrecting the Wild Man's sexuality will resurrect the Wild Man as seen in Shiva or the wild man as seen in Zeus.

Even though Bly (1990) insists that the wild man is "profoundly pagan" (see Arnold, 1991, p. x), Patrick Arnold (1991), in *Wildmen, Warriors, and Kings*, proposes that a number of masculine archetypes, including the wild man, are embodied in prominent and revered biblical figures. For example, Abraham is depicted as the Patriarch (the archetype of love, resolve, and magnamity, not the modern definition of patriarchy, which connotes male dominance and exploitation) and as the Pilgrim (possessing dynamic masculinity). Moses is seen as both Warrior (resistance to evil through bravery, self-sacrifice, stamina, skill, and heroic detachment) and Magician (resources of a man's inner psychic consciousness such as intuition and connecting with the pervasive force that guides all creation). The archetype of the sacred King (fosters creativity, nourishes intellectual endeavors, encourages and fosters the growth of the people) is found in Solomon. Elisha is the Healer (a warrior archetype who can overpower evil spirits by making alliances with higher spiritual powers), whereas Jeremiah is the Prophet archetype (a kind of spiritual Pilgrim who seeks and shares the deeper truths about God and the human experience). In Jonah, one finds the Trickster archetype (an elusive figure with at least three types: the primitive animal nature; the puerile, instinctive, mean, sinful, and earthy human character; and the divine god). Essentially, the Trickster is the "fool" who can make us laugh at ourselves and become wise.

For Arnold (1991):

> The Wildman is the spiritual archetype that connects men affectively to God as they experience nature in all its sheer wildness, beauty, and starkness. . . . The Wildman is also our psychic connection to the nature of the human body, its tidal rhythms, its hungers and lusts, its energy and fatigue, and its subtle wisdom that tell us what we genuinely need and really want rather than what someone else manipulates us into needing and wanting. (pp. 124-125).

Arnold states that all men were Wild Men at one time but Adam, who was fashioned by God directly from the earth, was the first biblical wild man. This connection between God and man, the Wild Man archetype, is also found, according to Arnold, in biblical scriptures relating to Ishmael, Esau, Samson, Amos, Elijah, and Jesus. Both Bly (1990) and Arnold describe John the Baptist as a Wild Man. And like Bly, Arnold urges men to find the power and freedom contained in the Wild Man hidden deep within each man.

## ❑ Mature Masculine Archetypes

Jungian psychoanalyst Robert Moore and mythologist Douglas Gillette (1990) are also at the forefront of the mythopoetic men's movement. They, like Bly (1990), propose that men have drifted from

embracing their heritage as mature men, as seen in various archetypes and as realized through traditional masculine rituals. Because
so many men are turning to mythopoetic men's movements that
seem to promise a resurgence of traditional masculinity, an examination of the offerings is warranted.

In 1913, Carl Jung broke with Sigmund Freud and established a
separate analytical psychology based on the premise that the psyche
was real, structured, and governed by laws and had its own method
of expression. This was in contrast to Freud's major hypothesis that
components of the psyche can be reduced to some type of instinct.
For Jung, the psyche was the totality of all psychic phenomena,
including the conscious and the unconscious. Although consciousness is only a small part of the total psyche, it is multidimensional
and can include a wide range of events from simple acts of perception, without elaboration, to acts of evaluation, elaboration, and understanding. The unconscious is much older than consciousness and contains all sorts of matter that has been subliminally perceived, repressed,
forgotten, felt, or thought about (personal unconscious) and matter
inherited from all our ancestors, such as reactions to typical human
situations regardless of ethnic group, socioeconomic status, or historic
era (collective unconscious). Dwelling deep inside the collective unconscious are motifs and symbols of the universal history of all humankind.
These symbols are eternal, contain a high energy charge, and exert a
dominant influence on the psyche. Initially, Jung called these symbols *primordial images*, but he later adopted the term *archetype*, mostly
from St. Augustine's definition of principle ideas.

Within Jungian psychology, archetypes represent an enormous
repository of ancient knowledge and the latent potential of all humans. Although the archetypes remain within all of us as inner
blueprints for positive human interactions, learning to access the
information comes from external sources such as adequate parenting
and important social rituals (e.g., initiating boys into manhood).
When the outer world fails to provide the nurturing, guidance, and
modeling necessary to access our benefactors of salvation and protection, immature and aberrant forms of the archetypes emerge.
According to Jung, archetypes must be taken seriously and any
violation of them can produce serious negative personal and social
consequences.

Moore and Gillette (1990) propose that four fundamental configu-
rations of archetypes—King, Warrior, Magician, and Lover—constitute

the deep structures of the mature male psyche. A key word here is "mature," as Moore and Gillette also emphasize the difference between what they identify as "boy psychology" and "man psychology." For example, boy psychology dominates men who have not had the initiations necessary for the important transition from boyhood to manhood. The result, according to Moore and Gillette, is:

> abusive and violent acting-out behaviors against others, both men and women; passivity and weakness, the inability to act effectively and creatively in one's own life and to engender life and creativity in others (both men and women); and, often, an oscillation between the two—abuse/weakness, abuse/weakness. (p. xvi)

On the other hand, man psychology is nurturing and generative, not destructive and wounding. This occurs when boys (or men with boy psychology) learn to connect with and access the instinctual energy potentials as seen in the mature masculine archetypes. The process of the successful transition from boyhood to manhood typically occurs through some form of formal ritual process conducted by learned ritual elders (mature masculine role models). Moore and Gillette lament the fact that not only have traditional initiatory rituals been replaced by pseudoinitiation processes or abandoned altogether, but our current culture lacks adequate models of men with mature masculinity.

What are the archetypes that represent mature masculinity and what do they have to do with the development of male sexuality? Although four distinct categories of archetypes (King, Warrior, Magician, Lover) are described, each may have some characteristics of the other three types. For example, a good and generative King also excels as a Warrior, Magician, and Lover. In addition, each archetype has an active-passive bipolar shadow structure that represents the failure to achieve or access the mature masculine energy of the archetype. Although each of the four archetypes has a destructive bipolar shadow, successfully accessing the mature masculine energy of the King within every man draws from the other archetypes to produce a generative, not destructive, man. According to Moore and Gillette (1992),

> The fully manifested archetypal King . . . consolidates the functions of the other mature masculine archetypes. The

Warrior aids him in setting, defending, and extending boundaries. The Magician helps order his thought, and provides
ideas on how to materialize them. Both the Magician and the
Warrior help develop the psychospiritual machinery a man
needs before the King can incarnate within him. And the
Lover ensures that incarnation will be life-enhancing and
joyful. (pp. 145-146)

The true King, therefore, should exhibit mature and benevolent
attitudes in all spheres, including sexuality. To appreciate the mythopoetic view of male sexuality, therefore, it is important to understand each of the archetypes and their respective shadows.

### ■ The King

According to Moore and Gillette (1990), the King archetype "is
primal in all men. It comes first in importance, and it underlies and
includes the rest of the archetypes in perfect balance. . . . And yet,
with most of us, the king comes on line last" (p. 49). The King
archetype is the primal masculinity in all men and comes close to
being God in a masculine form. The King energy is central to the
successful transition from boy psychology and man psychology and
includes two primary functions. The first is organizing, ordering, and
defining the universe or world. From these activities, laws and
civilizations are created based on some form of "divine world."
Chaos, noncreation, and the demonic lie beyond the organized and
created world. Without this function, we may be faced with disorder
and chaos.

The second function of King energy is to provide fertility and
blessing. Fertility is provided not only in the form of taming chaotic
earth forces so that plants and animals may flourish, but the King
archetype also engages in, and produces progeny from, sexual activities with other deities, as well as female mortals. As examples, Moore
and Gillette (1990) mention the ancient Egyptian deity Amun-Ra,
famous for establishing a heavenly harem, and the infamous ancient
Greek god Zeus.

This was not just frivolous sexuality but sexual behavior with
additional import: "As the mortal King went, so did the realm, both
its order and fertility. If the King was lusty and vigorous sexually,
could service his often many wives and concubines and produce

many children, the land would be vital" (Moore & Gillette, 1990, p. 59). Moore and Gillette explain that the mortal King, the embodiment of the King energy, was symbolically wedded to the land, the embodiment of feminine energies. In this way, a conduit between the divine world and the earthly world was established. Thus, a mortal king's sexuality played a vital role in maintaining creative energies in the kingdom. The Biblical King David, with his many wives and concubines, is given as one example of this type of fertility function flowing from the King archetype energies.

Moore and Gillette (1990) point out that few of us have experienced the king energy in its fullness. Instead, the bipolar darker versions, the tyrant and the weakling, seem to prevail. The tyrant King is not creative and generative, only destructive. He may see threats to his kingdom everywhere and will respond quickly with whatever means necessary to eliminate the perceived dangers to his power and sovereignty. The tyrant also exploits others' weaknesses and vulnerabilities. Sexually, the tyrant King will use the same forceful means to gain sexual gratification as he does in ruling his kingdom. He perceives all females as his and will use his property in any way he sees fit. Resistance will be met with threats and coercion. Rivals will be eliminated.

The passive pole of the shadow King is the weakling. The weakling is a coward who lacks inner security yet demands that others worship and adore him. His fears of disloyalty become so strong that he slips into paranoia. Moore and Gillette (1990) do not address the weakling's sexual responses.

■ **The Warrior**

The Warrior form of masculine energy "is concerned with skill, power, and accuracy, and with control, both inner and outer, psychological and physical" (Moore & Gillette, 1990, p. 83). A man who has accessed the Warrior archetype shows loyalty, courage, extraordinary mental discipline, economy of energy, mastery of weapons, the ability to take decisive actions, and the willingness to accept responsibility for his behavior. The true Warrior does not attempt to gratify personal needs but aspires, instead, to serve a higher spiritual edict. Warrior energy can be found in the religion of Islam and in the Jesuit order in Christianity, according to Moore and Gillette.

A key part of accessing the Warrior archetype is to embrace the emotional detachment necessary to act decisively and efficiently.

Without mediation from the other archetypes, the pure Warrior remains emotionally detached even in situations where it is clearly inappropriate to do so. For example, Warriors tend to view women as objects with which to have fun, not as people with whom to form intimate relationships. Military Warriors often express their sexuality in nonintimate ways such as engaging prostitutes and raping the enemy's women. Nonmilitary warriors, such as overly dedicated professionals, often place their intimate relationships second to their work and may engage in emotionally detached sexual contact with women other than their intimate partners.

If the pure Warrior's sexuality tends to be emotionally detached and destructive, what happens when the darker side of the Warrior archetype, the shadow Warrior, enters the sexual arena? Although Moore and Gillette (1990) do not address this issue directly, they discuss the shadow Warrior as either a sadist or a masochist. The sadist is essentially an insecure adolescent who may become a passionless and cruel killing machine. He often struggles with the power of the feminine and may strike out against women with physical and emotional abuse. On the other hand, the masochist is a self-punishing coward who does not defend himself adequately and allows others to best him until he can no longer tolerate the abuse. He then may revert to the sadist side with explosive outbursts of anger, culminating with verbal abuse and physical violence. Although sexual abuse is not specifically mentioned regarding the sadist or masochist, one can easily assume that any expression of sexuality from these bipolar sides of the shadow Warrior can only be an extension and exacerbation of the emotionally detached sexual attitudes embodied in the Warrior archetype.

### ■ The Magician

Moore and Gillette (1990) describe the Magician archetype as an initiate of secret and hidden knowledge who monitors information from within and outside to make decisions that will be beneficial to himself and others. The Magician channels the psyche's energies toward achieving maximum benefits through, in part, thoughtfulness and reflection. Magician energy can be found in witch doctors, shamans, professionals, clergy, technicians, and others who are consciously using their knowledge to benefit others and themselves. It can also be found in crisis situations when clarity of thought and "hidden" knowledge suddenly come to the fore to help solve the immediate problem.

The Magician archetype also has a bipolar darker side. The active pole takes the form of an emotionally detached manipulator who maneuvers people for his own benefit by withholding or polluting information potentially beneficial for the other person. The passive pole, the denying "innocent" one, is seen in individuals who hide behind a smoke screen of innocence while attempting to block others from using mature Magician energy to help others. The innocent one hides his hostility, irresponsibility, and lack of life energy by feigning naivete when challenged. Moore and Gillette (1990) mention nothing about the mature Magician or the shadow Magician's role in sexuality.

■  **The Lover**

The Lover is:

the primal energy pattern of what we could call vividness, aliveness, and passion. It lives through the great primal hungers of our species for sex, food, well-being, reproduction, creative adaptation to life's hardships, and ultimately a sense of meaning, without which human beings cannot go on with their lives. (Moore & Gillette, 1990, p. 120)

Thus, the Lover is sensually aware, connected to, and empathetically united with all aspects of the physical world. Lover energy is also the source of spirituality.

Examples of the Lover archetype are found in the Indian god Shiva, the Greek gods Priapus and Zeus, and the Egyptian god Osiris. Although Christianity and Judaism have a history of fearing Lover energy and persecuting those who express it, the Song of Solomon and the love of Yahweh for Israel are presented by Moore and Gillette (1990) as examples of biblical Lover energy.

Although the Lover is arguably a very positive archetype, its shadow side is a different matter. The bipolar sides of the shadow Lover are the addicted Lover and the impotent Lover. Moore and Gillette (1990) describe the addicted Lover as a man who becomes lost in and overwhelmed by his senses. He becomes a slave to and victim of his own feelings. The addicted Lover is always seeking something more without being clear about what he is seeking. Boundaries are his nemesis. He may be drawn into one sexual escapade after another or become trapped in destructive relationships seemingly without the resources to escape. The addicted Lover not only embarks on a never-ending quest for the illusive ultimate high or orgasm, but he may also express negative attitudes toward females through sexual humiliation and violence.

The impotent Lover is described as a man who is bored and listless and lacks enthusiasm for anything. He has no zest for life. Simply put, the impotent Lover is depressed and, well, impotent. The hallmark of the impotent Lover is withdrawal from intimacy and sexual activity.

## ❏ The New Male

Based on the works of Bly (1990) and others, seminars, workshops, and weekend retreats to assist men in restoring their masculine self-esteem through "gender journeys" are very popular throughout the United States and Canada. In spite of this popularity, social scientists express serious concerns regarding the potential effect of the mythopoetic men's movement on men and society (e.g., Betcher & Pollack, 1993; Kimmel & Kaufman, 1994; Levant, 1992). First, there is concern that any movement with a focus on some form of essential masculine identity is a return to the unsupported notions of masculinity proposed by the gender role identity paradigm. Second, by popularizing this notion and guiding men to this type of thinking, destructive antifeminist and promasculinist attitudes may be strengthened. Third, men should not be trying to separate more from women but should be attempting a closer connection with women. And most researchers doubt that weekend retreats such as those offered by mythopoetic workshop leaders can be much help in restoring a positive masculine self-image and resolving serious personal and social issues in a man's life, in spite of the emergence of the Wild Man. As Levant (1992) notes, "there is absolutely no evidence that weekend retreats help men address the unresolved issues in their lives and rebuild a positive self-image based on a reconstruction of masculinity" (p. 384). Journalist Asa Baber (1993) sees the men's movement as "self indulgent and inflated at its core" and the new male as "a crybaby, tree-hugger, softhearted, white-boy, wussie who sometimes dances around an open fire at night and pretends he was a caveman" (p. 42).

Many critics of the new men's movements align themselves with the feminist viewpoint regarding masculinity and the negative influence of traditional patriarchy on women. For example, Kimmel and Kaufman (1994) state,

> Men have been made to feel bad about traditional masculinity, about men's violence, rape, pornography, battery, and a litany of other feminist accusations. Their response is not to enlist in the feminist struggle against these excesses of manly behavior but to declare themselves tired of listening. (p. 286)

These authors also quip, "We need more Ironing Johns, not more Iron Johns" (p. 272). Betcher and Pollack (1993) write,

> We admire Robert Bly's poetry and acknowledge his contribution to the new psychology of men. But although his mythopoetic approach does reach down to more primitive developmental levels, his solutions tend to obscure the complexity of the issues and can easily encourage macho-like, antifeminist sentiment. (p. 21)

It is easy to see why profeminists of either gender would express concern over any kind of movement that may appear to be a resurgence of masculinst notions about men, women, and power. Traditionally, men have used men-only social and spiritual activities to establish and maintain power differentials between women and men. The call to bring back sweat lodges, male initiation rites, and the like to reestablish "wild man masculinity" strikes fear in a lot of people who have been oppressed by this type of gendered spatial separation. In nonindustrialized societies, women's status is lowest when male-only rituals are strongest (Spain, 1992). And traditional ideas that women are somehow inferior to men often bring about sexual exploitation, even in industrialized and so-called modern societies.

Bly (1990, 1994), on the other hand, has been steadfast in his denial that his call for men to rediscover their masculinity is also a call for men to return to antifeminist or masculinst ideology. Yes, it is true that he describes men who have gotten in touch with their feminine side as unhappy men who lack energy and experience considerable grief and anguish, but he also states, "The journey many

American men have taken into softness, or receptivity, or 'development of the feminine side,' has been an immensely valuable journey, but more travel lies ahead" (1990, p. 4).

Less known, but certainly no less important, are the men's movements developing within the scientific and applied professions. Leading advocates for men's studies such as psychologists Ron Levant, Gary Brooks, and others express concern that mythopoetic-based men's movements may ultimately produce more problems than solutions for males in search of the meaning of being male. Proposed is an approach to examining and reconstructing masculinity based more on established research principles and clinical experience than on some form of warrior's journey, psuedopsychoanalysis, or mythical masculine archetypes (see Brooks, 1991; Levant, 1992).

Levant (1995; Levant & Kopecky, 1995) suggests a reconstruction based on identifying, separating, and celebrating aspects of the traditional male role that appear valuable and constructive; and, at the same time, identifying, separating, and targeting for change those aspects of the male role that appear to be obsolete and destructive. He identifies examples of possible positive attributes already included in the male socialization process: a man's ability to withstand hardship and pain for others, problem-solving skills, logical thinking, loyalty, stick-to-it-tiveness, self-reliance, risk taking, ability to stay calm in the face of danger. Some examples of negative or obsolete attributes, which also remain in the current socialization milieu, are overall emotional restrictiveness except for anger, experiencing sexuality as separate from relationships, and difficulties in forming full partnerships with partners regarding domestic and parental roles. Essentially, the positive attributes seem to relate to skills of provision and protection, whereas the negative aspects of the socialization process seem related to producing destructive emotional deficits.

Another offering from the scientific and therapeutic community is the "gender role journey workshop" developed by psychologist James O'Neil (1996). Using journey as a metaphor, the workshop combines traditional lecturing with psychoeducational group interventions to help men and women "examine how early gender role socializaation experiences and sexism have affected their lives" (p. 194). After a decade of leading gender role journey workshops, O'Neil found that more than 87% of the participants reported a continuing positive influence on their consciousness about gender roles. The ability to resolve gender role conflict was also greatly enhanced (see O'Neil, 1996; O'Neil, Good, & Holmes, 1995).

Amid all the controversy about the new men's movements, what is being said about male sexuality? Very little. On the one hand is a focus on separating from females and returning to some form of masculine essence. On the other is a call to embrace feminism and reconstruct masculinity along less traditional concepts. Curiously, issues about sexuality are not addressed directly by any of the mythopoetic writers or their critics. Instead, there are assumptions. Proponents of mythopoetic warrior journeys seem to promise, "Find your Wild Man and your life as a man will significantly improve." That is, if men restore their positive masculine role as defined by traditional or archetypical concepts, they will effect improvement in their personal, social, and business lives. The assumption is that a man's sexual life will also be swept along with this tidal wave of improvements. But nobody says, "Find your Wild Man or become a true King and you will also find sexual paradise." Critics warn that many traditional masculine values about sexuality have been harmful to both males and females; they worry about releasing ancient Wild Men on women and society. Proposed instead is a studied approach to reconstructing masculinity and resolving conflicts created by traditional gender roles. Perhaps the "New Warrior" prototype is not yet complete.

# 10

# Achieving True Manhood

## Reconstructing Male Sexuality

In the late 1800s and again in the 1960s, a gender war broke out in the United States. Fueled by feminist discontent over sexual discrimination, the first war was waged primarily to gain access, through the vote, to the male-dominated political process. The purpose of the second war was to expose and eliminate all forms of sexism in America. In both cases, the enemy was identified as the self-proclaimed and religiously ordained superior sex: the male heterosexual. Or, more accurately, the enemy was prevailing masculine ideologies supporting the notions that males are inherently superior and dominant, but females are inherently weaker and subservient. Although the first war was won by the women's suffrage movement and some battles have been won by feminists since, the second war against male domination and sexual discrimination rages on.

At the heart of the debate over gender differences and male superiority appears to be an insidious form of biological determinism contained in religious dogma and legitimized by scientific inquiry conducted mostly by males. Although it is a sad commentary that religion and science may have joined forces to maintain male dominance over females, some of the counterarguments appear equally spurious. For example, the studies of the genetic and biological factors leading to sex differentiation point to a female template until fetal male hormones intervene to produce a biological male. In the absence of these biological juices, a female is produced. This process seems straightforward and devoid of any sociopolitical malevolence. But some feminists take issue with this portrayal of female development because it seems to reinforce the cultural stereotype of the passive female. Some are also critical of the notion that females develop as a function of lacking something, another cultural stereotype of the inferior woman (see Fausto-Sterling, 1985).

Although I agree that women have been subjected to all forms of discrimination and have unjustly and unnecessarily been portrayed in negative ways by a sometimes less-than-objective scientific community, it seems a bit of a stretch to point to the role of fetal testosterone as a major contributing factor to the perpetuation of negative cultural stereotypes of women. An equally strong argument supporting the superiority of females could be made using the same information about the biological process of sexual differentiation. At the very least, the entire argument about fetal testosterone and sexual differentiation appears counterproductive.

If one looks at the research on fetal sexual development, it becomes clear that the design is extraordinary, cost-effective, but not sexist. For starters, both sexes derive from the same material and both sexes remain genetically bipotential until about the 6th week. With the introduction of specialized hormones, these magnificent tissues transform into one gender or the other. What does it matter politically that hormones from the fetal testes or ovaries are involved in the growth of sexual structures? Are males and females reduced to squabbling about the relative value of fetal testosterone versus estrogen as a means of "proving" male or female superiority? If so, we have lost sight of the most important aspect of this issue: We are different by design. Difference does not equal superiority, just difference. Without this difference, the human species as we know it would soon perish. Recent studies have also pointed to gender differences in brain structures related to sexual orientation and behavior. It is also believed that some of these differences may have a genetic foundation. The grand design appears to favor diversity rather than gender superiority. Perhaps it is time to celebrate this diversity rather than use it as a weapon in an ongoing gender and sexual orientation war.

An examination of developmental variables strongly suggests that American culture is repressive regarding sexual behavior in general, but even more so when it comes to young people, females, and the elderly. It is as though we treat the elderly the same way we treat children. Because our culture tells us that children are not yet prepared to make intelligent decisions about sex, even about normal childhood sexual exploration activities, guardians make the decisions for them in the form of admonishments, threats, and punishments. People in our society seem to believe that the elderly somehow lose the ability to make intelligent decisions about themselves and sexual behavior; besides, elderly sex is seen as an aberration and something to be banned the same way we ban child sex. The major cultural techniques of admonishments, threats, and punishments are employed. Often we keep children segregated by gender when the possibility of sexual contact exists. We often do the same for the elderly who find themselves unable to maintain independent living and must seek assistance through nursing homes or other similar facilities. As a resident of such a facility, one must obey the rules. The rules often forbid sexual activities among the residents even if the couples are married (Pratt & Schmall, 1989). Unfortunately, the abuse of sexuality follows the child into adulthood and into the silver years.

In America, the application of a double standard regarding gender and sexual behavior begins very early. For example, when faced with information about a male's propensity for erections, even before birth, some, mostly females, immediately label this behavior as negative: "It's just like a male, always going around with a hard-on." Or "No wonder they can't keep it in their pants, they are born like that." Others, mostly male, interpret this physiological phenomenon with typical male phallocentric pride: "What a man." Or "He is going to be quite the lady-killer."

Faced with information about a similar "sexual" response in infant females, many people are shocked that baby girls lubricate and have clitoral erections. But seldom do we hear comments like "Man, she's got a hot pussy" or "You better watch that one when she grows up." Although our society in general and parents in particular worry about displays of sexual arousal in children, especially very young children, these displays are not related to some form of sociosexual erotic stimulation (Martinson, 1981). The point is this: Sexual development may be just like any other developmental task, such as locomotion and language, requiring certain biological structures and reflexes to be in place and operational for the child to accomplish successfully the developmental tasks that lie ahead. Inappropriate labeling of these structures or their functions may create undue pressure on the child to conform to unrealistic expectations. Or worse, the child may be thwarted from accomplishing the developmental task at all.

Most everyone agrees that children should receive some information about sexual matters, but there is little agreement about who should provide the information, what type of information should be offered, or at what developmental stage sex education should begin. Many parents are adamant about reserving the family's role as the provider of information about sexuality to their children. "Sex education is a family matter. Stay out of it," they shout at those who propose alternative plans. Although I agree that the primary purveyor of accurate sexual information should be members of the child's family, research shows that parents, especially fathers, simply are not doing the job. For example, a majority of Americans failed a test of basic sexual knowledge administered by the Kinsey Institute a few years ago (Reinisch, 1990). This suggested that most Americans do not receive accurate sexual information. When participants were asked to identify the childhood sources of their information about sexual matters, only 29% indicated mothers and a meager 12% said fathers. As suspected, the highest percentage (42%) of participants indicated that they went to friends, not parents, for information about sex. Many received their information from books (22%) and magazines (13%). In the absence of adequate parental tutoring, children will look elsewhere. It appears that society's ignorance and fear related to sexual matters lead to the continued neglect of the needs of the child regarding fostering informed healthy sexuality.

Most of the ammunition used by feminists in the ongoing gender war comes from studies supporting the idea that the practice of patriarchy in the United States is largely responsible for intimate violence against women by heterosexual men. Wife abuse is viewed as another form of domination and control of women by men (see Browne, 1987; Dobash & Dobash, 1979; Martin, 1976; Pharr, 1988; Schecter, 1982; Walker, 1979). Although studies seem to support the feminist position regarding most cases of opposite-sex domestic abuse, they do not address the issue of same-sex intimate violence.

Until recently, studies of gay and lesbian domestic violence were virtually absent from the interpersonal violence research literature, leaving questions about this area unanswered. Now that studies of interpersonal dynamics in same-sex relationships are consistently finding that gay and bisexual male, as well as lesbian, domestic violence often equals or surpasses heterosexual wife abuse, the foundation for feminist domestic violence theory, gender oppression (male victimizers and female victims), is being challenged (Coleman, 1994; Letellier, 1994). Dutton (1994) systematically dismantles contemporary feminist analyses of gender socialization and its role in wife assault by pointing out that studies of cross-cultural variables, homosexual relationships, female violence, and men raised in identifiable patriarchal systems found no direct relationship between power and violence within couples and no direct relationship between structural patriarchy and wife assault. Dutton concludes:

> Hence, patriarchy does not elicit violence against women in any direct fashion. Rather, it may provide the values and attitudes that personality-disordered men can exploit to justify their abuse of women. This distinction is an important one: It explains why the majority of men remain nonviolent and how they differ in at least one essential and nontautological aspect from violent men. (p. 176)

These findings are important to the development of male sexuality and the problems many men experience in negotiating this developmental milestone successfully. Earlier in this volume, I argued that the cultural messages about male heterosexuality are a toxic brew containing dogma and misinformation. I also documented and discussed many sociocultural ideologies and their negative influence on males. Central to this presentation is that the Judeo-Christian belief in male superiority and female inferiority provides the foundation for an overall disproportionate power base and many of the inappropriate notions about sexual behavior perpetuated by Western culture. Bem (1993) describes this process as looking through culture's gender lenses of androcentrism, gender polarization, and biological essentialism. She argues that by looking at, not through, these lenses we will be better able to understand and effect a correction in the distorted perceptions. I also agree with the recent call to establish an integrated, multidimensional theory of intimate violence instead of continuing to focus almost exclusively on the role male socialization variables play in cases of domestic violence (see Renzetti, 1994). This process should help in establishing a more objective analysis of gender differences, sociopolitical influences, personal differences, interpersonal relationships, and the development of sexual behavior. In the meantime, males must begin to learn ways of coping better with faulty lenses and the "witches' brew." It is to this end that I offer the following suggestions regarding reconstructing male hetero-sexuality. I begin by looking at some major cultural concepts about sexuality that are in disrepair and sorely need reconstruction.

## ❑ Cultural Reconstruction

Although I doubt that what I am about to propose will have much immediate effect on the Judeo-Christian influence in our cul-ture regarding gender differences and sexual behavior, it needs to be said. It is my hope that by planting the ideas now they will, over time, germinate and take root—not like a weed to be snatched from the ground, but like a newly developed medicinal plant with beautiful blossoms and a lovely scent. Polyandrous? Perhaps. But let's proceed anyway.

First, let's look at the positive side of Western thought about sexuality. This shouldn't take long. Essentially, Judeo-Christian ide-ology is not totally sex negative because it condones sexual behavior in some situations. At least sex is not completely verboten (except for devotees of some religious orders who are permitted to teach sexu-ality but not practice it). Monogamy is also a positive component because monogamous relationships generally provide more stability for the couple and their progeny, as well as offering a lifestyle with a lowered risk for acquiring sexually transmitted diseases.

If everyone could fit into this scheme nicely, the problem with sex in America would be eradicated. But that is the problem. Naturally occurring sexual diversity defies the culturally established standard. Western thought has established a number of rationalizations and rules to control sexual behavior and force it into narrowly defined categories: good sex (heterosexual sex in marital relationships for the purpose of producing children) and bad sex (everything else). It may be that the ideal is not such a bad idea. But the rigidity of the concept leads to a number of unfounded and unnatural notions about human sexuality and a need to shame and persecute those who do not, or cannot, meet the standard. It is a form of "ism" I like to call *sexualityism*. That is, if your sexuality fits the standard, you are accepted. If it does not, you experience cultural discrimination in the form of derision and exclusion.

Let's now look at the negative side of Western thought regarding sexuality and some suggestions for change. This may take a bit longer. First, our culture must deconstruct the notions that women are inferior to men and men must, therefore, be dominant in all matters, including sexual behavior. Although I do not believe that this concept alone causes men to force women into unwanted sexual activities, it provides another insidious rationalization for some sexually immature and disordered men to justify their inappropriate actions. I also believe that our ancestors who constructed this standard out of some ancient interpretation of divine will did not intend for it to be used in this manner but did not have the foresight to see the potential dangers of such an idea. Now that we have had thousands of years of experience with this notion and sufficient data supporting its negative effect on both genders in our society, perhaps it is time for a reinterpretation of divine will and a reconstruction of this concept. Imagine if each gender felt equal and could express sexuality consistent with feelings of equality rather than some form of domination. That is a standard with which we could all learn to live.

Next, it is time for our culture to recognize that the grand scheme includes the development of sexual beings. This process begins at conception and progresses through a number of developmental milestones throughout the life cycle. It is natural for both genders and does not produce superior sexuality in either gender, only variations on the overall theme. Our culture must begin to view sex in this manner instead of assigning sex the legacy of lust and sin left to us from the interactions of Adam, Eve, and a serpent. By taking the myth out of sex, we open the opportunity to study the real development of sexuality in the human species. We could all become more enlightened about this vital function. Armed with more factual information, our culture would be in a better posture to offer guidance related to developing healthy and responsible sexual behavior. This process would be similar to information-based procedures used to nurture other developmental skills such as mobility, language, and higher-order cognition. Proposed is a positive approach to developing healthy sexuality rather than the present cultural emphasis on thwarting sexuality through negative methods such as repression, shame, and retribution.

In spite of the overall repressive attitudes found in the cultural underpinnings of sex in America, a different standard is established for males than for females. This double standard sets the role of the male as the sexual aggressor and the female as the paragon of chastity. Males are encouraged at some level, if not openly, to seek out females for sexual favors to prove their manhood (e.g., a real man fucks women), but females are cautioned to withhold sex to maintain their status in the mainstream social community (e.g., virginity and immaculate conception are the ideal, only bad girls have sex). The point is this: Too much emphasis is placed on the act of sex as an indicator of one's worth in this society. Neither males nor females should be placed in a position of having to prove their worth through the initiation or withholding of sexual behavior. Most sexual functions are regulated by noncortical areas of the brain; if the wiring and plumbing are intact, the system will probably function without much effort. Why, then, is a "no-brainer" activity so important to society's view of a person's status? Again, Western culture needs to put sex in a better perspective by generating messages devoid of connections between sexual behavior and personal worth.

Now I turn to Western thought regarding sexual orientation and how messages about other-than-heterosexual behavior are so terribly harmful for each gender regardless of sexual orientation. Nonheterosexual behaviors have been with us forever. These activities, although not as common as male-female sexual attraction, are clearly part of the overall diverse nature of homo sapiens as a species. With the work by LeVay (1991, 1993), Bailey and Pillard (1991), Bailey, Pillard, Neale, and Agyer (1993), and others, we may yet discover the basis for all sexual behavior coded in some manner in our DNA. But Western thought about other-than-heterosexual behavior remains predominantly focused on labeling these activities abhorrent and people who engage in them as perverse. Homophobia becomes a social disease that affects us all in negative ways.

As a reaction to this form of discrimination and in hopes of eliminating the bigotry, many nonheterosexual individuals have become very vocal in their protests. Some groups have even taken to the streets to flaunt their "perverse" sexuality as a form of shock therapy for society, a display of sexuality frowned on by more conservative gay and lesbian groups. None of these actions would be necessary if our culture would recognize sexual diversity rather than trying to eliminate it. Diverse does not mean perverse.

Cultural reconstruction would include disgorging the misinformation about nonheterosexuality, incorporating contemporary research literature findings into its collective unconscious, and embracing the idea that other-than-heterosexual behavior is also part of the grand scheme, not an evil perversion. It makes no more sense to discriminate on the basis of sexual orientation than it does to discriminate based on biological gender, skin color, eye color, color blindness, or anything else willed to use by our genetic pool and biological juices. The notion that individuals who engage in other-than-heterosexual behavior are "that way" because they want to be and they could become heterosexuals if only they really wanted to is absurd (see Bell, Weinberg, & Hammersmith, 1981; Gonsiorek & Weinrich, 1991).

## ❏ Reconstructing Male Heterosexuality

I begin the task of reconstructing male heterosexuality by revisiting Levant's recommendations regarding the reconstructing of masculinity (Levant, 1992; Levant & Kopecky, 1995). He points out that men need to validate the positive attributes they already possess, such as problem-solving skills, the ability to be a team member, risk taking, the ability to remain calm in the face of danger, and assertiveness. Moderating the tendency to indulge in self-sacrifice and sacrifice-indulge behavior, as well as reducing defensive autonomy and a sense of entitlement, would pave the way for a less harmful lifestyle. Developing additional skills such as empathy, emotional self-awareness, and the ability to express emotions appropriately will help round out the picture. These components of reconstructed masculinity provide the foundation for allowing men to take the next step: reconstructing masculine sexuality.

The first task is to strip away many layers of distorted ideas left by a series of ancient philosophers and spiritual leaders who seemed to have had good intentions but failed Human Sexuality 101. Many of these notions about sexuality are now formalized into beliefs and standards by which men feel compelled to judge themselves. As with any measurement, if the scale is not true, the result will not be accurate. Zilbergeld (1992) identifies several culturally driven destructive myths men hold about sexuality. Men who are seduced by these distorted ideas display problems with intimacy and expressing "nonmasculine" feelings. They also interact with females according to misinformation about gender differences and unrealistic expectations of sexual behavior. Popular myths are poor standards for healthy sexual relationships.

Men must assume the responsibility for seeking accurate information about sexual matters and begin to transform this information into pleasurable, healthy, and responsible sexual behavior. Because heterosexual males remain a powerful group within our society, their efforts to reconstruct harmful attitudes about sex may provide the impetus needed for the overall cultural reconstruction discussed earlier. To assist in this process, I have attempted to identify a majority of distorted and harmful ideas about male sexuality. They seem to fall within six categories: phalocentricism, performance, promiscuity, paternity, phobia, and playfulness.

## ■ Phalocentricism

The penis was deified in antiquity and remains central to the development of myths about masculinity and male sexuality. As Thorn (1990) notes, "consciously or unconsciously, the penis is the very center of human life: love, sex passion, lust, procreation, off-spring—all these and more—pass through his amazing urge or the absence of it" (p. 20). Much of what a man believes about his masculinity and sexuality is connected to myths associated with penis size and worth. A man with a large penis is afforded a special place in masculine society. Some even become legends. A man with a below-average penis is often shamed by other men with comments such as, "An inch more and you might be a man. An inch less and you are a woman." At the very least, nearly all men display angst about the size of their penis and look for some form of standard. Naked boys in locker rooms look at other naked boys to make comparisons, a practice often continued into manhood. This only further confuses males because the size of a penis at rest has no relationship at all to the size of the organ once aroused. Even the smallest of organs can transform into a mighty male tool.

Phalocentricism is also perpetuated by some females who take pride in describing their partner's "magnificent member" and how wonderful it feels to be "all filled up." All this in spite of the research that suggests that the size of the penis is less important than the sexual acumen of the owner. That is, a smaller tool under the control of a master craftsman can create greater satisfaction than a larger one in the hands of a clumsy oaf.

But it is not just concern over the size of the penis that creates problems for men, it is the general concept that the penis (masculinity) is the center of the universe. In ancient times, men were required to grasp their genitals while swearing the truth or taking an oath. The word *testimony* comes from the Latin word *testes*, meaning testicles and witness. Pledging one's genitals as collateral for the truth is risky business. Swearing by the penis of God was also required in some ancient civilizations. I suppose using God's penis for collateral is even more of a risk, assuming that God has a penis. And we still equate male genitals with power and courage. For example, men who have performed acts of courage and daring may be told that they have "balls of steel" or "balls the size of a dinosaur."

Although I believe much of the contemporary focus on male genitals as the seat of power in the universe can be seen by most males as just a humorous look at masculinity, the misguided ideas about masculine superiority and domination appear embedded in our culture and continue to be perpetuated unconsciously through phallic myths. Many males continue to accept these notions as truths and guide themselves accordingly. Males must be ready to identify and change these ideas instead of perpetuating them. Men can change, and they can do so without pledging their genitals.

The following story illustrates some men's ability to change. I am a member of a group of men who have been playing poker on a regular basis for several years. A few years ago, a charter member of our group vacated his chair when he moved to another city. We were approached by the wife of a mutual friend with a request to join the group. Because she was an accomplished poker player, she was accepted without much ado, although some members indicated that they did not intend to use different language or behave in any way different from established male poker group etiquette. Early in the course of the woman's introduction into our games, we continued to use terms familiar to most men without paying much attention to the effect. One night, our newest member displayed an absolutely brilliant but quite risky poker maneuver. As she was raking in a substantial pot of money, we showed our admiration by telling her she had just made a "ballsy" call. She laughed while informing us that she had actually made an "ovarian" call. The term was quickly adopted by the rest of the previously all-male (but never masculinist) group. A number of women have played in the group since then, and we have all learned from each other. In a playful manner, we have gradually identified and skewered many myths about sexuality perpetuated by both genders.

### ■ Performance

Once a male discovers his penis, he must learn how to use it and how to use it well. It is time to show his stuff. It is time to perform. Not only are impromptu performances expected, but the performance must be award winning as well. Although most males fear any type of "failure" in sexual matters, they continue to perpetrate the myth connecting manhood and the ability to perform sexually. Related to this issue is the male myth that the only problems real men have with sex is that there are never enough female sexual partners available. This is one way males continue to connect sexuality with other matters, such as maintaining status within the male community and sustaining a positive self-image. Because it is highly improbable that all males can give award-winning sexual performances consistently, or ever, for that matter, males often keep their failures a secret and lie to themselves and other males about their sexual prowess. This practice effectively removes many males from the opportunity to learn how to deal with sexual problems effectively.

It is time to incorporate accurate information about the male's sexual abilities and normal limitations into the male psyche. Excluded in this new concept of male sexuality will be references to performance expectations and failures. Excluded also will be all the lies males tell each other about the size and power of their penis, the length of time they were able to maintain heavy thrusting while their partners screamed in sexual ecstasy, the amount of ejaculate produced, and the number of times they were able to get it up following orgasms. (But, just for fun, maybe a few little white lies will be allowed.)

### ■ Promiscuity

An integral part of growing up male is to take as many female sexual partners as possible. Men who have many successful sexual conquests are often revered by other men who look to them as models of manhood and real-man sexuality. A young man can prove his manhood by having numerous "notches in his belt" or "notches on his bedpost" representing successful sexual conquests. A close friend of mine, during singledom, kept a diary listing the women with whom he had sex, their physical attributes, and a rating of the experience. He would often boast about the large number of entries in his log. Other males keep little black books with similar information and telephone numbers. Perhaps this practice may be harmless, but some males interpret the macho creed too literally and set off on an unending quest to prove manhood through compulsive or other forms of inappropriate sexual behavior. In addition to the potential harm to sexual targets, promiscuity is personally harmful because it significantly increases the risk of encountering and contracting sexually transmitted diseases, some of which are fatal.

Some young males view sexual conquest as a sporting event and organize games in which the person who "scores" the most is declared the winner and official stud. A good example of this is a group of male teenagers in California called the "Spur Posse." These young men took the sexual conquest game seriously and seldom gave in to female resistance, even from preteens. They were verbal about their conquests and passionate about their standing in the group. Often they referred to some of their scores in derogatory language such as "sluts" and "whores," even when the girls had been inexperienced and were coerced into sexual activities. Although some people thought that this case was just another example of "boys will be boys," a lot of misery for a large number of young females was created by the boys' inappropriate sexual behavior. Adult males must begin mentoring younger males to recognize that this type of sexual behavior is driven by the need to fulfill a myth of masculine sexuality. It is neither necessary nor appropriate. Sex is not a game.

Promiscuity also becomes a threat to a male's ability to establish and maintain a stable and nurturing relationship with one partner. Even so, many males feel compelled to seek out what Zilbergeld (1992) calls "fresh flesh" to live up to masculine notions of what constitutes a real man. When a man appears to be afraid to cheat on his partner or dominated by her, he is often called "pussy whipped." The terms are even more derogatory and shameful for males who, for whatever reason, have not been successful in sexual conquests with women.

During one of my presentations at a national conference, I asked members of the audience how many heard of the 4-F Club (not the 4-H Club). About 90% of the men began smirking and raised their hands. Most of the women looked puzzled. Only a couple of women raised their hands. They were not smirking. I was not surprised by the results of my informal poll because the 4-F Club is a mythical organization of self-proclaimed male studs. It is the Find Them, Feel Them, Fuck Them, and Forget Them Club. To become a member, a male must subscribe to the club's credo and play it out by seducing a large number of females. Only real men need apply.

These are just some examples of the types of messages males give males regarding the role promiscuity plays in achieving true masculinity. To assist in developing a more healthy approach to sexuality, males must begin to dismantle these traditional concepts equating sex (lots of sex) and manhood. Sexuality and masculinity should be placed in separate categories. That is, men in our society must allow a young male to achieve manhood even if he has chosen not to make the pursuit of vaginal juices his lifetime occupation.

### ■ Paternity

One of the most serious consequences of male heterosexual behavior is the creation of another human being. Perhaps this is some form of primordial urge to produce as many progeny as possible, thus assuring that our essence will remain an integral part of the gene pool. Whatever the reason, producing children has become another badge of manhood for some males. That is, part of the masculine message about manhood and sexuality is that real men not only fuck women, they also impregnate them. The belief is that a man's virility and sexuality are assured if he can produce a large number of children. Unfortunately absent from this conceptualization of sexuality is the idea that a real man should also be prepared to assume responsibility for the child. Caring for children remains a feminine not a masculine role, even though overall messages about paternity point to the father's role as provider and protector.

For immature males of any age, the badge of manhood they pin on themselves when they procreate is a false symbol of anything remotely resembling true manhood. It represents only the simple biological ability to plant viable sperm in somebody, nothing else. The underpinnings of mature masculinity, which I believe contain the elements of caring, responsibility, and a true desire to be a father to the child rather than just to father a child, are absent. Although most mature males will tell you that they look forward to producing and raising children, immature males will refer only to a desire to get somebody pregnant.

Paternity can be very confusing for males because cultural messages are often a strange mix of Judeo-Christian dogma about procreation and misinformation about masculinity and sexuality. Males are told that they must prove their manhood by having sex with lots of females. Although most males are told not to get anyone pregnant in this process, some males are warned about the sinful nature of effective birth control methods. Many males are also told that producing children by several females will bring them more status within the male subculture. Lost in all this are the needs of the child. Not only is the rate of premature pregnancies soaring in this country, immature males and females are thrust into the role of rearing children when they do not have the skills to rear themselves. Immature males typically absent themselves and take up with other receptive females. Females are left to care for the child as best they can. No one is taking responsibility for their actions and the children, who have become pseudosymbols of manhood, suffer the consequences.

The reconstructed sexual male will have accurate information about sexuality, procreation, and child rearing necessary to make an informed choice about paternity. He will also be mature enough to resist the voices that tell him that real men produce children regardless of the consequences for the child. If he cannot resist the urge to engage in sexual activities, he will at least use effective birth control techniques until he can truly be a father to his child. Adult males must begin to provide younger males with more appropriate messages in this regard. As mentors, adult males must show younger males how to assume a responsible role in sexual matters and procreation. Males must also begin to model nurturing parenting attitudes and behavior. It is irresponsible for males in our society to ignore this problem and continue to perpetuate it by not emphasizing the role of a real man as sexually responsible and a good father to his progeny. Perhaps we need to resurrect the positive aspects of patriarchy as seen in colonial days, when men seemed to take responsibility for their actions and their children.

## ■ Phobia

Although many cultural messages about male sexuality are confusing, one is very clear: Real men do not have sex with real men. Heterosexuality is so revered, and nonheterosexuality so hated, by mainstream society that males become fearful of feeling or exhibiting anything remotely resembling nonheterosexuality (nonmasculinity). Like most irrational fears, homophobia produces unnecessary and unproductive reactive behavior.

Many males engage in a form of hyperheterosexuality to assure others and themselves that they are real men. This may take the form of embracing and displaying all the emblems of traditional manhood such as wearing only real-man clothing, driving only real-man vehicles, drinking only real-man beverages, and using only real-man language. Engaging in dangerous activities and compulsive womanizing are also important components of the scenario. Some fearful and insecure male heterosexuals attempt to prove their manhood by using society's fear and rejection of nonheterosexuality as a rationalization for either harassing or physically assaulting homosexuals, whom they have labeled as perverts and a threat to society. Some homosexuals, on the other hand, try to hide their sexual orientation, fearing society's wrath. Others engage in futile attempts to change sexual orientation in hopes of finding acceptance.

None of this would be necessary if all men would reject the notion that male heterosexuality is the only path to manhood. Accepting sexual diversity as the norm precludes the need for men to be fearful of other-than-heterosexual behavior.

### ■ Playfulness

The fabric of sex in America is woven with constriction and procreation, not experimentation and recreation. Although some religious malcontents have attempted to change this notion, many males continue to feel guilty about engaging in something that seems to feel natural but is deemed by most religious leaders as sinful, dirty, disgusting, and bad. This guilt often comes into conflict with other feelings associated with more permissive double-standard messages applied to masculine sexual behavior. As one of the results, much sexual behavior is driven underground or diverted to other nonhealthy channels. Faced with restricted natural sexual experimentation and playfulness, many males develop secret sex lives replete with all sorts of harmful sexual activities. Some seek help in the psychotherapist's office. Most go untreated.

Dispelling myths and operating from a solid base of factual information can produce less anxiety and a more healthy approach to sex. Instead of sexual sports and gender wars, perhaps we can learn to view sex in a mature manner and be more playful in our approach. Once we have established trust that men are not going to use sex as a weapon, perhaps we can joke about sexual matters in a manner similar to recounting humorous events in our everyday lives. We can feel free to explore and experiment with consenting partners without fear of societal reprisal or being damned to hell for eternity. We can also learn to accept the sexuality of others even though it may be different from our own. Males will not have to prove their manhood through numerous sexual conquests and fathering children they have no interest in other than to use as some form of sexual merit badge. And, once and for all, males will no longer have to brag about the size of their penis.

## ❏ Sex and the New Real Man

Reconstructing harmful concepts related to the development of masculinity and male sexuality appears essential to the development of a new and better functioning real man. But reconstructing an ancient edifice with a deteriorating superstructure and a faulty foundation may be more risky than pledging genitals. The work will require considerable thought, time, and energy. Contemporary custodians of the institution will not take kindly to anyone meddling in "their" affairs; they will not easily relinquish control of the property. But if the reconstruction project is successful, members of our society will be rewarded with a well-designed structure rebuilt using sound principles of architecture and reliable materials rather than from plans derived from myths and misinformation. I leave you with an outline of my vision of the reconstructed real man and his new approach to sexuality.

- The new real man will know as much about true masculine sexuality as he does about other internal combustion engines.
- The new real man will know as much about true female sexuality as he does about football or other sports.
- The new real man will refrain from using power and position to extract sexual favors from others in more vulnerable positions.
- The new real man will release, remove, and destroy the coupling between sex and violence.

- The new real man will become a true father by producing only children he wishes to parent and has the means to care for properly.
- The new real man will be a real man regardless of level of sexual desire.
- The new real man will be a real man regardless of sexual orientation.
- The new real man will find satisfaction in exploring sexuality in playful ways.
- The new real man will mentor younger males in the art of becoming a true real man.
- The new real man will scoff at myths of masculinity.

# References

Abel, G. G., Becker, J. V., Cunningham-Rathner, J., Mittelman, M., & Rouleau, J. L. (1988). Multiple paraphiliac diagnoses among sex offenders. *Bulletin of the American Academy of Psychiatry and the Law, 16*(2), 153-168.

Abel, G. G., Becker, J. V., Murphy, W. D., & Flanagan, B. (1981). Identifying dangerous child molesters. In R. B. Stuart (Ed.) *Violent behavior: Social learning approaches to predicting management and treatment* (pp. 116-137). New York: Brunner/Mazel.

Abel, G. G., Mittelman, M. S., & Becker, J. V. (1985). Sexual offenders: Results of assessment and recommendation for treatment. In M. H. Ben-Aron, S. J. Huckle, & C. D. Webster (Eds.), *Clinical criminology: The assessment and treatment of criminal behavior* (pp. 191-205). Toronto: M & M Graphic.

Abou-David, K. (1967). Epidemiology of carcinoma of the cervix uteri in Lebanese Christians and Moslems. *Cancer, 20*, 1706-1714.

*Action Comics.* (1938). Issue number 1. New York: DC Comics.

Adams, B., Gold, A. R., & Burt, A. D. (1978). Rise in female-initiated sexual activity at ovulation and its suppression by oral contraceptives. *New England Journal of Medicine, 299*(21), 1145-1150.

Ade-Ridder, L. (1985). Quality of marriage: A comparison between golden-wedding couples and couples married less than fifty years. *Lifestyles, 7*, 224-237.

*The Adventures of Superman.* (1995). Issue number 15. New York: DC Comics.

Alan Guttmacher Institute. (1991). *Teenage sexual and reproductive behavior* (Facts in Brief). New York: Author.

Albin, R. S. (1977). Psychological studies of rape. *Signs: Journal of Women in Culture and Society, 3*, 423-435.

Alexander, R. D. (1980). *Darwinism and human affairs*. Seattle: University of Washington Press.

Allen, C. M. (1990). Women as perpetrators of child sexual abuse: Recognition barriers. In A. L. Horton, B. L. Johnson, L. M. Roundy, & D. Williams (Eds.), *The incest perpetrator: A family member no one wants to treat* (pp. 108-125). Newbury Park, CA: Sage.

Allen, L. S., & Gorski, R. A. (1992). Sexual orientation and the size of the anterior commissure in the human brain. *Proceedings of the National Academy of Sciences of the USA, 89*, 7199-7202.

American Academy of Pediatrics. (1975). Committee on Fetus and Newborn: Report of the Ad Hoc Task Force on Circumcision. *Pediatrics, 56*, 610-611.

American Academy of Pediatrics. (1984). *Care of the uncircumcised penis.* Grove Village, IL: Author.

American Psychiatric Association. (1994). *Diagnostic and statistical manual of mental disorders* (4th ed.). Washington, DC: Author.

Ames, M. A., & Houston, D. A. (1990). Legal, social, and biological definitions of pedophilia. *Archives of Sexual Behavior, 19*, 333-342.

Anand, K. J. S., & Hickey, P. R. (1987). Pain and its effects in the human neonate and fetus. *New England Journal of Medicine, 317*, 1321-1326.

Arnold, P. M. (1991). *Wildmen, warriors, and kings: Masculine spirituality and the Bible.* New York: Crossroad.

Atwater, L. (1982). *The extramarital connection: Sex, intimacy, and identity.* New York: Irvington.

Austrom, D., & Hanel, K. (1985). Psychological issues of single life in Canada. *International Journal of Women's Studies, 8*, 12-23.

Baber, A. (1993, September). Wake-up call. *Playboy*, p. 42.

Bailey, J. M., & Pillard, R. C. (1991). A genetic study of male sexual orientation. *Archives of General Psychiatry, 48*, 1089-1096.

Bailey, J. M., Pillard, R. C., Neale, M. C., & Agyei, Y. (1993). Heritable factors influence sexual orientation in women. *Archives of General Psychiatry, 50*, 217-223.

Bain, J., Langevin, R., Dickey, R., & Ben-Aron, M. (1987). Sex hormones in murderers and assaulters. *Behavioral Sciences and the Law, 5*(1), 95-101.

Ballard, D. T., Blair, G. D., Devereaux, S., Valentine, L. K., Horton, A. L., & Johnson, B. L. (1990). A comparative profile of the incest perpetrator: Background characteristics, abuse history, and use of social skills. In A. L. Horton, B. L. Johnson, L. M. Roundy, & D. Williams (Eds.), *The incest perpetrator: A family member no one wants to treat* (pp. 43-64). Newbury Park, CA: Sage.

Banmen, J., & Vogel, N. (1985). The relationship between marital quality and interpersonal sexual communication. *Family Therapy, 12,* 45-58.

Banning, A. (1989), Mother-son incest: Confronting a prejudice. *Child Abuse and Neglect, 13,* 563-570.

Barash, D. P. (1979). *The whisperings within: Evolution and the origin of human nature.* New York: Harper & Row.

Barbaree, H. E., & Marshall, W. L. (1991). The role of male sexual arousal in rape: Six models. *Journal of Consulting and Clinical Psychology, 59,* 621-630.

Barlow, D. H. (1986). Causes of sexual dysfunction: The role of anxiety and cognitive interference. *Journal of Consulting and Clinical Psychology, 54,* 140-148.

Barlow, D. H., Sakheim, D. K., & Beck, J. G. (1983). Anxiety increased sexual arousal. *Journal of Abnormal Psychology, 92,* 49-54.

Baxter, D. J., Barbaree, H. E., & Marshall, W. L. (1986). Sexual responses to consenting and forced sex in a large sample of rapists and nonrapists. *Behaviour Research and Therapy, 17,* 215-222.

Beach, F. A. (1974). Human sexuality and evolution. In W. Montagna & W. Sadler (Eds.), *Reproductive behavior* (pp. 333-365). New York: Plenum.

Beach, S. R. H., Jouriles, E. N., & O'Leary, K. D. (1985). Extramarital sex: Impact on depression and commitment in couples seeking marital therapy. *Journal of Sex and Marital Therapy, 11,* 99-108.

Beck, J. G. (1988). *Love is never enough.* New York: Harper & Row.

Beck, J. G., & Barlow, D. H. (1984). Current conceptualizations of sexual dysfunction: A review and an alternative perspective. *Clinical Psychology Review, 4,* 363-378.

Bell, A. P., Weinberg, M. S., & Hammersmith, S. K. (1981). *Sexual preference: Its development in men and women.* Bloomington: Indiana University Press.

Bello, D. C., Pitts, R. E., & Etzel, M. J. (1983). The communications effects of controversial sexual content in television programs and commercials. *Journal of Advertising, 12*(3), 32-42.

Bem, S. L. (1993). *The lenses of gender.* New Haven, CT: Yale University Press.

Bender, L., & Blau, A. (1937). The reaction of children to sexual relations with adults. *American Journal of Orthopsychiatry, 7,* 500-518.

Bender, L., & Grugett, A. (1952). A follow-up report on children who had atypical sexual experiences. *American Journal of Orthopsychiatry, 22,* 825-837.

Bennett, N. G., Blanc, A. K., & Bloom, D. E. (1988). Commitment and the modern union: Assessing the link between premarital cohabitation and subsequent marital stability. *American Sociological Review, 53,* 127-138.

Benson, D. J., & Thomson, G. E. (1982). Sexual harassment on a university campus: The confluence of authority relations, sexual interest, and gender stratification. *Social Problems, 29,* 236-251.

Berger, K. S. (1988). *The developing person through the life span.* New York: Worth.

Berkowitz, L. (1984). Some effects of thoughts on anti- and prosocial influence of media events: A cognitive neoassociation approach. *Pscychological Bulletin, 95,* 410-427.

Berlin, F. S., & Coyle, G. S. (1981). Sexual deviation syndromes. *The Johns Hopkins Medical Journal, 149,* 119-125.

Bernard, J. (1982). *The future of marriage.* New Haven, CT: Yale University Press.

Berscheid, E. (1988). Some comments on love's anatomy: Or, whatever happened to old-fashioned lust? In R. J. Sternberg & M. L. Barnes (Eds.), *The psychology of love* (pp. 359-374). New Haven, CT: Yale University Press.

Berscheid, E., & Walster, E. (1978). *Interpersonal attraction.* Reading, MA: Addison-Wesley.

Betcher, W., & Pollack, W. (1993). *In a time of fallen heroes: The re-creation of masculinity.* New York: Macmillan.

Blair, C. D., & Lanyon, R. I. (1981). Exhibitionism: Etiology and treatment. *Psychological Bulletin, 89,* 439-463.

Block, J. H. (1976). Debatable conclusions about sex difference. *Contemporary Psychology, 21,* 517-522.

Blumstein, P., & Schwartz, P. (1983). *American couples: Money, work, sex.* New York: William Morrow.

Blumstein, P., & Schwartz, P. (1990). Intimate relationships and the creation of sexuality. In D. P. McWhirter, S. A. Sanders, & J. M. Reinsch (Eds.), *Homosexuality/heterosexuality: Concepts of sexual orientation* (pp. 307-320). New York: Oxford University Press.

Bolton, F. G., Morris, L. A., & MacEachron, A. E. (1989). *Males at risk: The other side of child sexual abuse.* Newbury Park, CA: Sage.

Bly, R. (1990). *Iron John: A book about men.* New York: Random House.

Bly, R. (1994, August). Where are men now? In R. F. Levant (Chair), *On men: Acolloquy.* Paper presented at the 102nd annual convention of the American Psychological Association, Los Angeles.

Boutilier, M. A., & SanGiovanni, L. (1983). *The sporting woman.* Champaign, IL: Human Kinetics.

Bowlby, J. (1969). *Attachment and loss* (Vol. 1). London: Hogarth.

Bradford, J. M. W. (1983). Research on sex offenders: Recent trends. *Psychiatric Clinics of North America, 6,* 715-731.

Bradford, J. M., & McLean, D. (1984). Sexual offenders, violence and testosterone: A clinical study. *Canadian Journal of Psychiatry, 29*(4), 335-343.

Brandt, R. S. T., & Tisza, V. B. (1977). The sexually misused child. *American Journal of Orthopsychiatry, 47,* 80-90.

Braude, A. I., Davis, C. E., & Fierer, J. (Eds.). (1986). *Infectious diseases and medical microbiology* (2nd ed.) Philadelphia: W. B. Saunders.

Brecher, E. M., and the Editors of Consumer Reports Books. (1984). *Love, sex, and aging.* Boston: Little, Brown.

Bretl, D. J., & Cantor, J. (1988). The portrayal of men and women in U.S. television commercials: A recent content analysis and trends over 15 years. *Sex Roles, 18,* 595-609.

Bretschneider, J., & McCoy, N. (1988). Sexual interest and behavior in healthy 80- to 102-year-olds. *Archives of Sexual Behavior, 17,* 109.

Briere, J., & Malamuth, N. M. (1983). Self-reported likelihood of sexually aggressive behavior: Attitudinal vs. sexual explanations. *Journal of Research in Personality, 17,* 315-323.

Briere, J., & Runtz, M. (1989). University males' sexual interest in children: Predicting potential indices of "pedophilia" in a non-forensic sample. *Child Abuse and Neglect, 13,* 65-75.

Briere, J., & Smiljanich, K. (1993, August). *Childhood sexual abuse and subsequent sexual aggression against adult women.* Paper presented at the 101st annual convention of the American Psychological Association, Toronto.

Bright, S. (Ed.). (1988). *Herotica.* Burlingame, CA: Down There.

Bright, S., & Blank, J. (Eds.). (1992). *Herotica 2.* New York: Plume.

Brigman, W. (1986). Pornography as political expression. *Journal of Popular Culture, 17*(2), 129-134.

Brod, H. (1985, April). Reply to Bly. *AHP Perspective.* New York: Association for Humanistic Psychology.

Brooks, G. (1995). *The centerfold syndrome.* San Francisco: Jossey-Bass.

Brooks, G. R. (1991). Men's studies and psychotherapy: A current perspective on the status of the men's movement. *Psychotherapy Bulletin, 26*(2), 19-22.

Brooks, L., & Perot, A. R. (1991). Reporting sexual harassment: Exploring a predictive model. *Psychology of Women Quarterly, 15,* 31-47.

Brooks-Gunn, J., & Furstenberg, F. F. (1989). Adolescent sexual behavior. *American Psychologist, 44*(2), 249-257.

Brooks-Gunn, J., & Matthews, W. S. (1979). *He and she: How children develop their sex-role identity.* Englewood Cliffs, NJ: Spectrum.

Brown, L. S. (1988). Harmful effects of posttermination sexual and romantic relationships with former clients. *Psychotherapy, 25,* 249-255.

Brown, M., Amoroso, D., & Ware, E. (1976). Behavioral aspects of viewing pornography. *Journal of Social Psychology, 98,* 235-245.

Browne, A. (1987). *When battered women kill.* New York: Free Press.

Browne, A., & Finkelhor, D. (1986). Impact of child sexual abuse: A review of the research. *Psychological Bulletin, 99*(1), 66-77.

Brownmiller, S. (1975). *Against our will: Men, women, and rape.* New York: Simon & Schuster.

Bryant, J., & Brown, D. (1989). Uses of pornography. In D. Zillmann & J. Bryant (Eds.), *Pornography: Research advances and policy considerations* (pp. 25-55). Hillsdale, NJ: Lawrence Erlbaum.

Burnstein, J. G. (1983). *Handbook of drug therapy in psychiatry*. Boston: John Wright, PSG.

Burt, M. R. (1980). Cultural myths and supports for rape. *Journal of Personality and Social Psychology, 38*, 217-230.

Burton, R. F. (Trans.). (1962). *The Kama sutra of Vatsyayana*. New York: E. P. Dutton.

Butler, R. M., & Lewis, M. I. (1976). *Sex after sixty*. New York: Harper & Row.

Byrne, D. (1977). The imagery of sex. In J. Money & H. Musaph (Eds.), *Handbook of sexology* (pp. 327-350). New York: Elsevier/North Holland.

Calderone, M. S., & Johnson, E. W. (1989). *Family book about sexuality* (Rev. ed.). New York: Harper & Row.

Calderwood, D. (1987). The male rape victim. *Medical Aspects of Human Sexuality, 21*(5), 53-55.

Calhoun, A. W., & Atkeson, B. M. (1991). *Treatment of rape victims: Facilitating social adjustment*. Elmsford, NY: Pergamon.

Calhoun, L. G., Selby, J. W., & Warring, L. J. (1976). Social perception of the victims' causal role in rape: An exploratory examination of four factors. *Human Relations, 29*, 517-526.

Cameron, D. W., Simonsen, J. N., & D'Costa, L. (1989). Female to male transmission of human immunodeficiency virus type 1: Risk factors for seroconversion in men. *Lancet, 2*, 403-407.

Cann, A., Calhoun, L. G., & Selby, J. W. (1979). Attributing responsibility to the victim of rape: Influence of information regarding past experience. *Human Relations, 32*, 57-67.

Caputi, J., & MacKenzie, G. O. (1992). Pumping "Iron John." In K. L. Hagan (Ed.), *Women respond to the men's movement* (pp. 69-81). San Francisco: HarperCollins

Carnes, P. J. (1990). Sexual addiction. In A. L. Horton, B. L. Johnson, L. M. Roundy, & D. Williams (Eds.), *The incest perpetrator: A family member no one wants to treat* (pp. 126-146). Newbury Park, CA: Sage.

Carney, P. A., Bancroft, J., & Matthews, A. (1978). The combination of hormone and counseling in the treatment of female sexual unresponsiveness. *British Journal of Psychiatry, 133*, 339-346.

Centers for Disease Control. (1989a). *Summaries of identifiable diseases in the United States*. Washington, DC: Author.

Centers for Disease Control. (1989b). Treatment guidelines for sexually transmitted diseases. *Morbidity and Mortality Weekly Report, 38*, No. S-8.

Centers for Disease Control. (1990a). Prevalence of HIV infection in childbearing women in the United States: Surveillance using newborn blood samples. *Journal of the American Medical Association, 265*, 1704-1708.

Centers for Disease Control. (1990b). Progress toward achieving the 1990 objectives for the nation for sexually transmitted diseases. *Morbidity and Mortality Weekly Report, 39*, 53-57.

Centers for Disease Control. (1991a). Mortality attributable to HIV infection/AIDS—United States, 1981-1990. *Journal of the American Medical Association, 265,* 848.

Centers for Disease Control. (1991b). Summary of notifiable diseases, United States, 1990. *Morbidity and Mortality Weekly Report, 39,* 1-53.

Centers for Disease Control. (1992). *HIV infection and AIDS: Are you at risk?* Atlanta: Author.

Check, J. V. P. (1985). *The effects of violent and nonviolent pornography.* Report to the Department of Justice, Ottawa.

Check, J. V. P., & Guloien, J. (1989). Reported proclivity for coercive sex following repeated exposure to sexually violent pornography, nonviolent dehumanizing pornography, and erotica. In D. Zillmann & J. Bryant (Eds.), *Pornography: Research advances and policy considerations* (pp. 159-184). Hillsdale, NJ: Lawrence Erlbaum.

Check, J. V. P., & Malamuth, N. M. (1983). Sex-role stereotyping and reactions to depictions of stranger versus acquaintance rape. *Journal of Personality and Social Psychology, 45,* 344-356.

Cherlin, A. J. (1981). *Marriage, divorce, remarriage.* Cambridge, MA: Harvard University Press.

Christiansen, J. R., & Blake, R. H. (1990). The grooming process in father-daughter incest. In A. L. Horton, B. L. Johnson, L. M. Roundy, & D. Williams (Eds.), *The incest perpetrator: A family member no one wants to treat* (pp. 88-98). Newbury Park, CA: Sage.

Christiansen, K., & Winkler, E.-M. (1992). Hormonal, anthropometrical, and behavioral correlates of physical aggression in !Kung San men of Namibia. *Aggressive Behavior, 18*(4), 271-280.

Chu, S. Y., Buehler, J. W., & Berkelman, R. L. (1990). Impact of the human immunodeficiency virus epidemic on mortality in women of reproductive age, United States. *Journal of the American Medical Association, 264,* 225-229.

Clayton, R. R., & Voss, H. L. (1977). Shacking up: Cohabitation in the 1970s. *Journal of Marriage and the Family, 39,* 273-283.

Cohen, R. J. (1993). Sex in advertising. In S. A. Rathus, J. S. Nevid, & L. Fichner-Rathus (Eds.), *Human sexuality in a world of diversity* (pp. 632-633). Boston: Allyn & Bacon.

Coleman, V. E. (1994). Lesbian battering: The relationship between personality and the perpetration of violence. *Violence and Victims, 9*(2), 139-152.

Coles, R., & Stokes, G. (1985) *Sex and the American teenager.* New York: Harper & Row.

Comfort, A. (1963). *Sex in society.* London: Duckworth.

Comings, D. E., & Comings, B. G. (1982). A case of familial exhibitionism in Tourette's syndrome successfully treated with haloperidol. *American Journal of Psychiatry, 139,* 913-915.

Commission on Obscenity and Pornography. (1970). *The technical report of the Commission on Obscenity and Pornography.* Washington, DC: Government Printing Office.

Conte, J. R. (1985). Clinical dimensions of adult sexual use of children. *Behavioral Sciences and the Law, 3,* 341-354.

Conte, J. R. (1990). The incest offender: An overview and introduction. In A. L. Horton, B. L. Johnson, L. M. Roundy, & D. Williams (Eds.), *The incest perpetrator: A family member no one wants to treat* (pp. 19-28). Newbury Park, CA: Sage.

Conte, J., & Schuerman, J. (1987). The effects of sexual abuse of children: A multidimensional view. *Journal of Interpersonal Violence, 2,* 380-390.

Cooper, A. J. (1981). A placebo-controlled trial of the antiandrogen cyproterone acetate in deviant hypersexuality. *Comprehensive Psychiatry, 22,* 458-465.

Cowan, G., & O'Brien, M. (1990). Gender and survival vs. death in slasher films: A content analysis. *Sex Roles, 23,* 187-196.

Cucchiari, S. (1981). The gender revolution and the transition from bisexual horde to patrilocal band: The origins of gender hierarchy. In S. B. Ortner & H. Whitehead (Eds.), *Sexual meanings: The cultural construction of gender and sexuality* (pp. 31-79). Cambridge, UK: Cambridge University Press.

Cunningham, G., Cordero, E., & Thornby, J. (1989). Testosterone replacement with transdermal therapeutic systems. *Journal of the American Medical Association, 261,* 2525-2531.

Cutrona, C. E. (1983). Causal attributions and perinatal depression. *Journal of Abnormal Psychology, 92,* 161-172.

Dabbs, J. M., Frady, R. L., Carr, T. S., & Besch, N. F. (1987). Saliva testosterone and criminal violence in young adult prison inmates. *Psychosomatiac Medicine, 49*(2), 174-182.

Dabbs, J. M., Jurkovic, G. J., & Frady, R. L. (1991). Salivary testosterone and cortisol among late adolescent male offenders. *Journal of Abnormal Child Psychology, 19*(4), 469-478.

Dabbs, J. M., & Morris, R. (1990). Testosterone, social class, and antisocial behavior in a sample of 4,462 men. *Psychological Science, 1,* 1-3.

Dabbs, J. M., Ruback, R. B., Frady, R. L., & Hopper, C. H. (1988). Saliva testosterone and criminal violence among women. *Personality and Individual Differences, 9*(2), 269-275.

Darling, C. A., & Davidson, J. K., Sr. (1986). Coitally active university students: Sexual behaviors, concerns, and challenges. *Adolescence, 21,* 403-419.

Darwin, C. (1958). *On the origin of species by means of natural selection.* New York: Mentor. (original work published 1859)

Dawkins, B. J. (1990). Genital herpes simplex infections. *Primary Care: Clinics in Office Practice, 17,* 95-113.

*The Death of Superman.* (1992). New York: DC Comics.

Deitz, S. R., & Byrnes, L. E. (1981). Attribution of responsibility for sexual assault: The influence of observer empathy and defendant occupation and attractiveness. *Journal of Psychology, 108,* 17-29.

Department of Justice. (1986). *Attorney General's commission on pornography: Final report.* Washington, DC: Government Printing Office.

Department of Justice, Federal Bureau of Investigation. (1990). *Uniform crime reports. Rape statistics.* Washington, DC: Government Printing Office.

Derogatis, L. R. (1980). Etiologic factors in premature ejaculation. *Medical Aspects of Human Sexuality, 14,* 32-47.

deYoung, M. (1982). *Sexual victimization of children.* Jefferson, NC: McFarland.

Dimock, P. (1988). Adult males sexually abused as children: Characteristics and implications for treatment. *Journal of Interpersonal Violence, 3*(2), 203-221.

Dobash, R. E., & Dobash, R. (1979). *Violence against wives: A case against the patriarchy.* New York: Free Press.

Donaldson, S. (1993). *Rape of incarcerated males in the USA: A preliminary statistical look.* Ft. Bragg, CA: Stop Prisoner Rape.

Donnerstein, D. (1980). Aggressive erotica and violence against women. *Journal of Personality and Social Psychology, 39,* 169-277.

Donnerstein, D., & Berkowitz, L. (1981). Victim reactions in aggressive erotic films as a factor in violence against women. *Journal of Personality and Social Psychology, 41,* 710-724.

Donnerstein, D., Berkowitz, L., & Linz, D. (1986). *Role of aggressive and sexual images in violent pornography.* Unpublished manuscript, University of Wisconsin-Madison.

Donnerstein, D., Linz, D., & Penrod, S. (1988). *The question of pornography: Research findings and policy implications.* New York: Free Press.

Draper, P. (1975). !Kung women: Contrasts in sexual egalitarianism in foraging and sedentary contexts. In R. R. Reiter (Ed.), *Toward an anthropology of women* (pp. 77-109). New York: Monthly Review.

Dutton, D. G. (1994). Patriarchy and wife assault: The ecological fallacy. *Violence and Victims, 9*(2), 167-182.

Dziech, B. W., & Weiner, L. (1984). *The lecherous professor.* Boston: Beacon.

Edgley, C. (1989). Commercial sex: Pornography, prostitution, and advertising. In K. McKinney & S. Sprecher (Eds.), *Human sexuality: The societal and interpersonal context* (pp. 370-424). Norwood, NJ: Ablex.

Ehrhardt, A., & Baker, S. W. (1978). Fetal androgens, human central nervous system differentiation, and behavior sex differences. In R. Friedman, T. M. Richart, & R. L. Vande Wiele (Eds.), *Sex differences in behavior* (pp. 33-51). Huntington, NY: Krieger.

Ehrhardt, A., & Meyer-Bahlburg, H. R. L. (1979). Prenatal sex hormones and the developing brain. *Annual Review of Medicine, 30,* 417-430.

Ehrhardt, A., & Meyer-Bahlburg, H. R. L. (1981). Effects of prenatal sex hormones on gender-related behavior. *Science, 211,* 1312-1317.

Elliot, D. S., & Morse, B. J. (1989). Delinquency and drug use as risk factors in teenage sexual activity. *Youth and Society, 21,* 32-60.

Ellis, L., & Ames, M. A. (1987). Neurohormonal functioning and sexual orientation. A theory of homosexuality-heterosexuality. *Pscyhological Bulletin, 101,* 233-258.

Ember, C. R., & Ember, M. (1990). *Anthropology.* Englewood Cliffs, NJ: Prentice Hall.

Englander-Golden, P., Change, H. S., Whitmore, M., & Dienstbier, R. (1980, March). Female sexual arousal and the menstrual cycle. *Journal of Human Stress,* pp. 42-48.

Faller, K. C. (1990). *Understanding child sexual maltreatment.* Newbury Park, CA: Sage.

Farley, A. U., Hadler, J. L., & Gunn, R. A. (1990). The syphilis epidemic in Connecticut: Relationship to drug use and prostitution. *Sexually Transmitted Diseases, 17,* 163-168.

Farley, L. (1978). *Sexual shakedown: The sexual harassment of women on the job.* New York: McGraw-Hill.

Faulkner, R. O. (1985). *The ancient Egyptian book of the dead.* London: British Museum.

Fausto-Sterling, A. (1985). *Myths of gender: Biological theories about women and men.* New York: Basic Books.

Feild, H. S. (1978). Attitudes toward rape: A comparative analysis of police, rapists, crisis counselors, and citizens. *Journal of Personality and Social Psychology, 36,* 156-179.

Fejes, F. J. (1992). Masculinity as fact: A review of empirical mass communication research on masculinity. In S. Craig (Ed.), *Men, masculinity, and the media* (pp. 9-22). Newbury Park, CA: Sage.

Feldman-Summers, S., & Jones, G. (1984). Psychological impacts of sexual contact between therapists or other health care professionals and their clients. *Journal of Consulting and Clinical Psychology, 52,* 1054-1061.

Finkelhor, D. (1980). Sex among siblings: A survey of prevalence, variety, and effects. *Archives of Sexual Behavior, 9,* 171-194.

Finkelhor, D. (1984). *Child sexual abuse: New theory and research.* New York: Free Press.

Finkelhor, D. (1986). *A sourcebook on child sexual abuse.* Beverly Hills, CA: Sage.

Finkelhor, D., & Yllö, K. (1985). *License to rape: Sexual abuse of wives.* New York: Free Press.

Fisher, H. E. (1983). *The sex contract: The evolution of human behavior.* New York: Quill.

Fisher, H. E. (1987, October). The four-year itch. *Natural History, 96*(10), 22-23.

Fitzgerald, L. F. (1992). *Sexual harassment in higher education: Concepts and issues.* Washington, DC: National Education Association.

Fitzgerald, L. F. (1993). Sexual harassment: Violence against women in the workplace. *American Psychologist, 48,* 1070-1076.

Fitzgerald, L. F., & Shullman, S. L. (1993). Sexual harassment: A research analysis and agenda for the 1990s. *Journal of Vocational Behavior, 42,* 5-27.

Fitzgerald, L. F., Shullman, S. L., Bailey, N., Richards, M., Swecker, J., Gold, A., Ormerod, A. J., & Weitzman, L. (1988). The incidence and dimensions of sexual harassment in academia and the workplace. *Journal of Vocational Behavior, 32,* 152-175.

Ford, C. S., & Beach, F. A. (1951). *Patterns of sexual behavior.* New York: Harper & Row.

Forman, B. (1982). Reported male rape. *Victimology: An International Journal, 7*(1-4), 235-236.

Fox, R. (1980). *The red lamp of incest: What the taboo can tell us about who we are and how we got that way.* New York: E. P. Dutton.

Frayser, S. (1985). *Varieties of sexual experience: An anthropological perspective on human sexuality.* New Haven, CT: Human Relations Area Files.

Freeman, E. W., & Rickels, K. (1993). *Early childbearing: Perspectives of black adolescents on pregnancy, abortion, and contraception.* Newbury Park, CA: Sage.

Freeman-Longo, R. E. (1986). The impact of sexual victimization on males. *Child Abuse and Neglect, 10,* 411-414.

Freeman-Longo, R. E., & Wall, R. V. (1986, March). Changing a lifetime of sexual crime. *Psychology Today,* pp. 58-64.

Freund, K. (1980). Therapeutic sex drive reduction. *Acta Psychiatrica Scandinavica, 62,* (Suppl. 287), 5-38.

Friedan, B. (1963). *The feminine mystique.* New York: Norton.

Friedan, B. (1995, April). Why men die young and why you'll live longer. *Playboy,* pp. 62-152.

Friedrich, W. N. (1995). *Psychotherapy with sexually abused boys.* Thousand Oaks, CA: Sage.

Frieze, I. H. (1983). Investigating the causes and consequences of marital rape. *Signs: Journal of Women in Culture and Society, 8,* 532-552.

Fromuth, M. E., & Burkhart, B. R. (1987). Childhood sexual victimization among college men: Definitional and methodological issues. *Violence and Victims, 2,* 241-253.

Fromuth, M. E., & Burkhart, B. R. (1989). Long-term psychological correlates of childhood sexual abuse in two samples of college men. *Child Abuse and Neglect, 13,* 533-542.

Fulero, S. M., & Delara, C. (1976). Rape victims and attributed responsibility: A defensive attribution approach. *Victimology: An International Journal, 1,* 551-563.

Funk, R. E. (1990, November). *Male rape survivors.* Workshop presented at the Third National Conference on Male Survivors, Tucson, AZ.

Funk, R. E. (1993). *Stopping rape: A challenge for men.* Philadelphia: New Society.

Furstenberg, F. F., Morgan, S. P., Moore, K. A., & Peterson, J. L. (1987). Race differences in the timing of adolescent intercourse. *American Sociological Review, 52,* 511-518.

Gabbard, G., & Pope, K. (1989). Sexual intimacies after termination: Clinical, ethical, and legal aspects. In G. Gabbard (Ed.), *Sexual exploitation in professional relationships* (pp. 115-127). Washington, DC: American Psychiatric Press.

Gadpaille, W. J. (1975). *The cycles of sex.* New York: Scribner.

Gaffney, G. R., & Berlin, F. S. (1984). Is there hypothalamic-pituitary-gonadal dysfunction in pedopilia? *British Journal of Psychiatry, 145,* 657-660.

Gaffney, G. R., Laurie, S. F., & Berlin, F. S. (1984). Is there familial transmission of pedophilia? *Journal of Nervous and Mental Disease, 172,* 546-548.

Gagne, P. (1981). Treatment of sex offenders with medroxyprogesterone acetate. *American Journal of Psychiatry, 138,* 644-646.

Garfinkel, P. (1985). *In a man's world: Father, son, brothers, friend, and other roles men play.* New York: Signet.

Gartrell, N., Herman, J., Olarte, S., Feldstein, M., & Localio, R. (1989). Prevalence of psychiatrist-patient sexual contact. In G. O. Gabbard (Ed.), *Sexual exploitation in professional relationships* (pp. 3-13). Washington, DC: American Psychiatric Press.

Gebhard, P. H., Gagnon, J. H., Pomeroy, W. B., & Christenson, C. V. (1965). *Sex offenders: An analysis of types.* New York: Harper & Row.

Gechtman, L. (1989). Sexual contact between social workers and their clients. In G. Gabbard (Ed.), *Sexual exploitation in professional relationships* (pp. 17-38). Washington, DC: American Psychiatric Press.

Gilgun, J. F., & Conner, T. M. (1990). Isolation and the adult male perpetrator of child sexual abuse: Clinical concerns. In A. L. Horton, B. L. Johnson, L. M. Roundy, & D. Williams (Eds.), *The incest perpetrator: A family member no one wants to treat* (pp. 74-87). Newbury Park, CA: Sage.

Girelli, S. A., Resick, P. A., Marhoefer-Dvorak, S., & Hutter, C. K. (1986). Subjective distress and violence during rape: Their effects on long-term fear. *Violence and Victims, 1,* 35-45.

Gitlin, M. J., & Pasnau, R. O. (1989). Psychiatric syndromes linked to reproductive function in women: A review of current knowledge. *American Journal of Psychiatry, 146,* 1413-1422.

Gladue, B. A., Beatty, W. W., Larson, J., & Staton, R. D. (1990). Sexual orientation and spatial ability in men and women. *Psychobiology, 18,* 101-108.

Glasner, P. D., & Kaslow, R. A. (1990). The epidemiology of human immunodeficiency virus infection. *Journal of Consulting and Clinical Psychology, 58,* 13-21.

Goldberg, H. (1976). *The hazards of being male: Surviving the myth of masculine privilege.* New York: Signet.

Goldberg. H. (1979). *The new male: From self-destruction to self-care.* New York: William Morrow.

Goldman, R., & Goldman, J. (1982). *Children's sexual thinking.* Boston: Routledge, Kegan Paul.

Goldsmith, M. (1986). Sexually transmitted diseases may reverse the "revolution." *Journal of the American Medical Association, 255,* 1665-1672.

Goldstein, M. J., & Kant, H. S. (1973). *Pornography and sexual deviance.* Berkeley: University of California Press.

Gonsiorek, J. C. (1993, August). Relationship of sexual abuse of males and sexual orientation confusion. In L. A. Morris (Chair), *Wounded warriors: Male survivors of childhood sexual abuse.* Paper presented at a symposium conducted at the 101st Annual Convention of the American Psychological Association, Toronto.

Gonsiorek, J. C., Bera, W. H., & LeTourneau, D. (1994). *Male sexual abuse: A trilogy of intervention strategies.* Thousand Oaks, CA: Sage.

Gonsiorek, J. C., & Weinrich, J. D. (Eds.). (1991). *Homosexuality: Research implications for public policy.* Newbury Park, CA: Sage.

Goodchilds, J., & Zellman, G. (1984). Sexual signaling and sexual aggression in adolescent relationships. In N. Malamuth & E. Donnerstein (Eds.), *Pornography and sexual aggression* (pp. 233-243). New York: Academic Press.

Goodchilds, J., Zellman, G., Johnson, P. B., & Giarrusso, R. (1988). Adolescents and their perceptions of sexual interactions. In A. W. Burgess (Ed.), *Rape and sexual assault* (Vol. 2, pp. 245-270). New York: Garland.

Grauerholz, E, & Koralewski, M. A. (1991). *Sexual coercion: A sourcebook on its nature, causes, and prevention.* Lexington, MA: Lexington.

Gregersen, E. (1994). *The world of human sexuality: Behavior, customs, and beliefs.* New York: Irvington.

Groth, A. N. (1979). *Men who rape: The psychology of the offender.* New York: Plenum.

Groth, A. N., & Birnbaum, H. J. (1978). Adult sexual orientation and attraction to underage persons. *Archives of Sexual Behavior, 7*(3), 175-181.

Groth, A. N., & Burgess, A. W. (1977). Sexual dysfunction during rape. *New England Journal of Medicine, 297,* 764-766.

Groth, A. N., Hobson, W. F., & Gary, T. (1982). The child molester. Clinical observations. In J. Conte & D. Shore (Eds.), *Social work and child sexual abuse* (pp. 129-144). New York: Haworth.

Gutek, B. (1985). *Sex and the workplace.* San Francisco: Jossey-Bass.

Hall, G. C. N. (1989). Sexual arousal and arousability in a sexual offender population. *Journal of Abnormal Psychology, 98,* 145-149.

Hall, G. C. N., & Hirschman, R. (1991). Toward a theory of sexual aggression: A quadripartite model. *Journal of Consulting and Clinical Psychology, 59,* 662-669.

Hall, G. S. (1904). *Adolescence: Its psychology and its relations to physiology, anthropology, sociology, sex crime, religion, and education* (2 vols.). New York: Appeleton.

Halpern, C. T., Udry, J. R., Campbell, B., & Suchindran, C. (1993). Testosterone and pubertal development as predictors of sexual activity: A panel analysis of adolescent males. *Psychosomatic Medicine, 55*(5), 436-447.

Hamer, D. H., Hu, S., Magnuson, V. L., Hu, N., & Pattatucci, A. M. L. (1993). A linkage between DNA markers on the X-chromosome and male sexual orientation. *Science, 261*, 321-337.

Handsfield, H. H. (1988). Questions and answers: "Safe sex" guidelines: Mycoplasma and chlamydia infections. *Journal of the American Medical Association, 259*, 2022.

Harahap, M., & Siregar, A. (1988). Circumcision: A review and a new technique. *Journal of Dermatology and Surgical Oncology, 14*, 383-386.

Harding, J. J. (1989). Postpartum psychiatric disorders: A review. *Comprehensive Psychiatry, 30*, 109-112.

Hardy, J. B., & Zabin, L. S. (1991). *Adolescent pregnancy in an urban environment: Issues, programs, and evaluation.* Washington, DC: Urban Institute Press.

Harney, P. A., & Muehlenhard, C. L. (1991). Rape. In E. Grauerholz & M. A. Koralewski (Eds.), *Sexual coercion: A sourcebook on its nature, causes, and prevention* (pp. 3-16). Lexington MA: Lexington.

Harris, L. (1988). *Inside America.* New York: Vintage.

Harrison, J. B., & Morris, L. A. (1996). Group therapy for adult male survivors of child sexual abuse. In M. P. Adronico (Ed.), *Men in groups: Insights, interventions, and psychoeducational work* (pp. 339-356). Washington, DC: American Psychological Association.

Harrison, P. J., Downes, J., & Williams, M. D. (1991). Date and acquaintance rape: Perceptions and attitude change strategies. *Journal of College Student Development, 32*, 131-139.

Hass, A. (1979). *Teenage sexuality.* New York: Macmillan

Hatfield, E. (1988). Passionate and companionate love. In R. J. Sternberg & M. L. Barnes (Eds.), *The psychology of love* (pp. 191-217). New Haven, CT: Yale University Press.

Hatfield, E., Sprecher, S., & Traupman, J. (1978). Men's and women's reaction to sexually explicit films: A serendipitous finding. *Archives of Sexual Behavior, 7*, 583-592.

Havemann, E., & Lehtinen, M. (1990). *Marriages and families: New problems, new opportunities* (2nd ed.). Englewood Cliffs, NJ: Prentice Hall.

Hayashino, D. S., Wurtele, S. K., & Klebe, K. J. (1995). Child molesters: An examination of cognitive factors. *Journal of Interpersonal Violence, 10*, 106-116.

Hefner, H. M. (1979a, January). The Playboy philosophy. *Playboy,* pp. 81-89.

Hefner, H. M. (1979b, January). [Untitled]. *Playboy,* p. 3.

Hefzallah, I. M., & Maloney, W. (1979). Are there only six kinds of TV commercials? *Journal of Advertising Research, 19*(4), 57-62.

Hegeler, S., & Mortensen, M. (1977). Sexual behavior in elderly Danish males. In R. Gemme & C. Wheeler (Eds.), *Progress in sexology* (pp. 285-292). New York: Plenum.

Heiby, E., & Becker, J. D. (1980). Effect of filmed modeling on the self-reported frequency of masturbation. *Archives of Sexual Behavior, 9*, 11-20.

Hein, K., DiGeronimo, T. F., & the Editors of Consumer Reports Books. (1989). *AIDS: Trading fears for facts.* Mount Vernon, NY: Consumers Union.

Hein, N. (1981). Sexual behavior of castrated sex offenders. *Archives of Sexual Behavior, 10*, 11-19.

Hendrick, C., & Hendrick, S. (1986). A theory and method of love. *Journal of Personality and Social Psychology, 50*, 392-402.

Hendrick, S. S., Hendrick, C., & Adler, N. L. (1988). Romantic relationships, love, satisfaction, and staying together. *Journal of Personality and Social Psychology, 54*, 980-988.

Herbst, A. (1979). Coitus and the fetus. *New England Journal of Medicine, 301*, 1235-1236.

Herdt, G. (1987). *The Sambia: Ritual and gender in New Guinea.* New York: Holt, Rinehart & Winston.

Herrell, J. M. (1975). Sex differences in emotional responses to "erotic literature." *Journal of Consulting and Clinical Psychology, 43*, 921.

Highwater, J. (1990). *Myth and sexuality.* New York: Penguin.

Holt, R. E. (1971a). *Little "dirty" comics.* San Diego: Socio Library.

Holt, R. E. (1971b). *More little "dirty" comics.* San Diego: Socio Library.

Horton, A. L., Johnson, B. L., Roundy, L. M., & Williams, D. (Eds.). (1990). *The incest perpetrator: A family member no one wants to treat.* Newbury Park, CA: Sage.

Hunt, M. (1974). *Sexual behavior in the 1970s.* Chicago: Playboy.

Hunter, M. (1990). *Abused boys: The neglected victims of sexual abuse.* Lexington, MA: Lexington.

Hunter, M. (1993, August). Males who have experienced childhood sexual abuse: Recovery issues. In L. A. Morris (Chair), *Wounded warriors: Male survivors of childhood sexual abuse.* Paper presented at symposium conducted at the 101st Annual Convention of the American Psychological Association, Toronto.

Imperato-McGinley, J., Guerrero, R., Gautier, T., & Peterson, R. E. (1974). Steroid 5 reductase deficiency in man: An inherited form of male pseudohermaphroditism. *Science, 186*, 1213-1215.

Imperato-McGinley, J., Miller, M., Wilson, J. D., Peterson, R. E., Shackleton, C., & Gajdusek, D. C. (1991). A cluster of male pseudohermaphrodites with 5-alpha-reductase deficiency in Papua New Guinea. *Clinical Endocrinology, 34,* 293-298.

Imperato-McGinley, J., Peterson, R. E., Gautier, T., & Sterla, E. (1979). Androgens and the evolution of male-gender identity among male pseudohermaphrodites with 5-alpha-reductase deficiency. *New England Journal of Medicine, 300,* 1233-1237.

Janoff-Bulman, R., Timko, C., & Carli, L. L. (1985). Cognitive biases in blaming the victim. *Journal of Experimental Social Psychology, 21,* 161-177.

Jenkins, M. J., & Dambrot, F. H. (1987). The attribution of date rape: Observer's attitudes and sexual experiences and the dating situation. *Journal of Applied Social Psychology, 17,* 875-895.

Justice, B., & Justice, R. (1979). *The broken taboo: Sex in the family.* New York: Human Sciences.

Kammeyer, K. C. W. (1990). *Marriage and family: A foundation for personal decisions* (2nd ed.). Boston: Allyn & Bacon.

Kammeyer, K. C. W., Ritzer, G., & Yetman, N. R. (1990). *Sociology: Experiencing changing societies.* Boston: Allyn & Bacon.

Kane, M. (1988). Media coverage of the female athlete before, during, and after Title IX: "Sports Illustrated" revisited. *Journal of Sports Management, 2,* 87-99.

Kanekar, S., & Kolsawalla, M. B. (1980). Responsibility of a rape victim in relation to her respectability, attractiveness, and provocativeness. *Journal of Social Psychology, 112,* 153-154.

Kanekar, S., & Nazareth, A. M. (1988). Attributed rape victim's fault as a function of her attractiveness, physical hurt, and emotional disturbance. *Social Behavior, 3,* 37-40.

Kanin, E. J. (1985). Date rapists: Differential sexual socialization and relative deprivation. *Arichives of Sexual Behavior, 14,* 219-231.

Kantner, J. F., & Zelnick, M. (1972). Sexual experience of young unmarried women in the United States. *Family Planning Perspectives, 4,* 9-18.

Kaplan, A. (1955). Obscenity as an esthetic category. *Law and Contemporary Problems, 20,* 552-559.

Kaplan, H. (1987). *The illustrated manual of sex therapy.* New York: Brunner/Mazel.

Kaplan, H. S. (1979). *Disorders of sexual desire.* New York: Brunner/Mazel.

Kasl, C. D. (1990). Female perpetrators of sexual abuse: A feminist view. In M. Hunter (Ed.), *The sexually abused male* (Vol. 1, pp. 259-274). Lexington, MA: Lexington Books.

Kaufman, A., DiVasto, P., Jackson, R., Voorhees, D., & Christy, J. (1980). Male rape victims: Noninstitutionalized assault. *American Journal of Public Health, 67,* 221-223.

Kemeny, M. E., Cohen, F., Zegans, L. S., & Conant, M. A. (1989). Psychological and immunological predictors of genital herpes recurrence. *Psychosomatic Medicine, 51,* 195-208.

Kempe, R. S., & Kempe, C. H. (1984). *The common secret: Sexual abuse of children and adolescents.* New York: Freeman.

Kemper, T. D. (1983). Predicting the divorce rate: Down? *Journal of Family Isssues, 4,* 507-524.

Kent, M. R. (1991). Women and AIDS. *New England Journal of Medicine, 324,* 1442.

Kimmel, M. S., & Kaufman, M. (1994). Weekend warriors: The new men's movement. In H. Brod & M. Kaufman (Eds.), *Theorizing masculinities* (pp. 259-288). Thousand Oaks, CA: Sage.

Kinsey, A. C., Pomeroy, W. B., & Martin, C. E. (1948). *Sexual behavior in the human male.* Philadelphia: W. B. Saunders.

Kinsey, A. C., Pomeroy, W. B., Martin, C. E., & Gebhard, P. H. (1953). *Sexual behavior in the human female.* Philadelphia: W. B. Saunders.

Klapp, O. E. (1962). *Heroes, villains, and fools: The changing American character.* Englewood Cliffs, NJ: Prentice Hall.

Knopp, F. H. (1984). *Retraining adult sex offenders: Methods and models.* Syracuse, NY: Safer Society.

Knox, D. (1988). *Choices in relationships: An introduction to marriage and the family.* St. Paul, MN: West.

Knussman, R., Christiansen, K., & Couwenbergs, C. (1986). Relations between sex hormone levels and sexual behavior in men. *Arichives of Sexual Behavior, 15,* 429-445.

Koopman, P., Gubbay, J., Vivian, N., Goodfellow, P., & Lovell-Badge, R. (1991). Male development of chromosomally female mice transgenic for Sry. *Nature, 351,* 117-121.

Koss, M. P. (1985). The hidden rape victim: Personality, attitudinal, and situational characteristics. *Psychology of Women Quarterly, 9,* 193-212.

Koss, M. P. (1988). Hidden rape: Sexual aggression and victimization in a national sample of students in higher education. In A. W. Burgess (Ed.), *Rape and sexual assault* (Vol. 1, pp. 3-25). New York: Garland.

Koss, M. P., & Dinero, T. E. (1989). Predictors of sexual aggression among a national sample of male college students. *Human sexual aggression: Current perspectives, Annals of the New York Academy of Science, 528,* 113-146.

Koss, M. P., Goodman, L. A., Browne, A., Fitzgerald, L. F., Keita, G. P., & Russo, N. P. (1994). *No safe haven: Male violence against women at home, at work, and in the community.* Washington, DC: American Psychological Association.

Koss, M. P., & Harvey, M. R. (1991). *The rape victim: Clinical and community interventions.* Newbury Park, CA: Sage.

Koss, M. P., & Leonard, K. E. (1984). Sexually aggressive men: Empirical findings and theoretical implications. In N. M. Malamuth & E. Donnerstein (Eds.), *Pornography and sexual aggression* (pp. 213-232). New York: Academic.

Koss, M. P., Leonard, K. E., Beezley, D. A., & Oros, C. (1981, August). *Personality and attitudinal characteristics of sexually aggressive men.* Paper presented at the annual meeting of the American Psychological Association, Los Angeles.

Koss, M. P., Leonard, K. E., Beezley, D. A., & Oros, C. (1985). Nonstranger sexual aggression: A discriminate analysis of the psychological characteristics of undetected offenders. *Sex Roles, 12,* 981-992.

Kronhausen, E., & Kronhausen, P. (1964). *Pornography and the law.* New York: Ballentine.

LaChance, C. C., Chestnut, R. W., & Lubitz, A. (1978). The "decorative" female model: Sexual stimuli and the recognition of advertisements. *Journal of Advertising, 8,* 231-235.

Lafavore, M. (Ed.). *Men's health advisor 1993.* Emmaus, PA: Rodale.

Lang, R. A., Langevin, R., Bain, J., Frenzel, R. R., & Wright, P. (1989). An examination of sex hormones in genital exhibitionists. *Annals of Sex Research, 2,* 67-75.

Langevin, R. (1985). *Erotic preference, gender identity, and aggression in men: New research studies.* Hillsdale, NJ: Lawrence Erlbaum.

Lanyon, R. (1986). Psychological assessment procedures in court-related settings. *Professional Psychology, 17,* 260-268.

LaTour, M. S. (1990). Female nudity in print advertising: An analysis of gender differences in arousal and ad response. *Psychology and Marketing, 7,* 65-81.

Laws, D. R. (Ed.). (1989). *Relapse prevention with sex offenders.* New York: Guilford.

Lee, J. A. (1988). Love-styles. In R. J. Sternberg & M. L. Barnes (Eds.), *The psychology of love* (pp. 38-67). New Haven, CT: Yale University Press.

Leiblum, S., & Rosen, R. (Eds.). (1988). *Sexual desire disorders.* New York: Guilford.

Leitenberg, H., Greenwald, E., & Tarran, M. J. (1989) The relation between sexual activity among children during preadolescence and/or early adolescence and sexual behavior and sexual adjustment in young adulthood. *Archives of Sexual Behavior, 18,* 299-313.

Leshner, A. I. (1978). *An introduction to behavioral endocrinology.* New York: Oxford University Press.

Letellier, P. (1994). Gay and bisexual male domestic violence victimization: Challenges to feminist theory and responses to violence. *Violence and Victims: An International Journal, 9,* 95-106.

Lew, M. (1988). *Victims no longer: Men recovering from incest and other sexual child abuse.* New York: Nevraumont.

Lewis, M., & Kagan, J. (1965). Studies in attention. *Merrill-Palmer Quarterly, 2,* 95-127.

Lewisohn, R. (1958). *A history of sexual customs* (A. Mayce, Trans.). New York: Harper & Brothers.

Levine-MacCombie, J., & Koss, M. P. (1986). Acquaintance rape: Effective avoidance strategies. *Psychology of Women Quarterly, 10,* 311-320.

Levy, M. R., Dignan, M., & Shirreffs, J. H. (1987). *Life and health* (5th ed.). New York: Random House.

Levant, R. F. (1992). Toward the reconstruction of masculinity. *Journal of Family Psychology, 5,* 379-402.

Levant, R. F. (1995). Toward the reconstruction of masculinity. In R. F. Levant & W. S. Pollack (Eds.), *A new psychology of men* (pp. 229-251). New York: Basic.

Levant, R. F., Hirsch, L. S., Celentano, E., Cozza, T. M. , Hill, S., MacEachern, M., Marty, N., & Schnedeker, J. (1992). The male role: An investigation of contemporary norms. *Journal of Mental Health Counseling, 14,* 325-337.

Levant, R. F., & Kopecky, G. (1995). *Masculinity reconstructed: Changing the rules of manhood—At work, in relationships, and in family life.* New York: E. P. Dutton.

LeVay, S. (1991). A difference in hypothalamic structure between heterosexual and homosexual men. *Science, 153,* 1034-1037.

LeVay, S. (1993). *The sexual brain.* Cambridge: MIT Press.

Lindesay, J. (1987). Laterality shift in homosexual men. *Neuropsychologia, 25,* 965-969.

Liebow, E. (1967). *Tally's corner.* Boston: Little, Brown.

Lindsey, R. (1988, February 1). Circumcision under criticism as unnecessary to newborn. *New York Times,* p. A1.

Linz, D. (1989). Exposure to sexually explicit materials and attitudes toward rape: A comparison of study results. *Journal of Sex Research, 26,* 50-84.

Linz, D., Donnerstein, E., & Adams, S. M. (1989). Physiological desensitization and judgments about female victims of violence. *Human Communication Research, 15*(4), 509-522.

Linz, D., Donnerstein, E., Bross, M., & Chapin, M. (1986). Mitigating the influence of violence on television and sexual violence in the media. In R. Blanchard (Ed.), *Advances in the study of aggression* (Vol. 2, pp. 165-194). New York: Academic.

Linz, D., Donnerstein, E., & Penrod. S. (1988). The effects of long-term exposure to violent and sexually degrading depictions of women. *Journal of Personality and Social Psychology, 55,* 758-767.

Lisak, D. (1991). Sexual aggression, masculinity, and fathers. *Signs: Journal of Women in Culture and Society, 16,* 238-262.

Lisak, D. (1993, September). *Research on male victims of childhood abuse: What do we know and what do we need to know?* Paper presented at the Fifth Annual National Conference on Male Survivors, Bethesda, MD.

Lisak, D., & Roth, S. (1990). Motives and psychodynamics of self-reported, unincarcerated rapists. *American Journal of Orthopsychiatry, 60,* 268-280.

Livingston, J. A. (1982). Responses to sexual harassment on the job: Legal, organizational, and individual actions. *Journal of Social Issues, 38,* 5-22.

Longo, D. J., & Clum, G. A. (1989). Psychosocial factors affecting genital herpes recurrences: Linear vs. mediating models. *Journal of Psychosomatic Research, 33,* 161-166.

Lovdal, L. T. (1989). Sex role messages in television commercials: An update. *Sex Roles, 21,* 715-724.

Lovejoy, C. O. (1981). The origin of man. *Science, 211,* 341-350.

Loy, P. H., & Stewart, L. P. (1984). The extent and effects of sexual harassment of working women. *Sociological Focus, 17,* 31-43.

Lucie-Smith, E. (1991). *Sexuality in western art.* New York: Thames & Hudson.

Maccoby, E. E. (1990). Gender and relationships: A developmental account. *American Psychologist, 45,* 513-520.

Maccoby, E. E., & Jacklin, C. N. (1974). *The psychology of sex differences.* Stanford, CA: Stanford University Press.

Maccoby, E. E., & Jacklin, C. N. (1980). Sex differences in aggression: A rejoinder and reprise. *Child Development, 51,* 964-980

MacKinnon, C. A. (1979). *Sexual harassment of working women.* New Haven, CT: Yale University Press.

Macklin, E. D. (1978). Review of research on nonmarital cohabitation in the United States. In B. I. Murstein (Ed.), *Exploring intimate life styles* (pp. 197-243). New York: Springer.

Maihoff, N., & Forrest, L. (1983). Sexual harassment in higher education: An assessment study. *Journal of the NAWDAC, 46,* 3-8.

Majors, R., & Billson, J. M. (1992). *Cool pose: The dilemmas of black manhood in America.* New York: Lexington.

Malamuth, N. M. (1981). Rape proclivity among males. *Journal of Social Issues, 37,* 138-157.

Malamuth, N. M. (1986). Predictors of naturalistic aggression. *Journal of Personality and Social Psychology, 50,* 953-962.

Malamuth, N. M. (1989). The Attraction to Sexual Aggression Scale: Part 2. *Journal of Sex Research, 26,* 324-354.

Malamuth, N. M., & Ceniti, J. (1986). Repeated exposure to violent and nonviolent pornography: Likelihood of raping ratings and laboratory aggression against women. *Aggressive Behavior, 12,* 129-137.

Malamuth, N. M., Check, J., & Briere, J. (1986). Sexual arousal in response to aggression: Ideological, aggressive, and sexual correlates. *Journal of Personality and Social Psychology, 50,* 330-340.

Malamuth, N. M., Sockloskie, R., Koss, M. P., & Tanaka, J. (1991). The characteristics of aggressors against women: Testing a model using a national sample of college students. *Journal of Consulting and Clinical Psychology, 59,* 670-681.

Maletzky, B. M. (1991). *Treating the sexual offender.* Newbury Park, CA: Sage.

Malovich, N. J. , & Stake, J. E. (1990). Sexual harassment on campus: Individual differences in atitudes and beliefs. *Psychology of Women Quarterly, 14,* 63-81.

Martens, M., & Faro, S. (1989, January). Update on trichomoniasis: Detection and management. *Medical Aspects of Human Sexuality*, 73-79.

Martin, D. (1976). *Battered wives*. New York: Simon & Schuster.

Martin, D. H. (1990). Chlamydial infections. *Medical Clinics of North America, 74,* 1367-1387.

Martinson, F. M. (1981). Eroticism in infancy and childhood. In L. L. Constantine & F. M. Martinson (Eds.), *Children and sex: New findings, new perspectives* (pp. 23-35). Boston: Little, Brown.

Masters, W. H., & Johnson, V. E. (1966). *Human sexual response*. Boston: Little, Brown.

Masters, W. H., & Johnson, V. E. (1970). *Human sexual inadequacy*. Boston: Little, Brown.

Masters, W. H., & Johnson, V. E. (1976). *The pleasure bond*. New York: Bantam.

Masters, W. H., & Johnson, V. E. (1979). *Homosexuality in perspective*. Boston: Little, Brown.

Masters, W. H., Johnson, V. E., & Kolodny, R. C. (1985). *Human sexuality* (2nd ed.). Boston: Little, Brown.

Masters, W. H., Johnson, V. E., & Kolodny, R. C. (1988a). *Crisis: Heterosexual behavior in the age of AIDS*. New York: Grove.

Masters, W. H., Johnson, V. E., & Kolodny, R. C. (1988b). *Masters and Johnson on sex and human loving*. Boston: Little, Brown.

Masters, W. H., Johnson, V. E., & Kolodny, R. C. (1994, March). Masters and Johnson: Adultery. *Playboy*, pp. 62-154.

Mathews, R., Matthews, J., & Speltz, K. (1990). Female sexual offenders. In M. Hunter (Ed.), *The sexually abused male* (Vol. 1, pp. 275-293). Lexington, MA: Lexington.

Matney, W., & Johnson, D. (Eds.). (1983). *America's black population 1970-1982: A statistical view*. Washington, DC: Department of Commerce, Bureau of Census.

McCabe, M. P., & Collins, J. K. (1984). Measurement of depth of desired and experienced sexual involvement at different stages of dating. *Journal of Sex Research, 20,* 377-390.

McCartney, J. (1966). Overt transference. *Journal of Sex Research, 2,* 227-237.

McCaul, K. D., Veltum, L. G., Boyechko, V., & Crawford, J. J. (1990). Understanding attributions of blame for rape: Sex, violence, and foreseeability. *Journal of Applied Social Psychology, 20,* 1-26.

McCormick, C. M., & Witelson, S. F. (1991). A cognitive profile of homosexual men compared to heterosexual men and women. *Psychoneuroendocrinolgy, 16,* 459-473.

McCormick, C. M., Witelson, S. F., & Kingstone, E. (1990). Left-handedness in homosexual men and women: Neuroendocrine implications. *Psychoneuroendocrinology, 15,* 69-76.

McMullen, R. J. (1990). *Male rape: Breaking the silence on the last taboo*. Boston, MA: Alson.

Mead, M. (1963). *Sex and temperament*. New York: Morrow. (Original work published 1935)

Meggitt, M. (1964). Male-female relationships in the highlands of Australian New Guinea. *American Anthropologist, 66*, 204-224.

Melvin, S. Y. (1990). Syphilis: Resurgence of an old disease. *Primary Care: Clinics in Office Practice, 17*, 47-57.

Mendel, M. P. (1995). *The male survivor: The impact of sexual abuse*. Thousand Oaks, CA: Sage.

Mertz, G. J. (1990). Genital herpes simplex virus infections. *Medical Clinics of North America, 74*, 1433-1454.

Meyer-Bahlburg, H. F. L. (1978). Aggression, androgens, and XYY syndrome. In R. C. Friedman, R. M. Richart, & R. L. Vande Wiele (Eds.), *Sex differences in behavior* (p. 447). Huntington, NY: Krieger.

Mezey, G., & King, M. (1989). The effects of sexual assault on men: A survey of 22 victims. *Psychological Medicine, 19*, 205-209.

Michael, R. T., Gagnon, J. H., Laumann, E. O., & Kolata, G. (1994). *Sex in America: A definitive survey*. Boston: Little, Brown.

Miller, B. C., Christopherson, C. R., & King, P. K. (1993). Sexual behavior in adolescence. In T. P. Gullotta, G. R. Adams, & R. Montemayor (Eds.), *Adolescent sexuality* (pp. 57-76). Newbury Park, CA: Sage.

Miller, B. C., McCoy, J. K., & Olson, T. D. (1986). Dating age and stage as correlates of adolescent sexual attitudes and behavior. *Journal of Adolescent Research, 1*, 361-371.

Milos, M., & Macris, D. (1992). Circumcision: A medical or human rights issue? *Journal of Nurse-Midwifery, 37* (Supplement), 87S-96S.

Money, J. (1968). *Sex errors of the body*. Baltimore: Johns Hopkins University Press.

Money, J. (1980) *Love and love sickness*. Baltimore: Johns Hopkins University Press.

Money, J. (1993). *Lovemaps: Clinical concepts of sexual/erotic health and pathology, paraphilia, and gender transposition in childhood, adolescence, and maturity*. New York: Irvington.

Money, J., & Ehrhardt, A. A. (1972). *Man and woman, boy and girl: The differentiation and dimorphism of gender identity from conception to maturity*. Baltimore: Johns Hopkins University Press.

Moore, K. A., Wenk, D., Hofferth, S. L., & Hayes, C. D. (1987). Statistical appendix, Table 3-1. In S. L. Hofferth & C. D. Hayes (Eds.), *Risking the future* (Vol. 2, pp. 414-415). Washington, DC: National Academy Press.

Moore, R., & Gillette, D. (1990). *King, warrior, magician, lover: Rediscovering the archetypes of the mature masculine*. New York: HarperCollins.

Moore, R., & Gillett, D. (1992). *The king within: Accessing the king in the male psyche*. New York: Avon.

Morris, D. (1969). *The naked ape: A zoologist's study of the human animal*. New York: McGraw-Hill.

Morris, L. A. (1993 September). *Socialization of the male sex role and the male survivor: Clinical issues.* Workshop presented at the Fifth Annual National Conference on Male Survivors, Bethesda, MD.

Morris, L. A. (1995). The need for a multidimensional approach to the treatment of male sexual abuse survivors. In M. Hunter (Ed.), *Adult survivors of sexual abuse: Treatment innovations* (pp. 154-173). Thousand Oaks, CA: Sage.

Mosher, D. L. (1988). Pornography defined: Sexual involvement theory, narrative context, and goodness-of-fit. *Journal of Psychology and Human Sexuality, 1,* 67-85.

Mott, F. L., & Haurin, R. J. (1988). Linkages between sexual activity and alcohol and drug use among American adolescents. *Family Planning Perspectives, 20*(3), 128-136.

Muehlenhard, C. L., & Falcon, P. L. (1990). Men's heterosocial skill and attitudes toward women as predictors of verbal sexual coercion and forceful rape. *Sex Roles, 23,* 241-259.

Muehlenhard, C. L., Friedman, D. E., & Thomas, C. M. (1985). Is date rape justifiable? The effects of dating activity, who initiated, who paid, and men's attitudes toward women. *Psychology of Women Quarterly, 9,* 297-310.

Muehlenhard, C. L., & Linton, M. A. (1987). Date rape and sexual aggression in dating situations: Incidence and risk factors. *Journal of Counseling and Psychology, 34,* 186-196.

Muller, U., & Urban, E. (1981). Reaggregation of rat gonadal cells *in vitro*: Experiments on the function of H-Y antigen. *Cytogenetics and Cellular Genetics, 31,* 104-107.

Muller, U., & Urban, E. (1982). Ovarian cells participate in the formation of tubular structures in mouse/rat heterosexual gonadal co-cultures. *Differentiation, 22,* 136-138.

Murdock, G. (1937, May). Comparative data on the division of labor by sex. *Social Forces,* 551-553.

Muuss, R. E. (1970). Adolescent development and the secular trend. *Adolescence, 5,* 267-284.

Nasjleti, M. (1980). Suffering in silence: The male incest victim. *Child Welfare, 59,* 203-215.

National Center for Health Statistics. (1988). *Advance report of final natality statistics, 1986* (Monthly Vital Statistics Report 37[3]). Hyattsville, MD: Department of Health and Human Services.

National Commission on AIDS. (1993). *Behavioral and social sciences and the HIV/AIDS epidemic.* Rockville, MD: CDC National AIDS Clearinghouse.

NEC Survey. (1990a, January/February). *New England Comics Newsletter.*

NEC Survey. (1990b, September/October). *New England Comics Newsletter.*

Nevid, J. S. (1993). *A student's guide to AIDS and other sexually transmitted diseases.* Boston: Allyn & Bacon.

Nieschlag, E. (1979). The endocrine functions of the human testes in regard to sexuality. In *Sex, hormones, and behavior* (Ciba Foundation Symposium 62; p. 183). New York: Excerpta Medica.

NOHARMM. (1992). *Male circumcision in America—Violating human rights: A consciousness raising primer and resource guide* (2nd ed.). San Francisco: Author.

Norton, A. J., & Moorman, J. E. (1987). Current trends in marriage and divorce among American women. *Journal of Marriage and the Family, 49,* 3-14.

O'Connell, M. A., Leberg, E., & Donaldson, C. R. (1990). *Working with sex offenders: Guidlines for therapist selection.* Newbury Park, CA: Sage.

O'Hara, M. W., Neunaber, D. J., & Zekoski, E. M. (1984). Prospective study of postpartum depression: Prevalence, course, and predictive factors. *Journal of Abnormal Psychology, 93,* 158-171.

Olson, P. E. (1990). The sexual abuse of boys: A study of the long-term psychological effects. In M. Hunter (Ed.), *The sexually abused male* (Vol. 1, pp. 137-152). Lexington, MA: Lexington Books.

Olweus, D., Mattsson, A., Schalling, D., & Low, H. (1988). Circulating testosterone levels and aggression in adolescent males: A causal analysis. *Psychosomatic Medicine, 50*(3), 261-272.

O'Neil, J. M. (1996). The gender role journey workshop: Exploring sexism and gender role conflict in a coeducational setting. In M. P. Andronico (Ed.), *Men in groups: Insights, interventions, psychoeducational work* (pp. 193-213). Washington, DC: American Psychological Association.

O'Neil, J. M., Good, G. E., & Holmes, S. (1995). Fifteen years of theory and research on men's gender role conflict: New paradigms for empirical research. In R. F. Levant & W. S. Pollack (Eds.), *A new psychology of men* (pp. 164-206). New York: Basic Books.

Overholser, J. C., & Beck, S. (1986). Multimethod assessment of rapists, child molesters, and three control groups on behavioral and psychological measures. *Journal of Consulting and Clinical Psychology, 54,* 682-687.

Padgett, V. R., & Brislin-Slutz, J. A. (1987). *Pornography, erotica, and negative attitudes towards women: The effects of repeated exposure.* Unpublished manuscript, Marshall University, Huntington, WV.

Padgett, V. R., Brislin-Slutz, J. A., & Neal, J. A. (1989). Pornography, erotica, and attitudes toward women: The effects of repeated exposure. *Journal of Sex Research, 26,* 479-491.

Padilla, E. R., & O'Grady, K. E. (1987). Sexuality among Mexican Americans: A case of sexual stereotyping. *Journal of Personality and Social Psychology, 52,* 5-10.

Pagels, E. (1988). *Adam, Eve, and the serpent.* New York: Random House.

Paikoff, R. L., & Brooks-Gunn, J. (1990). Physiological processes: What role do they play during the transition to adolescence? In R. Montemayor, G. R. Adams, & T. P. Gullotta (Eds.), *From childhood to adolescence: A transitional period?* (pp. 63-81). Newbury Park, CA: Sage.

Painter, K. (1987, October 27). Poll challenges Hite's figures on fidelity. *USA Today*, p. D1.

Palmore, E. (1981). *Social patterns in normal aging: Findings from the Duke Longitudinal Study*. Durham, NC: Duke University Press.

Patton, M. Q. (Ed.). (1991). *Family sexual abuse: Frontline research and evaluation*. Newbury Park, CA: Sage.

Peat, Marwick, & Partners. (1984). *A national population study of prostitution and pornography* (Working papers on pornography and prostitution, Report No. 6). Ottawa: Department of Justice.

Pecora, N. (1992). Superman/superboys/supermen: The comic book hero as socializing agent. In S. Craig (Ed.), *Man, masculinity, and the media* (pp. 61-77). Newbury Park, CA: Sage.

Perry, A. P. (1993 September). *The disclosure experience of the male victim of sexual abuse: Findings from a phenomenological study*. Paper presented at the Fifth Annual National Conference on Male Survivors, Bethesda, MD.

Persky, H., Leif, H., Strauss, D., Miller, W. R., & O'Brien, C. P. (1978). Plasma testosterone levels and sexual behavior of couples. *Arichives of Sexual Behavior, 7*(3), 157.

Petersen, J. P. (1979, November). Playboy interview: Masters and Johnson. *Playboy*, pp. 87-122.

Petrovich, M., & Templer, D. (1984). Heterosexual molestation of children who later become rapists. *Psychological Reports, 54*, 810.

Pharr, S. (1988). *Homophobia: A weapon of sexism*. Little Rock, AR: Chardon.

Pillard, R. C., & Weinrich, J. D. (1986). Evidence of familial nature of male homosexuality. *Archives of Sexual Behavior, 43*, 808-812.

Platt, R., Rice, P., & McCormack, W. (1983). Risk of acquiring gonorrhea and prevalence of abnormal adrenal findings among women recently exposed to gonorrhea. *Journal of the American Medical Association, 250*, 3205-3209.

*Playboy*. (1968, August, p. 14).

*Playboy*. (1968, May, pp. 67-202).

Pleck, J. H. (1981). *The myth of masculinity*. Cambridge: MIT Press.

Pleck, J. H., & Sawyer, J. (Eds.). (1974). *Men and masculinity*. Englewood Cliffs, NJ: Prentice Hall.

Poland, R. L. (1990). The question of routine neonatal circumcision. *New England Journal of Medicine, 322*, 1312-1314.

Pope, K. S. (1988). How clients are harmed by sexual contact with mental health professionals: The syndrome and its prevalence. *Journal of Counseling and Development, 67*, 222-226.

Pope, K. S. (1989). Therapists who become sexually intimate with a patient: Classifications, dynamics, recidivism, and rehabilitation. *Independent Practitioner, 9*(3), 28-34.

Pope, K. S. (1990a). Therapist-patient sex as sex abuse: Six scientific, professional, and practical dilemmas in addressing victimization and rehabilitation. *Professional Psychology: Research and Practice, 21,* 227-239.

Pope, K. S. (1990b). Therapist-patient sexual involvement: A review of the research. *Clinical Psychology Review, 10,* 477-490.

Pope, K. S., & Bajt, T. R. (1988). When laws and values conflict: A dilemma for psychologists. *American Psychologist, 43,* 828-829.

Pope, K. S., & Bouhoutsos, J. C. (1986). *Sexual intimacies between therapists and patients.* New York: Praeger.

Pope, K. S, Keith-Spiegel, P., & Tabachnick, B. G. (1986). Sexual attraction to clients: The human therapist and the (sometimes) inhuman training system. *American Psychologist, 41,* 147-158.

Porter, E. (1986). *Treating the young male victim of sexual assault: Issues & intervention strategies.* Syracuse, NY: Safer Society.

Porter, F. (1986). Neonatal pain cries: Effect of circumcision on acoustic features and perceived urgency. *Child Development, 57,* 790-802.

Porter, J. F., Critelli, J. W., & Tang, C. S. K. (1992). Sexual and aggressive motives in sexually aggressive college men. *Archives of Sexual Behavior, 21,* 457-468.

Posner, R. A. (1992). *Sex and reason.* Cambridge, MA: Harvard University Press.

Postman, N. (1979). *Teaching as a conserving activity.* New York: Delacorte.

Postman, N., Nystrom, C., Strate, L., & Weingartner, C. (1987). *Myths, men, and beer: An analysis of beer commercials on broadcast television.* Falls Church, VA: AAA Foundation for Traffic Safety. (ERIC Document Reproduction Service No. ED 290 074.)

Pratt, C., & Schmall, V. (1989). College students' attitudes toward elderly sexual behavior: Implications for family life education. *Family Relations, 38,* 137-141.

Pratt, W. F., & Eglash, S. (1990). *Premarital sexual behavior, multiple partners, and marital experience.* Paper presented at the annual meeting of the Population Association of America, Toronto.

Prentky, R. A., & Knight, R. A. (1991). Identifying critical dimensions for discriminating among rapists. *Journal of Consulting and Clinical Psychology, 59,* 643-661.

Press, A., et al. (1986, July 14). A government in the bedroom. *Newsweek,* pp. 36-38.

Prokopis, A. M. (1990, November). *The sexual politics of male rape.* Workshop presented at the Third National Conference on Male Survivors, Tucson, AZ.

Pryor, J. B. (1987). Sexual harassment proclivities in men. *Sex Roles, 17,* 269-290.

Pryor, J. B., LaVite, C. M., & Stoller, L. M. (1993). A social psychological analysis of sexual harassment: The person/situation interaction. *Journal of Vocational Behavior, 42,* 68-83.

Rada, R. T. (Ed.) (1978). *Clinical aspects of the rapist.* New York: Grune & Stratton.

Ramsey-Klawsnik, H. (1990a, April). *Sexual abuse by female perpetrators: Impact on children.* Paper presented at the National Symposium on Child Victimization, Atlanta, GA.

Ramsey-Klawsnik, H. (1990b, November). *Sexually abused boys: Indicators, abuser and impact of trauma.* Paper presented at the Third National Conference on Male Survivors, Tucson, AZ.

Rando, R. F. (1988). Human papilloma virus: Implications for clinical medicine. *Annals of Internal Medicine, 108,* 628-630.

Reinisch, J. M. (1981). Prenatal exposure to synthetic progestins increases potential for aggression in humans. *Science, 211,* 1171-1173.

Reinisch, J. M. (1990). *The Kinsey Institute new report on sex.* New York: St. Martin's.

Reinisch, J. M., Sanders, S. A., & Ziemba-Davis, M. (1988). The study of sexual behavior in relation to the transmission of human immunodeficiency virus: Caveats and recommendations. *American Psychologist, 43,* 921-927.

Reiss B. F. (1988, Spring/Summer). The long-lived person and sexuality. *Dynamic Psychotherapy, 6,* 79-86.

Remondino, P. C. (1974). *History of circumcision from the earliest times to the present.* New York: AMS. (Original work published 1891).

Renzetti, C. M. (1994). On dancing with a bear: Reflections on some of the current debates among domestic violence theorists. *Violence and Victims, 9,* 195-200.

Renzetti, C. M., & Curran, D. J. (1989). *Women, men, and society: The sociology of gender.* Boston: Allyn & Bacon.

Richardson, D. (1988). *Women and AIDS.* New York: Routledge, Chapman & Hall.

Riche, M. (1988, November 23-26). Postmarital society. *American Demographics, 60.*

Risin, L. I., & Koss, M. P. (1987). The sexual abuse of boys: Prevalence and descriptive characteristics of childhood victimizations. *Journal of Interpersonal Violence, 2,* 309-323.

Risman, et al. (1981). Living together in college: Implications for courtship. *Journal of Marriage and the Family, 43,* 77-83.

Roche, A. F. (1979). Secular trends in stature, weight, and maturation. In A. F. Roche (Ed.), *Secular trends in human growth, maturation, and development (Monographs of the Society for Research in Child Development, 44,* Whole No. 179).

Rolfs, R. T., Goldberg, M., & Sharrar, R. G. (1990). Risk factors for syphilis: Cocaine use and prostitution. *American Journal of Public Health, 80,* 853-857.

Rolfs, R. T., & Nakashima, A. K. (1990). Epidemiology of primary and secondary syphilis in the United States: 1981 through 1989. *Journal of the American Medical Association, 264,* 1432-1437.

Romeo, S. (1978, June). Dr. Martin Shepard answers his accusers. *Knave, 19,* 14-38.

Roper Organization. (1985). *The Virginia Slims American Women's Poll.* New York: Author.

Rosenthal, M. (1973, January). Gay Talese is hard on the trail of "the greatest joy in the world." *Gallery,* pp. 74-76.

Rotundo, E. A. (1993). *American manhood.* New York: Basic.

Rubin, L. J., & Borgers, S. B. (1990). Sexual harassment in universities during the 1980s. *Sex Roles, 23,* 397-411.

Russell, D. E. H. (1975). *The politics of rape.* New York: Stein & Day.

Russell, D. E. H. (1982). *Rape in marriage.* New York: Macmillan.

Russell, D. E. H. (1984). *Sexual exploitation: Rape, child sexual abuse, and workplace harassment.* Beverly Hills, CA: Sage.

Sabo, D., & Jansen, S. C. (1992). Images of men in sport media: The social reproduction of gender order. In S. Craig (Ed.), *Men, masculinity, and the media* (pp. 169-184). Newbury Park, CA: Sage.

Salter, A. C. (1988). *Treating child sex offenders and victims: A practical guide.* Newbury Park, CA: Sage.

Samuels, M., & Samuels, N. (1986). *The well pregnancy book.* New York: Simon & Schuster.

Sanders, G., & Ross-Field, L. (1986). Sexual orientation and visuo-spatial ability. *Brain and Cognition, 5,* 280-290.

Sanford, L. (1980). *The silent children.* Garden City, NY: Doubleday.

Schecter, S. (1982). *Women and male violence: The visions and struggles of the battered women's movement.* Boston: South End.

Schiavi, R. C., Theilgaard, A., Owen, D. R., & White, D. (1988). Sex chromosome anomalies, hormones, and sexuality. *Archives of General Psychiatry, 45,* 19-24.

Schiavi, R. C., Schreiner-Engle, P., Mandeli, J., Schanzer, H., & Cohen, E. (1990). Healthy aging and male sexual function. *American Journal of Psychiatry, 147,* 766-771.

Schmidt, G., Sigusch, V., & Schafer, S. (1973). Responses to reading erotic stories: Male-female differences. *Archives of Sexual Behavior, 2,* 181-199.

Schreiner-Engle, P., & Schiavi, R. (1986). Lifetime psychopathology in individuals with low sexual desire. *Journal of Nervous and Mental Diseases, 174,* 646-651.

Scott, J. (1985). *Violence and erotic material: The relationship between adult entertainment and rape.* Paper presented at the meeting of the American Association for the Advancement of Science, Los Angeles, CA.

Scully, D., & Marolla, J. (1983). *Incarcerated rapists: Exploring a sociological model* (Final Report for Department of Health and Human Services). Washington, DC: National Institutes for Mental Health.

Segal, Z. V., & Marshall, W. L. (1985). Heterosexual social skills in a population of rapists and child molesters. *Journal of Consulting and Clinical Psychology, 53,* 55-63.

Seidner, A. L., & Calhoun, K. S. (1984, August). *Childhood sexual abuse: Factors related to differential adult adjustment.* Paper presented at the Second National Conference for Family Violence Researchers, Durham, NH.

Seligman, C., Brickman, J., & Koulack, D. (1977). Rape and physical attractiveness: Assigning responsibility to victims. *Journal of Personality, 45,* 554-563.

Severn, J., Belch, G. E., & Belch, M. A. (1990). The effects of sexual and non-sexual advertising appeals and information level on cognitive processing and communications effectiveness. *Journal of Advertising, 19,* 14-22.

Sheehy, G. (1976). *Passages: Predictable crises of adult life.* New York: E. P. Dutton.

Shepard, M. (1971). *The love treatment: Sexual intimacy between patients and psychotherapists.* New York: Wyden.

Sherfey, M. J. (1972). *The nature and evolution of female sexuality.* New York: Random House.

Shields, N., & Hanneke, C. R. (1983). Battered wives' reactions to marital rape. In D. Finkelhor, R. J. Gelles, G. T. Hotaling, & M. A. Straus (Eds.), *The dark side of families* (pp. 132-148). Beverly Hills, CA: Sage.

Simenauer, J., & Carroll, D. (1982). *Singles: The new Americans.* New York: New American Library.

Simon, R. I. (1989, February). Sexual exploitation of patients: How it begins before it happens. *Psychiatric Annals, 19,* 104-112.

Simonsen, J. N., Cameron, D. W., & Gakinya, M. N. (1988). Human immunodeficiency virus infection among men with sexually transmitted diseases: Experience from a center in Africa. *New England Journal of Medicine, 319,* 274-278.

Sinclair, A. H., Berta, P., Palmer, M. S., Hawkins, J. R., Griffiths, B. L., Smith, U. J., Foster, J. W., Frischauf, A. M., Lovell-Badge, R., & Goodfellow, P. N. (1990). A gene from the human sex-determining region encodes a protein with homology to a conserved DNA-binding motif. *Nature, 346,* 240-242.

Smith, E. A. (1989). A biosocial model of adolescent sexual behavior. In G. R. Adams, R. Montemayor, & T. P. Gullotta (Eds.), *Biology of adolescent behavior and development* (pp. 143-167). Newbury Park, CA: Sage.

Smith, E. A., & Udry, J. R. (1985). Coital and non-coital sexual behaviors of white and black adolescents. *American Journal of Public Health, 75,* 1200-1203.

Sonenstein, F. L., Pleck, J. H., & Ku, L. C. (1989). Sexual activity, condom use, and AIDS awareness among adolescent males. *Family Planning Perspectives, 21,* 152-158.

Sonenstein, F. L., Pleck, J. H., & Ku, L. C. (1990, May). *Patterns of sexual activity among adolescent males.* Paper presented at the Annual Meeting of the Population Association of America, Toronto.

Sonenstein, F. L., Pleck, J. H., & Ku, L. C. (1991). Levels of sexual activity among adolescent males in the United States. *Family Planning Perspectives, 23*(4), 162-167.

Sonne, J., Meyer, C. B., Borys, D., & Marshall, V. (1985). Clients' reactions to sexual intimacy in therapy. *American Journal of Orthopsychiatry, 55,* 183-189.

Sorenson, R. C. (1973). *Adolescent sexuality in contemporary America.* New York: World.

Spain, D. (1992). *Gendered spaces.* Chapel Hill: University of North Carolina Press.

Spector, I. P., & Carey, M. P. (1990). Incidence and prevalence of the sexual dysfunctions: A critical review of the empirical literature. *Archives of Sexual Behavior, 19,* 389-408.

Spock, B., & Rothenberg, M. B. (1992). *Dr. Spock's baby and child care* (6th ed.). New York: Simon & Schuster.

Starr, B. D., & Weiner, M. B. (1982). *The Starr-Weiner report on sex and sexuality in the mature years.* New York: McGraw-Hill.

St. Antoine, A. (1991, November). Specialty file: Toyota 5FGC25 Forklift. *Car and Driver,* pp. 126-130.

Sternberg, R. J. (1988). *The triangle of love: Intimacy, passion, commitment.* New York: Basic Books.

Strate, L. (1992). Beer commercials: A manual on masculinity. In S. Craig (Ed.), *Men, masculinity, and the media* (pp. 78-92). Newbury Park, CA: Sage.

Straus, S. E. (1985). Herpes simplex virus infections: Biology, treatment, and prevention. *Annals of Internal Medicine, 103,* 404-419.

Stock, W. E. (1991). Feminist explanations: Male power, hostility, and sexual coercion. In E. Grauerholz & M. A Koralewski (Eds.), *Sexual coercion: A sourcebook on its nature, causes, and prevention* (pp. 61-73). Lexington, MA: Lexington Books.

Struve, J. (1990). Dancing with the patriarchy: The politics of sexual abuse. In M. Hunter (Ed.), *The sexually abused male* (Vol. 1, pp. 3-46). Lexington, MA: Lexington Books.

*Superman.* (1993). Issue number 30. New York: DC Comics.

*Superman in Action Comics.* (1993a). Issue number 12. New York: DC Comics.

*Superman in Action Comics.* (1993b). Issue number 20. New York: DC Comics.

Symons, D. (1979). *The evolution of human sexuality.* New York: Oxford University Press.

Tang, C. S. K., Critelli, J. W., & Porter, J. F. (1993). Motives in sexual aggression: The Chinese context. *Journal of Interpersonal Violence, 8,* 435-445.

Tavris, C., & Sadd, S. (1977). *The Redbook report on female sexuality.* New York: Delacorte

Taylor, J. (1991, May). *The prepuce: What exactly is removed by circumcision?* Paper presented at the Second International Symposium on Circumcision, San Francisco.

Teens express themselves. (1988, May 3). *The State* [Columbia, SC], p. 2A.

Terris, M., Wilson, F., & Nelson, J. H. (1973). Relation of circumcision to cancer of the cervix. *American Journal of Obstetrics and Gynecology, 117,* 1056-1066.

Thompson, A. P. (1983). Extramarital sex: A review of the research literature. *Jounrnal of Sex Research, 19,* 1-22.

Thorn, M. (1990). *Taboo no more: The phallus in fact, fantasy, and fiction.* New York: Shapolsky.

Thornton, A. (1990). The courtship process and adolescent sexuality. *Journal of Family Issues, 11,* 239-273.

Thornton, B., Robbins, M. A., & Johnson, J. A. (1981). Social perception of the rape victim's culpability: The influence of respondents' personal, environmental causal attribution tendencies. *Human Relations, 34,* 225-237.

Tieger, T. (1980). On the biological basis of sex differences in aggression. *Child Development, 51,* 943-963.

Tieger, T. (1981). Self-rated likelihood of raping and the social perception of rape. *Journal of Research in Personality, 15,* 147-158.

Tiger, L. (1970). The possible biological origins of sexual discrimination. *Impact of Science on Society, 20,* 29-44.

Tollison, C. D., & Adams, H. E. (1979). *Sexual disorders: Treatment, theory, and research.* New York: Gardner.

Toomey, K. E., & Barnes, R. C. (1990). Treatment of chlamydia trachomatis genital infection. *Reviews of Infectious Diseases* (Suppl. 6), S645-S655.

Touchette, N. (1991). HIV-1 link prompts circumspection of circumcision. *Journal of NIH Research, 3,* 44-46.

Udry, J. R. (1988). Biological predispositions and social control in adolescent sexual behaviors. *American Sociological Review, 53,* 709-722.

Udry, J. R. (1990). Biosocial models of adolescent problem behaviors. *Social Biology, 37*(1-2), 1-10.

Udry, J. R., & Billy, J. O. G. (1987). Initiation of coitus in early adolescence. *American Sociological Review, 52,* 841-855.

Udry, J. R., Billy, J. O. G., Morris, N. M., Groff, T. R., & Raj, M. H. (1985). Serum androgenic hormones motivate sexual behavior in adolescent boys. *Fertility and Sterility, 43*(1), 90-94.

Udry, J. R., Talbert, L. M., & Morris, N. M. (1986). Biosocial foundations for adolescent female sexuality. *Demography, 23*(2), 217-277.

Urquiza, A. J., & Capra, M. (1990). The impact of sexual abuse: Initial and long-term effects. In M. Hunter (Ed.), *The sexually abused male* (Vol. 1, pp. 105-136). Lexington, MA: Lexington Books.

U.S. Bureau of the Census. (1987). *Marital status and living arrangements: March 1987* (Current Population Reports, Series P-20, No. 423). Washington, DC: Government Printing Office.

U.S. Bureau of the Census. (1990). *Marital status and living arrangements: March 1990.* (Current Population Reports, Series P-20, No. 450). Washington, DC: Government Printing Office.

Vander Mey, B. J. (1988). The sexual victimization of male children: A review of previous research. *Child Abuse and Neglect, 12,* 61-72.

Walker, L. (1979). *The battered woman.* New York: Harper & Row.

Walker, L. (1984). *The battered woman syndrome.* New York: Springer.

Wallace, A. R. (1878). *Tropical Nature and other essays.* London: AMS.

Wallace, A. R. (1889). *Darwinism: An exposition of the theory of natural selection.* London: AMS

Wallack, L., Cassady, D., & Grube, J. (1990). *TV beer commercials and children: Exposure, attention, beliefs, and expectations about drinking as an adult.* Washington, DC: AAA Foundation for Traffic Safety.

Wallerstein, D. (1980). *Circumcision: An American health fallacy.* New York: Springer.

Walster, E., & Walster, G. W. (1978). *A new look at love.* Reading, MA: Addison-Wesley

Warner, E., & Strashin, E. (1981). Benefits and risks of circumcision. *Canadian Medical Association Journal, 125,* 967-976.

Warshaw, R. (1988). *I never called it rape.* New York: Harper & Row.

Waterhouse, J., Shanmugaramam, K., Muir, C., & Powell, J. (1982). Cancer incidences in five continents. *IARC Science Publications, 4,* 750-751.

Waxenburg, S. E., Drellich, M. G., & Sutherland, A. M. (1959). The role of hormones in human behavior: Changes in female sexuality after adrenalectomey. *Journal of Clinical Endocrinology and Metabolism, 19,* 193-202.

*Webtser's new world dictionary.* (1990). New York: Warner.

Weisz, M. G., & Earls, C. M. (1995). The effects of exposure to filmed sexual violence on attitudes toward rape. *Journal of Interpersonal Violence, 10,* 71-84.

Whatley, M. A., & Riggio, R. E. (1992). Atributions of blame for female and male victims. *Family Violence and Sexual Assault Bulletin, 8,* 16-18.

Whatley, M. A., & Riggio, R. E. (1993). Gender differences in attributions of blame for male rape victims. *Journal of Interpersonal Violence, 8,* 502-511.

Whitam, F. L., Diamond, M., & Martin, J. (1993). Homosexual orientation in twins: A report on 61 pairs and 3 triplet sets. *Archives of Sexual Behavior, 22,* 187-207.

Wilcox, B. L. (1987). Pornography, social science, and politics: When research and ideology collide. *American Psychologist, 42,* 941-943.

Williamson, P. S. (1984, February). Neonatal circumcision: Why and how to use a local anesthetic, *Consultant,* pp. 67-71.

Wille, R., & Beier, K. M. (1989). Castration in Germany. *Annals of Sex Research, 2,* 103-133.

Wilson, E. O. (1975). *Sociobiology: The new synthesis.* Cambridge, MA: Harvard University Press.

Wilson, G. D., & Cox, D. (1983). Personality characteristics of pedophile club members. *Personality and Individual Differences, 4,* 323-329.

Wilson, K. R., & Kraus, L. A. (1983). Sexual harassment in the university. *Journal of College Student Personnel, 24,* 219-224.

Winter, J. (1978). Prepubertal and pubertal endocrinology. In F. Falkner & J. Tanner (Eds.), *Human growth 2* (pp. 153-213). New York: Plenum.

Wolfe, J., & Baker, V. (1980). Characteristics of imprisoned rapists and circumstances of the rape. In C. G. Warner (Ed.), *Rape and sexual assault* (pp. 265-278). Germantown, MD: Aspen.

Wyatt, G. E., Peters, S. D., & Guthrie, D. (1988a). Kinsey revisited, Part I: Comparisons of the sexual socialization and sexual behavior of white women over 33 years. *Archives of Sexual Behavior, 17*(3), 201-209.

Wyatt, G. E., Peters, S. D., & Guthrie, D. (1988b). Kinsey revisited, Part II: Comparison of the sexual socialization and sexual behavior of black women over 33 years. *Archives of Sexual Behavior, 17*(4), 289-332.

Yalom, I., Green, R., & Fisk, N. (1973). Prenatal exposure to female hormones—Effect on psychosexual development in boys. *Archives of General Psychiatry, 28,* 554-561.

Yamaguchi, K., & Kandel, D. B. (1985). Dynamic relationships between premarital cohabitation and illicit drug use: An event-history analysis of role selection and role socialization. *American Sociological Review, 50,* 530-546.

Zabin, L. S., & Hayward, S. C. (1993). *Adolescent sexual behavior and childbearing.* Newbury Park, CA: Sage.

Zaslow, M. J., et al. (1985). Depressed mood in new fathers: Association with parent-infant interaction. *Genetic, Social, and General Psychology Monographs, 111*(2), 133-150.

Zbytovsky, M., & Zapletalek, M. (1979). Cyproterone actate in the therapy of sexual deviations. *Acta Nervosa Scandinavica Supplement (Praha), 21,* 162.

Zelnick, M., & Kantner, J. F. (1980). Sexual activity, contraceptive use, and pregnancy among metropolitan-area teenagers: 1971-1979. *Family Planning Perspectives, 12,* 230-237.

Zelnik, M., & Shah, F. K. (1983). First intercourse among young Americans. *Family Planning Perspectives, 15,* 64-70.

Zeman, N. (1990, Summer/Fall). The new rules of courtship. *Newsweek* (Special Edition), pp. 24-27.

Zilbergeld, B. (1992). *The new male sexuality: The truth about men, sex, and pleasure.* New York: Bantam.

Zillmann, D. (1989). Effects of prolonged consumption of pornography. In D. Zillmann & J. Bryant (Eds.), *Pornography: Research advances and policy considerations* (pp. 127-157). Hillsdale, NJ: Lawrence Erlbaum.

Zillmann, D., & Bryant, J. (1982, Autumn). Pornography, sexual callousness, and the trivialization of rape. *Journal of Communication,* 10-21.

Zillmann, D., & Bryant, J. (1984). Effects of massive exposure to pornography. In N. M. Malamuth & E. Donnerstein (Eds.), *Pornography and sexual aggression* (pp. 115-138). New York: Academic Press.

Zillmann, D., & Weaver, J. B. (1989). Pornography and men's sexual callousness toward women. In D. Zillmann & J. Bryant (Eds.), *Pornography: Research advances and policy considerations* (pp. 95-125). Hillsdale, NJ: Lawrence Erlbaum.

# Index

# About the Author

**Larry A. Morris** is a clinical psychologist with a private practice in Tucson, Arizona. He is a specialist in the evaluation and treatment of sexual disorders, childhood sexual abuse victims, adult victims of sexual assault, and sexual perpetrators. He has served as a consultant to, or an evaluation director of, several federally-funded social action programs designed to increase the information base and skills of prospective parents, to expand self-help programs for abusive parents, and to foster the cognitive and emotional growth of young children through family education programs.

Dr. Morris has made presentations at numerous conferences, conducted training seminars for child protective services staff, and provided workshops nationwide on treating male survivors of sexual victimization. He is one of the founding members of the newly formed National Organization on Male Sexual Victimization.

Dr. Morris serves on the editorial board of the *Journal of Child Sexual Abuse*. He is the author or coauthor of numerous articles, reports, and book chapters. He is also coauthor of the book, *Males at Risk: The Other Side of Child Sexual Abuse* (Sage, 1989).